Additional praise for *Rules to Break and Laws to Follow*

"For 70 years Carlson has been built on integrity and innovation, and sustained by its strong culture. In this groundbreaking book, Don and Martha deliver Twelve Laws that should be in the portfolio of every business manager hoping to achieve timeless leadership."
—Marilyn Carlson Nelson
Chairman & CEO, Carlson

"In too many businesses today, short-term thinking is exacting a long-term price. The relentless focus on making this quarter's numbers has suffocated innovation, eroded customer trust, and undermined employee engagement. Now two of our most distinguished business thinkers have charted an original and executable path out of the morass. This thoroughly researched and engagingly written book is a must-read for any business leader. Peppers and Rogers have done it again!"
—Daniel H. Pink,
Author of *A Whole New Mind*

"Balancing short- and long-term goals. Customers and shareholders. Innovation and efficiency. Culture and mission. Making a fair profit and building trust. It's all here. Peppers and Rogers bring together the best thinking from a variety of disciplines, and add their own experience and wisdom. The result is a terrific read that will help you make better decisions every day."
—Scott Dorsey
CEO, ExactTarget

"In today's technology-driven knowledge economy, leaders can no longer rely on business-as-usual. Rules to Break and Laws to Follow supports our belief that the key to growing a profitable customer base begins with deepening customer insight, choreographing customer interaction, and continuously improving customer outcomes. These customer-centered practices are the building blocks of customer trust."

—Jim Goodnight, Ph.D.
Co-founder & CEO, SAS

"Peppers and Rogers' latest book takes aim squarely at today's core business problem—the crisis of short-termism. Whoever reads it can no longer pretend that value is maximized by maximizing profits alone. Business success is a long-term proposition–based on trust, and driven by people. This book tells you why—and how."

—Charles H. Green
Author *Trust-Based Selling*, co-author *The Trusted Advisor*

"Highly readable and entertaining, this book provides a revolutionary insight on how critical customers are to business success as well as the impact customer and employee experience bears on today's business norms. Make sure everybody in your firm reads this book by last Friday."

—Dror Pockard
CEO, eglue

"Peppers and Rogers have hit on a key issue: balancing both short and long term priorities with a 'return on customer' lens. This is required reading for private and public companies to understand how focusing on customer value can truly build shareholder value."

—Jeffrey Bussgang
General Partner, IDG Ventures

"Score this work a victory for the future."

—David Norton
Co-founder of Balanced Scorecard Collaborative and co-author of *Strategy Maps: Converting Intangible Assets into Tangible Outcomes*

"Someday we will all look back and remember with distaste the decades we all spent worshipping at the altar of "quarterly numbers." And we'll remember this book as a fascinating read to help build a future of long-term profits, while at the same time create happier employees, and serve customers and shareholders."

—David J. Reibstein
William Stewart Woodside Professor, Wharton School of Business

"Don Peppers and Martha Rogers have a long history of challenging conventional business thinking. Fifteen years ago they rocked the marketing world with their seminal book, *The One to One Future*. Here and now, in *Rules to Break and Laws to Follow*, they once again provide unconventional—yet easily understood and highly actionable—insights about the wisest course to take in defining your future."

—B. Joseph Pine II and James H. Gilmore
Authors, *Authenticity: What Consumers Really Want*

RULES TO BREAK AND
LAWS TO FOLLOW

RULES TO BREAK AND LAWS TO FOLLOW

How Your Business can Beat the Crisis of Short-Termism

DON PEPPERS
MARTHA ROGERS, PH. D.

WILEY

John Wiley & Sons, Inc.

For general information on our other products and services, or technical support, please contact our Customer Care Department within the United States at 800-762-2974, outside the United States at 317-572-3993 or fax 317-572-4002.

Wiley also publishes its books in a variety of electronic formats. Some content that appears in print may not be available in electronic books.

For more information about Wiley products, visit our Web site at http://www.wiley.com.

Library of Congress Cataloging-in-Publication Data

Peppers, Don.
  Rules to break and laws to follow: how your business can beat the crisis of short-termism
  / Don Peppers, Martha Rogers.
      p.   cm.
  Includes bibliographical references and index.
  ISBN 978-0-470-22754-1 (cloth)
   1. Success in business. 2. Customer relations. I. Rogers,
Martha, Ph.D. II. Title.
   HF5386.P472 2008
   658.4'09–dc22
                                                    2007045706

Printed in the United States of America

10 9 8 7 6 5 4 3 2 1

To Marilyn Carlson Nelson
She has been honored by presidents and kings
Served tirelessly
Upheld and led genuine integrity
She is a visionary, CEO,
and our good friend

Other Books by Don Peppers and Martha Rogers, Ph.D.

The One to One Future: Building Relationships One Customer at a Time, 1993, revised 1997

Enterprise One to One: Tools for Competing in the Interactive Age, 1997

The One to One Fieldbook: The Complete Toolkit for Implementing a 1to1 Marketing Program (with Bob Dorf), 1998

The One-to-One Manager: Real-World Lessons in Customer Relationship Management, 1999

One to One B2B: Customer Development Strategies for the Business-to-Business World, 2001

Managing Customer Relationships: A Strategic Framework, 2004

Return on Customer: Creating Maximum Value from Your Scarcest Resource, 2005

Microsoft Executive Leadership Series: Series Foreword

The Microsoft Executive Leadership Series provides leaders with inspiration and examples to consider when forming business strategies to stand the test of time. As the pace of change quickens and the influence of social demographics, the impact of educational reform, and the impetus of national interests evolve, organizations that understand and embrace these underlying forces can build strategy on solid ground. Increasingly, information technology is bridging social, educational, and international distances, and empowering people to perform at their fullest potential. Organizations that succeed in the enlightened use of technology will increasingly differentiate themselves in the marketplace for talent, raw materials, and customers.

I talk nearly every day to executives and policy makers grappling with issues like globalization, workforce evolution and the impact of technology on people and processes. The idea for this series came from those conversations—we see it as a way to distill what we've learned as a company into actionable intelligence. The authors bring *independent* perspectives, expertise, and experience. We hope their insights will spark dialogues within organizations, among communities, and between partners about the critical relationship between people and technology in the workplace of the future.

I hope you enjoy this title in the Microsoft Executive Leadership Series and find it useful as you plan for the expected and unexpected developments ahead for your organization. It's our privilege and our commitment to be part of that conversation.

Daniel W. Rasmus

General Editor, Microsoft Executive Leadership Series

A Note About the Notes

We will be sharing two kinds of "notes" with our readers. Immediately following the Chapters, you'll find a list of "Notes," which are annotated in the text itself, and which provide additional information that would have broken the train of thought for the primary narrative. After the "Notes," you'll find a list of "References," which are simply citations for the sources of information, facts, quotes, and the like which we shared in the book. The "References" are listed by page number, and are not annotated in the main body of the book. You'll also find an index.

—Don Peppers and Martha Rogers

Contents

∼ 1 ∼

False Assumptions

The year is 1886. Gottlieb Daimler has just unhooked the horses from the front of a stagecoach and installed an engine in the back. He has created the first four-wheel automobile. But it's noisy, smelly, and smoky—mostly an oddity.[1] Daimler's company soon joined with Karl Benz and, early in the 1900s, the story goes, financial planners at the new Daimler Benz company attempted to forecast the eventual size of the world market for cars, looking ahead seven to ten decades. After careful analysis, they predicted that in another century there would be perhaps 1 million cars in use worldwide.

But this forecast, as audacious as it must have sounded at the time, was woefully inadequate, because by the year 2000, more than 600 million cars were already in use around the world. Nearly 60 million new cars were manufactured in that year alone.

Granted, this was a very long-term forecast, but still: How could Daimler's finance people have missed the number by a factor of nearly 1,000? It wasn't the time lapse that created the error. Nor was it sloppy calculation, nor the fact that in those days they had no electronic calculators or spreadsheet programs. Their error was due to a *completely false assumption*.

The planners predicted that in a hundred years, the world population of chauffeurs would be about a million, and this would be a de facto limitation on the growth of the horseless carriage industry. Their prediction about the world population of chauffeurs was surprisingly close to the mark, but their assumption that all cars would have to be operated by *chauffeurs* was dead wrong. The error was not in the accuracy of the measurement but in a false assumption about what they measured.

Assumptions just like this one—just as carefully and accurately measured and every bit as fallacious—are every day corroding decisions about what truly limits the growth of businesses—maybe yours.

Like Bell forecasting that the market for telephones would be limited by the availability of human operators to make the connections, or IBM's Tom Watson famously predicting that the world would never need more than about five large computers, it's not hard to be blinded by the current business model. Even when the model is for a brand-new product category.

For most of a century now, three unspoken assumptions have underpinned businesses' efforts to grow, meet financial goals, and make shareholders happy. But these three assumptions about how a business creates value are false, and we call them "Rules to Break."

RULES TO BREAK

1. The best measure of success for your business is current sales and profit.
2. With the right sales and marketing effort, you can always get more customers.
3. Company value is created by offering differentiated products and services.

What, are these Peppers and Rogers people nuts? Who could quarrel with the idea that the surest, most reliable indicator of any business's success is when sales and profit tick upward in the current period? When sales aren't that great, more effective marketing is what you need, right? Bring in more customers until you push the numbers up. And we all know that the most reliable way to do this is to offer products and services that have a clear point of difference, compared to competitors.

No, no, no. No to all of the above. These Rules to Break are really just assumptions about how business works, at the most basic level. They probably aren't written down anywhere in your strategy document, but they have almost certainly backed up your thinking and your company's actions for as long as you remember.

The problem is, each of these assumptions is *dead wrong*.

More than that. If you operate according to these false assumptions, not only will your business fail to create much value, but you'll also soon find yourself trapped in a *Crisis of Short-Termism*. Everything you do will be so furiously centered on making today's numbers that you will become increasingly blinded to everything else. Businesses swept up by this crisis find that even as they try to do the right thing for their shareholders, they end up destroying value rather than creating it. So while these Rules to Break may look no more dangerous than ordinary common sense, in truth they're deadly.

A "PERFECT STORM" OF NEW TECHNOLOGIES

Once upon a time, perhaps during the age of mass marketing but before the World Wide Web, these rules served as reasonable guides for running a successful business. But a number of new technologies have introduced capabilities and influences on business that have together created what you might call a "perfect storm" of radical change. Customers share their experiences electronically with millions of other customers. Business is transacted at the speed of wireless email. And the lowliest employee can leap tall corporate hierarchies with a single click. The technology of business has changed so radically that the old accepted wisdoms just don't work anymore.

In their place we're going to propose a whole new way of thinking about how to create real shareholder value in today's competitive environment, operating with today's technologies. As we explain the nuances of our proposed new way of thinking, we'll introduce 12 Laws to Follow— guidelines to ensure that your business can surmount the Crisis of Short-Termism smothering so many businesses today. No one knows how long these Laws to Follow will adequately guide your decisions, but one thing is certain: If you want to succeed, starting tomorrow morning and stretching out at least into the future we are capable of imagining today, then you'll have to start by standing the old assumptions on their collective head, because they've already become more destructive than helpful.

Which begs the question: If the Rules to Break are so wrong, why are they so widely accepted? Why is it that so many businesses pursue their goals this way, in just the way their executives learned in the MBA program, the same way they've always done it?

IMITATION, CIRCULAR MILLS, AND MYTHBUSTING

In a word: imitation. Imitation is one of life's most important defense mechanisms. Young deer learn to survive predators by imitating older deer that have survived predators. Birds learn to fly, wolves learn to hunt, beavers learn to build dams, and human beings learn to walk, talk, play, work, and flirt all by imitating others of their species.

Businesses, too, grow stronger and faster by carefully observing what has worked before and then imitating other successful businesses. Case studies, best practices, benchmarking, competitive reviews—call it what you want, there is no question that one company's success often becomes the object of imitation by others. (Listen, we believe imitation can be a good thing, in general. In fact, we're hoping you bought this book precisely because so many other people did.)

The problem is that imitation is so powerful, as both a learning tool and a survival mechanism, that when things get a bit out of kilter, the drive to imitate can sometimes lead to irrational and even self-destructive behavior. Army ants, for instance, are genetically programmed to follow each other in packs in order to find food, each army ant traipsing along in the footsteps of the ants in front of it. But occasionally naturalists have observed "circular mills" of army ants. These are battalions of several thousand ants that have somehow become separated from the main army, doubled back on each other, and are now marching around in a closed circle, because the leading foragers have chanced on the tail end of their own battalion and have begun following it.

When ants get themselves into circular mills, they will march around and around and around until they all die of weakness and starvation, literally *imitating each other to death.*

It seems to us that businesses have gotten into a kind of circular mill themselves—with each following the other in applying these three false assumptions despite the fact that these principles are no longer producing real growth. Most executives sense that business growth has become more difficult, yet their response to this challenge is to redouble their efforts and to apply these same false assumptions all the more diligently.

Businesses are doing the wrong things, for the wrong reasons, but doing them better, faster, more efficiently—even though what they are doing is based on assumptions as wrong as the belief 100 years ago that only a professional chauffeur would ever have the skills necessary to operate a motorcar.

The result is that businesses are following each other around and around, army-ant style, in a futile search for growth.

CRISIS OF SHORT-TERMISM: THE MOTHER OF ALL PROBLEMS

In our travels, we often ask chief executives and other decision makers what their biggest challenges are. We know this isn't a scientific poll, and we get a whole boatload of answers, but there is absolutely no question that the single most frequently cited problem is some form of this dilemma:

How can we do what's right for the company when the pressure to make our current-period numbers is so great?

The Crisis of Short-Termism is so all-consuming for businesses that it embodies many other problems, as well. Deep in our guts we all feel the need to "do what's right for the company," and we can usually grasp what the "right" thing is by paying close enough attention to our instincts, but the requirement to make the current numbers—to show concrete financial results *right now*—is so overwhelming that these instincts get submerged beneath a whole tidal wave of other concerns. The fallback position becomes "Make this quarter's numbers and the future will take care of itself," which sounds to us a lot like the tramp of army ants in a circular mill.

The most straightforward advice we can give business executives is to suggest that they change their mental models of what it means to succeed during the quarter or during any currently measured time period. And in this book we're going to do our best to give you a new mental model for business success, based on two very straightforward principles:

1. Customers will do business with you tomorrow only if they (and their friends) trust you today. Therefore, customer trust is a prerequisite for long-term business success.

2. Your employees will work to earn customer trust only if they trust you, their employer. So your job is to (a) motivate your employees to treat customers fairly and (b) enable them to do so by providing the right tools, training, and authority for taking action.

Obviously, this approach is going to be a lot easier for us to say than it will be for you to execute. But fortunately for all of us, the same breathtaking rush of technology that is driving businesses into ever shorter cycle times also makes it feasible to execute against this new mental model, today. To paint an accurate picture, we need to take account of how significantly technology has already transformed the business environment—and how the technology pouring toward us in the near future will drive more transformation:

- Technology makes possible sophisticated analytics to help companies calculate the current economic value of increased customer trust, which will be an important asset for beating the Crisis of Short-Termism.
- Technology subverts the power of hierarchies, which means corporate culture is now your most important management tool. The corporate culture that will give you the best chance to succeed will be centered on earning and keeping customer trust.

- Technology connects customers electronically with other customers, so bad news (and good news) travels at light speed. But because of the randomness inherent in how customer networks form, you can't "manage" them. All you can do is prepare for and encourage them.

- Technology undermines the advantages of new products, so business success requires constant innovation. To create a climate of innovation, you need to foster a culture of trust while harnessing the electronically networked intelligence of your employees.

QUESTIONS EVERY BUSINESS NEEDS TO ANSWER

To reexamine the false assumptions that seem to have governed business for so long, we will have to look carefully at some very basic issues. You can't come up with a new mental model for how to run your business today unless you can answer several questions:

- **How do companies create value?** Start with the simple and undeniable fact that every minute of every day, your company is going up or down in value. We're not talking about your stock value here but about your company's actual economic value as a business (i.e., how a perfectly efficient stock market *would* value your business if it really did know everything there was to know about it). Your business creates or destroys value with every decision it makes, every action it takes, every customer contact or interaction it has.

  The kind of value logged in your financial statements has to do with sales made, or revenue received, or costs incurred. But more often, value is created or destroyed when, as a result of some decision or action you take, the overall value of your company as a financial asset goes up or down. For instance, when a customer's complaint is not handled well, your actual value as a company declines just a bit, because the expected future cash flow from that customer declines. Until recently, it just hasn't been technologically feasible to track or project these small changes in the value of a company, and from our experience, the financial metrics are still pretty difficult. But it's no longer impossible, and the point is that even as a purely mental construct, this idea has some extremely important implications for how you manage your business.

- **Why do customers have more power?** People around the world are talking, blogging, texting, emailing, posting, and networking more than ever before, and in the future everyone will become even more connected to everyone else. One small aspect of this technologically enabled social development is that your customers now find it much easier to connect with other customers and share their opinions about your firm. In our first book, *The One to One Future*, published just before the World Wide Web arrived in the early 1990s, we predicted that when businesses became technologically capable of interacting with their customers in a cost-efficient way, they would use interactivity to try to build individual, one-to-one relationships.

The subtitle of that book was *Building Relationships One Customer at a Time*. However, now that customers are so effortlessly connected not just with the companies they do business with but also with *other customers*, you can no longer manage your business just in terms of one customer at a time. You have to think about the customer's friends, co-workers, family members, and anyone the customer has on speed-dial—the customer's social network. But guess what? Networks aren't as rational as people are, and are prone to highly unpredictable behavior. We'll explore some of the best recent work on the topic of social networks and delve into what it means for your business that your customers are becoming not only more demanding but less, well, manageable.

- **How can you use the network and your corporate culture to make better decisions?** As the entire world has become more cost-efficiently interconnected, most businesses (probably including yours) have begun relying on interactivity to run their operations more smoothly. Employees emailing other employees rather than phoning; invoices delivered electronically; orders submitted on the Web; business travel booked online; meetings held in self-service, password-protected conference calls; proposals, business plans, and other lengthy documents composed in sections and assembled effortlessly, without so much as a shuffled file folder. Many businesses have thinned out and flattened their organization charts, automating or outsourcing the vast majority of more routine business tasks that used to be handled by full-time employees.

  But while companies for the most part have used interactivity as a mechanism for streamlining and cost-cutting, the cleverer ones have also begun using it as a way to improve management decision making. Sociologists have long known that a group of people organized toward a common goal (such as a company's employees) is capable of making decisions that are better than any single group member could have made—better even than the sum of all the members' individual efforts. Employees electronically networked together can leverage this decision-making advantage and can easily come up with smarter decisions than all the "experts" at the top of the hierarchy. But it's tricky, because while networked employees may be capable of making better decisions, it's still the managers at the top of the hierarchy who have all the authority.

- **How do you stimulate more and better innovation?** It's not your imagination. The pace of change itself is accelerating, which means that creativity and innovation are more critical to your company's survival than ever before. Your organization must not only exploit its current opportunities fully but constantly explore for more, as well. No matter how innovative or interesting your product or service is today, tomorrow it will be a commodity. And tomorrow comes faster now than it used to.

To tap the combined creative powers of your employees and your customers, you have to create a climate of innovation that thrives on dissent, contrary points of view, and respectful disagreement. Doing this will require a corporate culture in which employees feel free to trust each other. It's the only way you can ensure that the pace of innovation at your firm keeps you ahead of the pack, supplying your company with more useful innovations, faster, than your R&D department would be able to manage by itself. It won't be easy, but the alternative is obsolescence, which will sneak up on you faster than you can text "LOL."

These are the themes you will find throughout this book. Each of these subjects is imperative for a leader of any size business to understand. There are numerous books written on each of these individual subjects, some of them quite good. Our goal, however, is to recognize that these ideas are themselves highly interconnected and then to weave them together, in order to help you think through a coherent and compelling new mental model for your business.

PRIMACY OF CUSTOMER TRUST

If you've followed our past writings, then you know full well how important we have always held customer trust to be. But with the technological developments and social trends just outlined, customer trust has become way more important and useful to a business than it was even a few years ago. We think this recognition of the power of trust will generate a much more fundamental shift in perspective than most people realize. In fact, we believe customer trust is probably the next big thing in business competition.

As we develop our argument, the many benefits of simply enjoying the trust and confidence of your customers should become more and more apparent:

- Customer trust will increase your financial value as a company, because customers who trust you will want to do more business with you and are also more likely to recommend you to friends or colleagues.
- Customer trust can serve as the basis for a corporate culture that will help you manage your organization more effectively, as technology renders hierarchical rules and structures less relevant.
- Having the trust of customers can help you reduce unpredictability when customers act together, as they do more and more often.
- Trust will speed up your company's operations by reducing organizational and bureaucratic friction, improving the decisions and actions of your electronically networked employees.
- Trust will allow your company to become more resilient, adaptable, creative, and innovative.

- Customer trust could be your saving grace if you have a bad moment, because when your credibility with other constituents hits bottom, it's the customers who trust you most who will come to your defense.

And most important of all, perhaps:

- Customer trust will help you beat the Crisis of Short-Termism by providing a guideline for action even if your financial metrics aren't sophisticated enough right now to be up to the task.

We'll develop these ideas throughout the book, but at the same time we will be proposing various tactics and strategies to help you earn and keep the trust of your customers. In other words, our goal here is not just to tell you why customer trust is so important but also to show you some best practices you can use to secure it.

Our first task? To consider the full implications of the three Rules to Break and then to terminate each of them with extreme prejudice.

~ 2 ~

"Value" Is the New "Profit"

If patience is a virtue, then few of us lead virtuous lives.

Think back to the last time you waited for a slow elevator. Did you find yourself hitting the button again—and again and again? Really think you sped that elevator up, even a little bit?

Don't worry. Patience may be a virtue, but that doesn't necessarily mean impatience is a vice. It's just an affliction, and it afflicts businesses as well as people.

The simple truth is that life really *is* moving faster these days than it used to. We all do more, we experience more, we buy more, and we go to more places than ever before. And, lest you think *you're* the one in life's fast lane, take a few minutes to observe how your kids do their homework while surfing online, texting their friends, listening to their iPods, following the television show, and . . .

Business is moving faster, as well. The same information technologies that have brought you more television channels, Web sites, customized services, mobile texting, interesting experiences, and time-saving conveniences have also increased the velocity of business, shortening the time between business initiatives and accelerating the rate of change and innovation. You can succeed or fail a lot faster now.

Economist Paul Romer says the speed of change is accelerating because information-based innovations and technologies have what amounts to their own network effect: The more technology improves, the faster it *can* improve, and since information now permeates nearly every product and service category, the run rate of change across many different industries is accelerating.[1] Because they are usually manipulating knowledge assets rather than physical assets, companies are operating on faster and faster "clockspeeds." These days, for instance, the time it takes GM to conceive and bring to market a new car has shrunk from 48 months to just 21 months. And Toyota can now customize an individual Scion car to your specifications in just two weeks, making dozens of changes to the car right on the dock where it arrives from Japan.

One of the most important benefits for an innovation is saving production time, which almost always cuts production costs, as well, whether the streamlining involves email-delivered invoices and electronic payments, or self-help check-in kiosks at airports, or cashless toll plazas, or FedEx drivers following computer-generated delivery routes that make fewer left turns, or Internet-based consumer research, or even phones that remember the last 100 numbers dialed.

And as information technology drives innovation, more economic activity consists of manipulating knowledge assets rather than physical ones. One of the innovations most responsible for driving the entire retail industry to an incredibly short-term orientation, for instance, was the laser scanner, which made product-specific sales figures available to retailers on a daily basis. According to one academic study, scanning data has led to the "widespread adoption of easy-to-harness, short-term measures," but the result has "made it more difficult for brand managers to maintain pricing power and compete in the market-place."

JABBING AT THE ELEVATOR BUTTON IN THE STOCK MARKET

The accelerating rate of change in business is reflected in the stock market, as well. Although the overall market is no more or less volatile than it was 50 years ago, the individual equity stocks that make it up are measurably more volatile. One study, for example, showed that the average life span of a company in the S&P 500 in 1935 was 90 years, while by 1975 this life expectancy had shrunk to just 30 years, and by 2005 it was estimated to be a mere 15 years. One result of all this volatility and change is that businesses and investors have begun to display the same level of impatience as we human beings. Instead of repeatedly pushing elevator buttons, however, the focus is on increasingly short-term financial results.

It doesn't help that today's investment community is largely driven by a relatively small set of highly competitive equity fund managers, usually benchmarked against their peers every 90 days. Fund managers have a strong incentive to get results as good as or better than their benchmark competitive set, so they regularly eliminate promising but currently underperforming stocks from their portfolios in order not to fall behind their peer group in any given quarter. The urge to do this has accelerated, of course, as competition among fund managers has sharpened over the years. In the 1950s, the average fund turned over about 20% of its portfolio each year, while today the *average* fund turnover rate is well over 100% a year. For a fund manager, it's better not to fall behind peers in the short term than to gamble on a long-term payoff, even a really promising one.

So the investment community puts intense and irrational pressure on companies to perform better in the short term, penalizing those that have good long-term prospects but don't generate immediate and demonstrable results. Paradoxically, this has been a complete and utter disaster for investors. Michael Mauboussin, chief investment strategist for Legg Mason Capital Management, says, "Short-termism is eating portfolio performance,"[2] and points to the fact that 90% of fund managers nowadays do worse than the most widely used general stock indexes. In other words, throwing darts at stocks and then holding those investments for the long run (not just for the short term) will yield a better return for the average investor than would be achieved with 9 out of 10 "professional" fund managers![3] (Ouch. We should have taken the stairs.)

For all these reasons, the "short-termism" problem for businesses has risen to a crisis level, driven first and foremost by our first Rule to Break:

RULE TO BREAK

The best measure of success for your business is current sales and profit.

Current sales and profit numbers are what the fund manager has to see, or she's going to drop your stock from her fund, and she'll do that even if she thinks you'll probably do better later. But when a business focuses exclusively on current-period sales and profit, it often will miss signs of weakness in the future. If anything, good current-period sales and profit numbers tend to reduce a company's responsiveness to the accelerating rate of change. And this is as true for a business-to-business (B2B) company as it is for a business-to-consumer (B2C) firm.

FOCUS ONLY ON THE SHORT TERM AND YOU'LL LOSE SIGHT OF THE LONG TERM

For years, thanks to its groundbreaking direct-to-consumer business model, Dell was the only major PC manufacturer making any money, with profit margins 10 points higher than its rivals. But according to *Business Week,* "Rather than use that cushion to develop fresh capabilities, Dell gave its admirers on Wall Street and the media what they want: the highest possible earnings."[4] Their false assumption? That as long as Dell continued to deliver satisfactory quarterly results, the long term would take care of itself. So by 2007, the original CEO, Michael Dell, had to be brought back to take over again and try to restore the company to its former luster. And within just a few months, the company announced that it would have to restate four years of earnings results because "unidentified senior executives and other employees manipulated company accounts to hit quarterly performance goals."

Dell certainly wasn't the first business to suffer because it tried to maximize quarterly earnings and profit, and it won't be the last.[5] U.S. automakers succumbed to a similar type of problem when they failed to plan for how newly available Japanese imports might alter consumers' tastes in cars. U.S. consumer electronics manufacturers made the same mistake with respect to their Pacific Rim competitors. Retailers that ignored the significance of Wal-Mart's new business model have yet to catch up. Most semiconductor manufacturers failed to embrace very large-scale integration (VLSI) chip technology when it replaced transistors, and their business was taken over by new entrants like Intel and Hitachi. In industry after industry, companies focused exclusively on current sales and profit fail to respond adequately to the innovations of their competitors and to the changes that those innovations inevitably precipitate. But as the speed of change increases, the penalties will be more serious and meted out more swiftly.[6]

Many executives recognize that their company's obsession with short-term results is fundamentally destructive but feel powerless to do anything about it. Others feel equally strongly that if they just focus relentlessly on immediate sales and profit, then the long term will be okay. But this is a false assumption, because the investment community's obsession with short-term performance is irrational and destructive. According to William Donaldson, former chairman of the Securities and Exchange Commission, "With all the attention paid to quarterly performance, managers are taking their eyes off of long-term strategic goals."[7] Focusing entirely on current sales and profit is a Rule to Break.

CUSTOMERS CREATE LONG-TERM VALUE, TOO

To begin extricating your own business from the Crisis of Short-Termism, first put on your customer hat and think about how customers create value for a company. With every interaction, a customer creates both short- and long-term value. In the short term, he represents revenue, since he may buy something, or cost, since you may have to use resources to serve him. These are the customer activities that get reflected in your quarterly sales and profit figures.

But customers also have memories. Each customer's decision whether to buy from you today will be based at least partly on his memory of any past experience he's had with you. Or perhaps on his impressions of you based on his friend's past experience. The important thing is that every time a customer has an experience with your business, his intention or likelihood of buying in the future is liable to change. Nice experience? Likely to buy more later. Might even talk about you with a friend. Bad experience? Likely not to buy much in the future. Also might talk about you with a friend.

When a customer's likelihood of buying in the future changes, or when his likelihood of sharing his experience with a friend changes, your likely future cash flow also changes—which means that your company itself goes up or down in value, as a company. But this kind of value creation (or destruction) is probably not captured in your financial statements—at least, not yet. Note, however, that the customer experience driving this increase or decrease in your value occurs today. While you may not realize the cash effect for days or weeks or months, the value itself is created or destroyed today, with the customer's current experience. This is happening whether you think about it or not, or whether your firm measures it or not, or whether anyone tries to manage it or not. The problem is that most firms' financial metrics just don't recognize this issue at all.[8]

There is a tension between creating value in the short term and creating it in the long term, because concentrating on either task can undermine the other. If you market too aggressively in order to build up current sales, you will almost certainly damage a customer's long-term value— maybe by cannibalizing sales you would have made in the future anyway, or perhaps by irritating the customer into not wanting to do business. Similarly, if you smother a customer in great service in order to maximize the future business he does with you—well, great service isn't free, and the money you have to spend today reduces whatever short-term value the customer creates. Therefore, you have to strike a balance, because your firm needs to create both short- and long-term value.

Unfortunately, for most businesses, the temptation to maximize the short term is nearly irresistible. Publicly held companies may have the excuse of investor pressures, but even nonpublic companies will succumb to the short-term temptation if they allow themselves to forget about the way customers really create value. Let's face it: Traditional measures of enterprise success drive short-term thinking and actions, but these measures do not account for all the ways shareholder value is actually created.

A friend whom we'll call "Fred" told us a story about his dry cleaner. He and his wife, both professionals, spend $100 a week on laundry and dry-cleaning services. Although the cleaner's regular discount coupon was technically good only on Tuesdays and Thursdays, the manager accepted a coupon any day of the week from Fred and finally got to the point where Fred didn't even have to surrender a coupon at all to get the discount. Fred was happy, and the manager was happy, too, making $5,000 a year from this one customer. All was well, until the owner found out about it and put a stop to this nonsense. If Fred came in on Saturday, he could pay the higher Saturday rates, and if he didn't clip a coupon, he would have to pay full price. What a clever owner! He saw a chance to take advantage of Fred's busy schedule to make a little bit more money. Wasn't long, though, before Fred figured out how to take his five grand in cleaning somewhere else. A few months after that, the manager found a new job where he'd be appreciated for treating good customers well. Short-term gain, long-term loss. You could see this coming the day the owner "fixed" everything.

THE SECRET LIFE OF COMPANIES: SHORT GAMES

Because customers create value in both the long term and the short term, you can think of customers as little financial assets. Each customer represents a bundle of likely future cash flows—costs and revenues tied to that particular customer's most likely future behavior. This is not a strange idea. There's a common term for the asset value of a customer: lifetime value (LTV). Sophisticated consumer marketing firms with databases of the transactional and other records regularly use statistical modeling techniques to forecast their customers' future behaviors in order to estimate their lifetime values. A customer's LTV is defined as the net present value of all the future cash flows attributable to that customer.

It's not an exact science, of course, and no matter how sophisticated the computer modeling becomes, it will never be completely accurate. Why? Because whenever you attempt to model LTV, you're essentially trying to predict the future, and in the end, you can't tell for sure what a customer's future behavior will be any more than you can forecast the future performance of a publicly traded stock, or the weather in March a year from now, or what fashion hits will really take off next fall. Nevertheless, the basic principle that a customer's asset value should be thought of in terms of the future cash flows he represents is very useful, especially when you consider how this asset value goes up and down on a daily basis with the customer's current experience.

The problem is that while LTV is a known and accepted concept in marketing circles, few marketers and even fewer finance people fully appreciate the real implications. Customers have memories and free will, so (unless you're the utilities monopoly) the treatment they receive from you today has a significant impact on the value they can be expected to yield not only today but also in the future. If a customer can be thought of as a financial asset, then *changes* in the value of this asset—changes in his LTV—are important. When a customer's opinion of a firm improves or deteriorates, based on his experience with the firm today, his lifetime value goes up or down, and the amount of this increase or decrease in LTV is real economic value that has been created or destroyed as a result of the customer's experience. In this light, changes in the lifetime value of a customer are every bit as important, financially, as the current-period sales or costs attributable to that customer and captured on financial statements.

Consider this analogy: Suppose your company has some physical asset, let's say a warehouse full of spare parts. Then suddenly the asset is rendered worthless by a disaster. Let's say a hurricane wipes out the warehouse, and you're not insured for the loss. If that were to happen, generally accepted accounting principles (GAAP) would require you to write down the value of that asset, and this quarter's income would be reduced by the amount of the write-down.*

Now think again about your customer's asset value. Suppose, instead of a hurricane wiping out a warehouse full of spare parts, you have some kind of customer service snafu, with the result that a very valuable customer becomes angry and upset with your firm. Because of this, his lifetime value plummets to zero (or even below zero, because he might communicate his bad feelings about you to his friends!). Didn't your company go down in value when that happened? Your future cash flow will certainly decline if that customer's opinion of you is not turned around again, right? Of course, the accounting treatment for this kind of "customer" event is quite different from that prescribed for the destruction of a physical asset carried on the balance sheet—but for now, don't focus on the accounting issues. Focus on the reality of the economic loss to your company.

Customers have memories.
They will remember you, whether you remember them or not.

---

*Yes, we know that the spare parts in the warehouse are already carried on your balance sheet, being the result of your investment of working capital to buy them, while the complaining customer's LTV is not carried on the balance sheet because the cost of building up that value was not capitalized but expensed as a cost of doing business. But this just proves our point! (For a more serious discussion of the accounting issues involved in LTV changes, see Appendices 2 and 3 of our book *Return on Customer: Creating Maximum Value From Your Scarcest Resource* [New York: Currency, 2005].)

What this comment means is that a customer's asset value will go up and down with her current experience, an experience that she'll remember later. You need a qualitatively different kind of thinking to deal with this concept, because your other assets don't have memories, do they?

- How you treat parts and supplies today will not affect the future cost of these supplies.
- But how you treat customers today will definitely affect your future profits from these customers.

The accounting courses you took in school didn't acknowledge customers as financial assets. But in the nonaccounting real world, a customer's experience with your company, its products, or its brands has an economic impact that goes beyond the current financial period. Any company that spends advertising money to improve its brand image is explicitly acknowledging this. Such a firm is investing money based on the assumption that customer intentions have a financial value. Affect those future intentions today and you will see the cash effect tomorrow, when customers spend more money (or don't).

Some companies have so internalized this view of the customer as a value-producing financial asset that it affects their whole philosophy of business. Amazon's Jeff Bezos says his firm would rather spend on free shipping, lower prices, and service enhancements than on advertising. "If you do build a great experience, customers will tell each other about that," he says.

One thing this means for a business is that, if you're talking about customers rather than products, the Crisis of Short-Termism won't be so much of a crisis. When you remember that a customer creates value not just in the short term, with her immediate purchases, but also in the long term, with her memory of her current experience, suddenly the push for short-term sales and profit can be seen for what it is: a destructively one-sided view of how your business actually creates value.

LAW TO FOLLOW

Long-term value is as important as current sales and profit.

———————— ⬿⬿ ————————

Our first Law to Follow points out a simple truth, and even though everyone knows it already, it still gets lost in the furious, frantic quest for short-term results. But no business can succeed for long by focusing exclusively on current-period sales and profit. Current sales and profit are simply one measure—an important measure, yes, but not the only measure—of a firm's value creation. Success for a business requires creating a balance of long-term as well as short-term value. Or, as John Stumpf, president and chief operating officer of Wells Fargo & Co., puts it: "Our responsibility is to leave the company better than we found it."

Creating long-term value for a business, so that you leave the company better than you found it, is the essence of good management and financial stewardship. The most direct way to ensure that this is, in fact, a goal pursued by your business is to focus relentlessly on the relationships you have with your customers—relationships that go on through time and extend across all your different operating units. Peter Wuffli, Group CEO for UBS in Zurich, puts it this way: "Our highest value is not in our balance sheet. It is in our business relationships."[9]

TAKE THE MONEY AND RUN

There are, unfortunately, many more examples of companies that have *not* internalized this view of their customers. And when a company doesn't see customers as having a long-term value that will be affected by its current actions, it is free to give in completely to the false assumption that its ultimate goal, as a business, is simply to maximize current sales and profit. Right now. The more impatient a company is for results, the more likely it becomes to engage in behavior that actually destroys value, because the more short term a company's focus becomes, the more impatient it is for immediate results. You can go ahead and jab at the buttons, but the elevator won't come any sooner.

The temptation to plunge full speed ahead and damn the long-term torpedoes is greatest when there is a big pot of short-term gains to be had or quick sales to be made, as was the case for Dell for so many years, or when a whole market or industry is in a rapid growth stage and competition heats up for a share of that growth. During the U.S. housing boom that accelerated with the rapid reduction of interest rates in 2002, there seemed to be no end of opportunity for reaping gains. Private investors were buying homes in droves, investing for speculation and rentals as well as for personal use. As the boom gained speed, a highly lucrative market developed for subprime mortgages—loans made to people who had little credit or a marginal financial history.

In January 2006, Ameriquest Mortgage Company, a lending firm with a national footprint that made a big business out of the subprime market, announced it had reached a legal agreement with a committee of state attorneys general. Termed a "final resolution" to the states' inquiry into the company's lending practices, the agreement required Ameriquest to allocate nearly $300 million in fees and restitution. Ameriquest's sin was a textbook example of short-term thinking: The company had enticed subprime borrowers into loans the borrowers couldn't afford, extracting large lending fees that were not fully disclosed, and locking consumers into loan agreements they really should never have undertaken. Then, as interest rates rose and the housing boom cooled, thousands of subprime borrowers began defaulting on their loans.

Following Ameriquest's agreement with the attorneys general, a class-action lawsuit was filed, and about a year later various Ameriquest employees began coming forward to talk about the shameful tactics they were pressured to use when enticing financially unsophisticated customers to borrow more than they could afford. According to one former employee, interviewed on National Public Radio, from the very first day he was hired, the company's training was aimed at showing him how to deceive potential borrowers and entice them to take the loans, right down to showing a segment of the movie *Boiler Room* during the training session and suggesting that the goal was to "make the sale at any cost." This ex-employee said that while he himself was honest with customers, many of his fellow employees were not. Often, for instance, an employee would white-out the income on a customer's W-2 and fill in a higher amount in order to qualify someone for a loan she wasn't actually eligible for. This was called "taking the loan application to the art department."

Because borrowers didn't want the low rates to go up, they were wary of adjustable-rate mortgages, which was Ameriquest's principal product, and the only product that could be sold at the rock-bottom introductory rates that were attracting so many subprime borrowers. But according to the employee, in order to ensure that deals went through without a hitch, some loan officers would print up fixed-rate documents and put them on the top of the big stack of papers the loan applicant had to sign at closing. The applicant would read the top documents more carefully but would soon simply sign all the documents (most of which were based on an adjustable-rate loan). Then, after the closing, the loan officer would just discard the fixed-rate documents!

Even as more companies than ever talk about "trust" and "ethics" and being "most admired," the obsession with current revenue and earnings at many firms has generated a pervasive culture of bad management. Poor succession planning. Over-the-top compensation deals. A refusal to hear bad news. Employee and customer discontent. Breaches of trust. Sometimes even, as in Ameriquest's case, outright fraud.[10]

BUSINESS MODELS BEHAVING BADLY

You don't have to be the victim of an outright fraud to encounter patently abusive behavior on the part of companies. You can run into that behavior every day because there are whole industries where the most successful business model is based on taking advantage of unwary, unknowing, or simply inattentive customers.

Too strong an indictment? Hardly. Consider these examples, for starters:

- **Mobile phone operators.** Do you know whether the cell phone pricing plan you signed up for is the right plan for you, based on your calling patterns? Pricing is extremely complex in this industry, and wherever there is pricing complexity, there is plenty of room for customers to make mistakes in their choices. Actually, someone does know exactly what the most economical plan for you is, and that's your service provider. But don't wait for them to take the initiative to save you money, because they won't, unless they can do so as a way to lock you in to a longer-term contract.

- **Credit cards.** Think of the consumers who are so financially strapped, undisciplined, or naive that they get themselves trapped into carrying large, rolling card balances, on which they pay exorbitant interest rates ranging from 15 to 25% or more (not even counting punitive monthly late fees). Get the picture? Of course, these consumers are actually the credit card

industry's *best customers*. Called on the carpet before
a parliamentary committee in the United Kingdom,
the chairman of one of that country's largest banks
admitted he advised his own children never to borrow
on credit cards because "they are too expensive."

• **Consumer electronics.** Here's an experiment you
can do on your own. Go into a consumer electronics
store and begin the purchase process for some big
item—say, a $1,500 washer and dryer pair. As you
near checkout your salesperson will ask if you
wouldn't also like to buy the "three-year, all-inclusive
extended warranty" for only a few hundred dollars
more. At this point, look him in the eye and ask, "If
you were buying these appliances, with your own
money, would *you* buy the warranty?" Watch his eyes
for that telltale shift, the flicker of doubt—because
the salesman almost certainly knows that the warranty
represents the highest-margin product sold by the
store and is rarely a good deal for the buyer.

SHORT-TERM GAIN, LONG-TERM LOSS

Often companies that might otherwise be well run and profitable will end up destroying customer value in the ordinary
course of business, simply because they don't have the policies in place to think more clearly about what they're doing.
Companies are large and complex organizations, and even
when everything runs smoothly, in the end there will be
situations you can't anticipate, problems you just can't plan
for in advance. The underlying business model itself—the
fundamental way profit is made—can be a kind of addic-
tion. And asking the addicts to admit themselves for rehab
probably won't effect a change. Generally, change will happen only when an industry is upended by a new contender
who, first, breaks all the rules.

Blockbuster Video has all but eliminated late fees (at least for company-owned stores and those franchisees who have bought in to the policy). This change was introduced in December 2004 despite the fact that late fees were expected to total some $250 million to $300 million in revenue the next year. The new policy should help the firm earn the trust of its customers, many of whom faulted it for making so much money on what amounts to "consumer error." Over the years, Blockbuster's late fees had provided plenty of fodder for competitors' ads and even late-night TV jokes. Still, it was a significant financial move, characterized by Larry Zine, the company's CFO, as a "double-gulp" moment.

"Any decision to give up profitability in the short term is kind of a big gulp," he said, but added that the company's marketers had told him late fees were the number-one consumer gripe with the brand.

Hold on, you say. Is this how it goes? We have to choose whether the customers love us or the shareholders do? Why would Blockbuster make such a financially destructive move?

Because, as Samuel Johnson said, "When a man knows he is to be hanged in a fortnight, it concentrates his mind wonderfully." And a financial hanging is exactly what Blockbuster faced. While the company wrung its hands over whether to make customers happy or to continue collecting high-margin late fees, a window opened for Netflix to enter the game with a hugely successful online, direct-to-home alternative with a completely new sales model.[11]

Nevertheless, Blockbuster eventually did get a handle on its own future and turned a weakness into a strength: With more than 5,000 retail sites nationwide, the company now offers the same online service as Netflix, plus the opportunity to swap your movie in person *at a store* if you want same-day service. Hollywood may turn out a nearly unlimited supply of movies, but only so many customers will rent six or more movies a month. Blockbuster, newly trusted, can now focus on getting the most business it can from each of the customers it has, over a long subscription period, rather than just renting videos to whatever consumers show up (and secretly hoping the movies don't come back on time). If only Blockbuster had fully understood the need to change its business model and had taken the big gulp two million customers earlier!

Now: Who wants to be first to upend the business model in credit cards? Or mobile phones? Or electronic sales and warranties? Or hotel check-in times? Or any other industry that is still doing it the way it has for years and annoying customers and employees all that time?

Look around your own shop. It should be easy to spot your trust vulnerabilities. Take a close look wherever customers are chronically resentful. Reexamine the most-hated employee activities. Try to identify the most resented fees. These are the places where your company may be making money today but leaking customer trust and destroying future value in the process.

In many industries, it must be difficult for employees to reconcile how their company treats customers with how they themselves would prefer to be treated, if they were the customer. We will talk more about this later in the book. But before casting too many stones at other businesses, you might want to examine your own company and ask yourself some hard questions about the degree to which your customers actually trust you.

Most firms will find that their market situations (and their own customers' expectations) evolve a good deal faster than the sales policies, marketing tactics, and service standards they use. For instance, does your company make special deals or extra-low "introductory" prices available exclusively to *new* customers? Do you pay sales commissions based on the profit margin of the product being sold rather than the profitability of the customer being sold to?

Here's another question you should ask yourself honestly: Does your company sell some products or services to customers that your own managers or employees probably wouldn't be willing to pay full price for, or hate selling? Do you make a large percentage of your profits from fees for services customers use only because they make a minor goof—such as turning in a DVD rental a day late, or overdrawing a checking account by a few dollars? If your own employees don't believe in some of your products and services but feel they have to sell them anyway, what does that say about your customers' ability to believe *anything* you or your employees say?

How do you find your way out before your competitors jump-start the process by cleaning up their act and exposing you for the bad guy your customers may already believe you are?

Has anything like this ever happened to you? An acquaintance of ours—we'll call this one "Jack"—told us he had been the customer of the same mobile phone company for just over 10 years, spending an average $100 or more per month—probably more than $12,000 in revenue for the phone company during his tenure. One day he called customer service about a $75 charge in his bill that he thought he shouldn't owe. He said the service rep, who was obviously working from a script about that particular problem, had been permitted no flexibility by the company, and actually apologized, saying "the system" left her no option other than to charge Jack the $75, sorry. Jack reminded the service rep that, long out of contract, he was free to take his business elsewhere. That he did, and ported his phone number over to a competitor, where he was able to take advantage of a special offer for new customers. Jack said he would have been happy to split the difference, but the rep didn't have the authority even to do that, and in the end it was the principle of the thing. The phone company had a script for the problem but no script for saving a valuable customer.

So the company lost all Jack's future business the minute no one could cope with a relatively small problem for a very valuable and loyal customer.

Which leads us to the question: Why does any company do anything so, well, *stupid*?

We think we know why. At that mobile phone company, as well as at many other firms, the customer contact person, the service manager, the product manager, and the CEO are all evaluated based on sales and profit *this quarter*. It is *the* overriding, primary, all-important goal, so much so that many businesses hardwire this short-term perspective right into their systems. You can almost hear the executive team saying "We *will* get those results, no matter what, and nothing will get in our way."

But financial straitjackets do not lead to financial discipline.

And meanwhile, who do you think is being held accountable at these companies for the thousands of dollars in future revenues put at risk to achieve the current goal? That's right: nobody.

STUPID IS AS STUPID DOES

What we've seen is that a relentless focus on this quarter's numbers produces one of three kinds of corporate behavior:

1. Bad: Stupid.
    Evidence: Decisions are good for current results but much worse for the overall business.
2. Worse: Unethical.
    Evidence: The business model depends on customers who are not paying attention to whether they're getting what's best for them.
3. Worst: Criminal.

Evidence: Someone settles with the prosecutors or maybe even goes to jail.

Note that this means "stupid" is as good as it gets when companies measure their own performance exclusively based on current numbers.[12] We cannot look around and find short-termism producing brilliant business results for more than a few quarters at a time. (Tell us again why companies are on the S&P 500 list for shorter stays than ever? Should we invest in "Just Visiting" signs?)

❧ 3 ❧

Customers Are a Scarce Resource

When you own a publicly traded stock for a period of time, there are all sorts of reasons why it goes up and down in value, including imperfect access to information, investors looking over their shoulders to see what other investors are doing, and even the way orders are queued into the limit-order book. The true value of a company, however—the economic basis for its stock price—is the net present value of the future stream of "free cash flow" the company is expected to produce. Fischer Black, one of the authors of the famous Black-Scholes equation for valuing stock options, once wrote that he would consider a market to be "efficient" if a firm's stock price was always between 50 and 200% of its true economic value. In other words, if the true economic value of a company would set its stock price at $100, Black would consider the stock market to be efficient as long as it didn't value the company's shares below $50 or higher than $200—which is a pretty wide margin of error, but given the fact that no one can truly know the future, perhaps it's not a bad guide.

This margin of error might not be a bad guide for evaluating customer lifetime values, either. We often write about lifetime values as if these future cash flows could somehow be calculated precisely, but the truth is there are way too many things going on in the future for us to be able to predict with total confidence any single customer's actual behavior. The pure randomness of any single customer's future behavior, as seen from the perspective of today, means that the only way a business can actually "calculate" customer lifetime value (LTV) is by applying statistical techniques to a large population of customers and inferring their likely future behaviors from their known historical patterns and other indications. The analysis can be very sophisticated but, as with stock markets, if your estimate of an individual LTV is no more than 50% less or 100% more than the actual, perhaps we should count it as accurate enough.

Still, this doesn't mean it's pointless to try to understand the factors that drive customer LTVs up and down. Far from it. To pursue the analogy with stock trading just a bit further, a smart investor will always try to pick stocks based on his understanding of a company's underlying value. The "inputs" to the investor's analysis may include such factors as the firm's competitors, its cost structure, market size, brand or reputation, management competency, and so forth. If one of these inputs changes—say, an unanticipated competitor emerges, or a new product launch fails (or succeeds) unexpectedly—then the investor will incorporate these new data points and revise his evaluation accordingly. The actual economic value of the company still may be different from the investor's analysis by 50 to 100%, one way or the other, but no matter what it's *true* value is, changing the inputs still will change the output in predictable ways.

In a similar fashion, if you want to understand how your company's actions today may influence the LTVs of your customers, then you need to have some knowledge of the inputs to these customers' LTVs. You need to know what kinds of things indicate higher or lower LTVs, for which kinds of customers. Then, by altering these inputs, you could conceivably alter the output in order to create new shareholder value.

For instance, if you operate a financial services firm, a media company, a mobile phone carrier, a Web site, or any other business that operates according to some type of "subscription" dynamic, then every year a certain proportion of your customers will defect to the competition or leave the franchise for some reason. If 25% of your customers leave each year, then we can assume there is a 25% chance that *any* given customer will leave in any given year. Your average customer lifetime value would take this churn rate into account, by reducing the amount of profit *expected* from the average customer by 25% each year. If, by improving service or changing the proposition in some way, you could reduce the churn rate from 25% to just 15% annually, then your average customer lifetime value would increase substantially.

New customer acquisition has always been the quintessential goal of traditional marketing and is something often trumpeted to shareholders. But raising your customers' lifetime values is just as important, because over and above whatever profit you are earning currently, increasing your customers' LTVs increases the value of your business.

This is an especially good thing to remember in view of the second false assumption in our list of three Rules to Break:

RULE TO BREAK

With the right sales and marketing effort, you can always get more customers.

Now, why would we label this a false assumption? Isn't the very purpose of sales and marketing to get more customers?

Well, yes and no. That may be the purpose of "marketing" the way most business executives have usually thought of it, but stop for a minute and consider the real constraints on growing your business. What really keeps you from growing faster? Is it a lack of products and services available to sell? Regulation? Is it insufficient working capital? Do you face a constricted or inadequate distribution system? If you're like most businesses, while any of these factors might play a role, the real explanation for why you can't grow your business faster is likely to be much simpler: not enough paying customers.

So the reason this is a Rule to Break is because you can't always get more customers. Much of what passes for "customer acquisition" activity is really just your firm trading customers with competitors. In reality, even in a world with billions of people, customers are still a scarce resource. For most businesses, in fact, customers are scarcer even than capital. And while it might technically be true that there's always another customer out there somewhere, the bigger truth is that the limited supply of customers probably hinders your business more than nearly any other constraint (although the limited supply of capable and skilled employees is a close second in many businesses!).

Despite all the lip service paid to "customer-centricity," this is still a difficult idea to accept. Lots of companies say they want to be more customer-centric, but in the final analysis, most still base their organizations, their planning, their management practices, and their metrics of success not on customers but on products and services.

Which leads to our third Rule to Break:

RULE TO BREAK

Company value is created by offering differentiated products and services.

Yet another false assumption. No matter how wonderful your products and services are, in the final analysis only customers pay you money. Said another way: All your company's income and all of its organic growth must originate from customers. Again, this is simply a well-established wisdom often forgotten. As early as 1954, in fact, Peter Drucker said it was "an ancient superstition" that a company's production process was what produced profits, famously going on to assert that "the purpose of the enterprise is to create a customer."

Don't get us wrong here. We're not saying that differentiated products and services aren't important, because they are. And we'll be talking quite a bit about innovation, because without constant innovation you can't have differentiated products for very long. But even if you have thousands of unique and innovative products on hand for immediate sale, you still won't make any money until you have a customer who wants to buy one of those products at a profit. By definition, all earned income must come from customers at some point—the customers you have today and the customers you will have tomorrow. You might call them customers, or clients, or patients, or students, or voters, or donors, or dealers, or members, or business customers, or end users. But "customers" are the only way you will ever get paid, they are the only source of earnings, and they are the only way you can develop your business. Period. The end.

Anne Mulcahy, CEO of Xerox, put it this way: "The customer is the center of our universe. Forget that and nothing much else matters. Employees lose jobs. Shareholders lose value. Suppliers lose business. The brand deteriorates. The firm spirals downward."

The problem is that, as businesspeople, most of us naturally think in terms of money and the efficiency with which we use our money to make more money. After all, ever since we set up our first lemonade stands, we've been taught that the scarcest resource we have is, of course, cash. So that's usually how businesses measure their success: return on investment, return on assets, payback period—some metric that tries to capture the rate at which money produces more money. But the implication of this thinking is that money itself is the biggest constraint on a business, which is simply not true.

While money definitely costs you something (that's your "cost of capital"), it's not nearly so limited as customers are. If you have a strong idea for making money but you need to invest something up front to make it happen, you can almost certainly get the funds required from somewhere: your board of directors, the division vice president, a San Mateo venture capitalist, the local bank, your Uncle Jim.

But there's no secondary market for customers. You can't just go to a bank, borrow some customers for a while, and pay them back with interest later. You can't clone them or create them out of thin air. No matter how much money you get from wherever you get it, there are still only so many hungry mouths within driving distance of your pizzeria, only so many children whose parents can afford your private school, only so many machine tool operators with a need for your lathe, only so many people with asthma and a need for your medication. Even if it's a *lot* of customers, it's still a finite number.

Unfortunately, most companies still base their operations on the dynamics of the industrial age, which, as one business journal put it, was an age "when capital was the scarce resource, interaction costs were high, and hierarchical authority and vertically integrated structures were the keys to efficient operation." But if you don't want to be like Daimler Benz basing its long-range industry forecast on the availability of chauffeurs, then shouldn't you recognize now that money is not as limiting a factor as "paying customers" are? And if money is not *the* most constrained resource you face, then perhaps you should be making your decisions differently.

USING UP CUSTOMERS

The constraint on the availability of customers is real, and there are important real-world implications to this line of thinking.

For instance, we know a multiline insurance company in the United States we'll call Company X. It sells auto, property, life, and health insurance through a network of its own agents, each having the authority to sell any of the company's products. Some of these products generate more profit than others. Life insurance, as one example, tends to sell at a higher margin and is less subject to fraud, when compared to auto insurance. To protect agent profitability and maintain order within the distribution channel, Company X doesn't allow any of its own agents to solicit clients from any of its other agents. So once an agent lands a new customer, no other agent from that company can ask that customer for additional business.

The problem is that for a variety of reasons—background, predisposition, expertise—some agents simply don't sell all of Company X's insurance products with equal enthusiasm and effectiveness. Consider an agent who has a fine track record for recruiting new auto insurance customers but then rarely if ever elects to sell any other line of insurance product to them. She has found that she can build herself a bigger book of business, faster, simply by concentrating on acquiring more and more auto insurance customers, a task she is exceedingly good at, rather than spending time and energy learning how to sell health or life or some other product to her existing customers. Of course, every new customer she recruits won't be buying any other type of insurance from Company X, because no other agent is allowed to solicit, while the agent herself is unlikely to suggest other products.

In effect, Company X is "using up" a whole customer whenever it sells an auto policy through this agent. If there were an unlimited supply of new or prospective customers, this wouldn't be a problem, but the supply is not unlimited. Even putting aside the fact that a single-product customer has a greater proclivity to wander away to a competitor, the real issue here is that every time the company gets a customer and does not get the most possible value from that customer, the company loses a real monetary opportunity. And it cannot simply make this opportunity up by finding more customers.[1]

With the right metrics and a thorough analysis, Company X might discover that the value this agent leaves on the table with each new customer recruited is more than the value generated by each auto policy sold. If that were the case, then this particular agent is not creating value for the company at all but destroying it! That's right: Company X may actually be destroying value every time this particular agent recruits a new customer.

Company X's business is based on the belief that as long as its sales and marketing effort is effective, it can always acquire more customers from somewhere. But this is a false assumption—a Rule to Break. Instead, to make the right decisions as a business, you must always take into consideration the population of customers and prospective customers truly available to you. After considering the whole population of customers and prospects, your job is to employ that population to create the most possible value for your firm.

Because customers are scarcer than other resources, using up customers is more costly than using up other resources.

If you let this thought sink in for a minute, you'll realize it requires you to adopt a different perspective on your business, and this perspective will lead you to make different decisions. Evaluating your business model, or your company's various sales and marketing and other activities, from the standpoint of return on investment or payback ratio or some other financial metric is important, but it's even more important to evaluate every action you take based on how many customers you have to use up to achieve the financial results you want.

WHICH DO YOU CHOOSE: CUSTOMERS OR MONEY?

Return on investment (ROI) measures how much value you can create for the money you have to use to create it. If you have to use $100 to fund an initiative, and you get that $100 back plus a $30 profit, then your ROI is 30%. If this is a better return than your cost of capital (the rate at which your company borrows and invests money), then it makes sense to take money out of the corporate bank account to pay for the initiative. If, however, your ROI were expected to be just 3%, which is almost certainly less than your cost of capital, then financially you would be better off just leaving the money where it is and letting it continue to earn interest.

However, because customers are the real constraint for most businesses when it comes to creating more value, if you make your decisions solely on the basis of ROI or other measures of *financial* efficiency, you may not be maximizing the value your company can actually create. No matter how carefully and accurately Daimler Benz projected the number of chauffeurs, that number could not provide the company with the guidance it needed about the real constraint on the business, simply because accurately measuring the wrong thing can't help you succeed.

Before burning us for heresy, consider this hypothetical case:

Suppose you and your leadership team are choosing between two different initiatives—code word for "internal investment," if you think about it. Each initiative will require

EXHIBIT 3.1 Which Initiative Is Better?

	Initiative A	Initiative B
Cost per customer	$10	$20
Profit per customer	$5	$7
Return on Investment	50%	35%

you to spend something in order to generate some type of response or behavior by your customers. A customer can be exposed only to one initiative or the other, but not both. And because this is hypothetical, let's make it really simple. Let's assume that each of the two initiatives has been tested already, so you know exactly what the results will be for each one. The only thing you have to decide is which initiative is better (see Exhibit 3.1).

- Initiative A requires you to spend $10 per customer, but it will return this $10 plus an additional $5 in profit per customer, for a 50% ROI.
- Initiative B requires you to spend $20 per customer, but will return this $20 plus an additional $7 in profit per customer, for a 35% ROI.

You know, of course, that "return on investment" should always be measured against the time value of the money invested, and in our hypothetical situation we haven't specified a time period. But solely for the purposes of evaluating this particular situation, let's assume there's almost no time lag between the money you spend on your initiative and the profit you make from the customer's response to it. Thus, for now at least, we can ignore the "cost" of the money required, although we'll come back to this issue very soon.

So, we have now completely defined a hypothetical choice your business needs to make. Which initiative would you choose, A or B? Be sure to select your answer before reading further.

Clearly, Initiative A generates a better financial return than B, because every dollar invested earns 50 cents in profit, compared to just 35 cents in profit per dollar invested in Initiative B. Yes, you do get a higher profit per customer with Initiative B, but it takes twice as much money per customer. So maybe you're thinking, for every $20 you could invest on a single customer in Initiative B, you'd be better off investing that same money in A, and applying it to each of two customers. Then for each $20 invested you'd get two times $5—or $10—back, rather than just $7.

But now here's the important question:

What if you only have *one* customer?

If you just don't have two customers, what would you do? In that case, even though Initiative A would give you a better financial return, Initiative B would put more dollars on your bottom line—a $7 profit compared to just $5 for Initiative A. And now suppose you discover that you do, in fact, have two customers (but that's all). Then you still have the same dilemma, right? Initiative A still yields the best return on the *funds* you use, but Initiative B yields the best return on the *customers* you use. In fact, it doesn't matter how many customers you have, does it? Your choice would be the same for three customers, or four, or four million.

As long as the number of customers you have is a finite number,
Initiative B creates more value.

So which decision makes more sense? The answer depends on whether you can get more money (probably yes) and whether you can get more customers (by definition, no). Given these constraints, you can choose either to earn a higher financial return but a smaller total profit (Initiative A) or to earn less on your money but a higher total profit (Initiative B). In both cases you will be "using up" all the available customers. Initiative B takes more working capital, but for a great return like this, the truth is you probably won't have any problem getting the additional money.

MONEY IS STILL THE ROOT OF ALL INVESTMENT

There's no such thing as a free picnic. To launch a new customer service initiative, or to develop an innovative workplace, or to undertake any kind of activity in your business at all, you do have to be able to commit funds, and the way you judge the attractiveness of your efforts is usually in terms of the ROI you expect.

As we've just shown, the availability of customers needs to be factored in to your evaluation. But we also need to consider the cost of the funds required whenever we undertake any activity at all. And the two initiatives in our hypothetical case require different initial investments. In fact, Initiative A costs half as much as Initiative B.

So, to take the cost of funds into account, and again making it very simple, let's assume that each of these initiatives requires exactly one year to produce its profit and that your cost of capital is, say, 10% per year. In other words, if you didn't have to commit $10 per customer for Initiative A for a whole year, you would be able to earn $1 on it just by keeping the money in the bank, or perhaps by not borrowing it in the first place. So, at a 10% cost of capital, the

EXHIBIT 3.2 Now Which Initiative Is Better?

	Initiative A	Initiative B
Initial investment per customer	$10	$20
Profit per customer	$5	$7
Financing cost per customer	$1	$2
Net profit per customer	$4	$5

financing cost for Initiative A is $1 per customer and the financing cost for B is $2 per customer. After deducting these costs from the profit produced by each initiative, however, Initiative B still generates more profit per customer than A, as you can see from Exhibit 3.2.

In other words, Initiative B still makes the most of your more constrained resource—customers—even after allowing for the additional investment required.*

LAW TO FOLLOW

Create the most possible value from the customers and prospects available to you.

———————————————— ⌇ ————————————————

When you analyze the "value" created by your customers, you have to factor in the cost of the money required. Once you do, you'll find that the primary constraint on your business is probably going to be the limited supply of customers and prospects available to you.

---

*We could have constructed the situation so that the cost of funds involved in Initiative B was greater than the difference in profit per customer, in which case Initiative A would have been the right choice after all. But in this particular scenario, Initiative B was better for your company even after financing costs.

WHAT'S IN YOUR BUDGET?

Because the prevailing philosophy at most organizations is that "cash is scarce," managers are given only one kind of budget: a monetary budget. Imagine that you are the marketing director for your division, and you're given a marketing budget of $15 million. Now, we all know why the budget is $15 million. Because that's what it was last year. Plus 10%. Or minus 10%, if you had a bad year. Or it's 2% of sales, or it's $500 per car sold, or it's last year's budget plus some increment for a planned new product launch. The point is, you are assigned custody of $15 million of your company's money based on some formula, and now your job is to make the most of it.

But—and this is important—as sacred as a monetary budget has always appeared to be, a "budget" is actually just an *artificial* scarcity of cash. It may seem very real when the CFO is breathing down your neck to stick to it, but deep down inside you know it's artificial, because you know if you had come up with a better plan, you probably could have gotten more money. But while your supply of money is an amount determined by your company, your supply of customers is fixed. Those customers and prospective customers are out there, already, right now. They're either doing business with you today or they're not, but there are only so many of them, and no matter how great you are at presenting your case to the CEO, there won't be any more of them. There is an *actual* scarcity of customers.

Perhaps you should think of the customers and prospects available to your company as a kind of *customer* budget. Then, rather than just focusing on the financial limits imposed by your marketing, sales, service, R&D, or any other monetary budget, if you want to maximize the value your company creates for shareholders, you should focus on the limits imposed by your *customer* budget. Because this is one budget that cannot be increased. Ten thousand customers and prospects? Twenty million? As long as the

ROI on whatever initiative or action you are considering is higher than your cost of capital, you will usually create more shareholder value by choosing the initiative that generates the most value from the customers and prospects available to you.

A financial budget is an <u>artificial</u> scarcity of cash, but a customer budget is an actual <u>scarcity</u> of customers.

Go back and think about Company X's situation. If the insurance agent is winning sales awards, then clearly she's doing just what the decision makers are asking her to do: selling more policies of any flavor to anyone who will buy them. It just so happens that the flavor she has chosen, for whatever reason, is concentrating solely on auto policies. But there are several things you could do if you were Company X, to deal with this problem. For instance:

- Instead of rewarding the agent only on current-period policy sales, why not also run some calculations to try to estimate the long-term value of each policyholder and then reward the agent for maximizing both short- and long-term value?

- You probably front-load agent compensation to encourage new customer acquisition, but why not also "back-load" compensation to ensure that the value of every policyholder, new or existing, is maximized for the company?

- Rather than rewarding the agent simply for how many policies she sells of any type (in her case, 100% auto), why not provide an extra incentive for selling a variety of different policies to each customer?*

---

*Even cross-selling incentives must have a customer-value component to avoid too-aggressive selling. See Naras Eechambadi, *High Performance Marketing: Bringing Method to the Madness of Marketing* (Kaplan Publishing, Chicago, 2005), p. 78.

- If you have a customer database and analytics capability, why not compensate the agent based partly on how much each of "her" customers is worth to the company overall, not just across all product lines, but also taking account of predicted future business?

Company X's situation shows that using up customers to make a financial profit has real-world consequences. Your business model needs to be set up so as to encourage employees and channel partners to act in ways that maximize the value to be created from each customer rather than maximizing the value that can be created through each channel or product line.

If you use up your financial budget before you achieve your goal, that's unfortunate, but with a strong business case, you can usually get more money to do it right the next time. Once you've exhausted your budget of customers, however, there is no appeal authority. When the customer budget is depleted, that's game-over. The only way to increase your customer budget is to get into a new line of work.

Our Law to Follow says concentrate on those business models and initiatives that will create the most possible value from the customers and prospects you have available—across all your different product and service lines, and including not just short-term but long-term value, as well. That would be the limit of shareholder value that can be created with the customer budget available to you. That's why the only way to create more value would be to start a different business.

From February to July 2006, the stock of Chico's FAS, Inc., fell more than 50%, as investment analysts reviewing the company's operations concluded that, in the *Wall Street Journal*'s words, Chico's "has been so successful that there may not be many new customers left to attract." Focused primarily on casual-to-dressy clothing for Baby Boomer women, the company rapidly grew to 500 stores with a very successful and highly admired retail formula. In 2006, however, investors concluded that the company may have begun to reach the limit of this market. For instance, one Piper Jaffray analyst pointed to the fact that Chico's was apparently finding it more difficult to get new sign-ups for its loyalty program, an important indicator of future business. The reason? Saturation. The company already had penetrated a large percentage of the population of available customers and prospects. The analyst pointed out that one in every three households with $75,000 or more in income now had a Chico's loyalty card, a substantial increase over the one in ten households that had the card just three years previously.

Chico's response to this market saturation has been to concentrate on developing three additional brands it created or acquired aimed at different types of women (mostly younger than today's Baby Boomers). It remains to be seen whether this will be a successful enough strategy to restore luster to the company's stock price.

RETHINKING YOUR WHOLE BUSINESS

Creating the most possible value from the customers and prospects available to you is not just a happy, customer-oriented bromide. When you try to put our second Law to Follow into practice, you'll find that it calls into question the whole organizing principle around brand management, channel management, product-based sales commissions, pricing policies, and service contracts. Customer scarcity strikes at the very heart of your company's reason for being. Just ask yourself how people at your firm would characterize the way your company goes about building its business. Is it:

- By finding more customers for the products and services you have available to sell? or
- By finding more products and services for the customers you have available to sell to?

The conflict introduced by this question is already faced by so many businesses in so many industries that it is, for all intents and purposes, universal. You confront it head on if you interact with your customers through more than one channel, for instance. If you offer customers both an on-line store and a retail store, or if your customer can buy either through a dealer or direct, then you have to "opti-mize" the customer experience across channels. When you sell more than one type of product or service to the same customer—a new car and a service contract, for instance, or a checking account and a loan, or a new IT application and the consulting services needed to integrate it into the system—each of these situations creates the same kind of customer optimization problem.

If customers really are your scarcest productive resource, then not only do you have to reorient your thinking, but you also have to reorient your *company*. Think about all the effort that now goes into making sure that every product line, every store or department, every factory, and every channel, is profitable. Does someone also make sure that every *customer* is profitable? And how exactly do you de-fine a customer's "profitability" anyway? Are you trying to estimate LTVs as well as *changes* in LTV?

You have brand managers, product managers, assembly-line managers, store managers, regional sales managers, ser-vice desk managers, and a "webmeister." These employees are crucial to the smooth operation and financial manage-ability of your business. You need them to oversee all the moving parts of your organization. But is there anyone in your firm today who is responsible for creating the most value possible from each of your *customers*?

At forward-thinking companies, "customer managers" can come with a variety of full or partial responsibilities. They could be called "segment managers," or "account managers," or "customer portfolio managers." If you set up this kind of an organization, you'll still need product managers and brand managers, but now the customers these managers serve should be internal—they should take their marching orders from customer managers, who are charged not only with generating current sales from their customers, but also with preserving and increasing their long-term values, as well.*

Clearly, making the most of the customers and prospective customers available to you is the best way to maximize the value you create for shareholders. But the organizational conflicts alone will require a great deal of attention because, so far at least, not very many businesses are structured so as to optimize their strategies around the individual customer experience, and yours probably isn't, either.

---

*For a comprehensive discussion of the organizational issues involved in customer management, see Don Peppers and Martha Rogers Ph.D., *Managing Customer Relationships: A Strategic Framework* (Hoboken, NJ: John Wiley & Sons, 2004), chap. 13, 359–409.

≈ 4 ≈

In the Long Term, the Good Guys Really Do Win

How's this for irony? At the very same time that businesses have become so concerned with short-term results that they resort to all types of tactics to pry open their customers' wallets, customers themselves have gotten smarter and expect more. And they're using interactive technologies not just to make themselves more knowledgeable with respect to your competitors, but also to talk to other customers who might know something about you (or your competitors). Thanks to blogs, customer review sites, online communities, and similar networking services, customers are now more in charge of commercial transactions than ever.

But don't take our word for it. Go ask one of your salespeople or one of the reps in your call center. In fact, ask any businessperson who's recently had responsibility for marketing, sales, or service functions and you'll learn that, for a number of reasons, customers are now more assertive, tougher in their negotiations, and generally more powerful than before.

So just at the moment that businesses are under more pressure than ever to deliver quarterly earnings, customers are suddenly and broadly empowered to do what works best for *them*.

Fortunately, however, we have a very simple Law to Follow that can help you deal with this new business environment. It is a kind of back-to-basics law, and it might sound old-fashioned, which it is. Nevertheless, we guarantee that this simple, one-step guide to policy setting and decision making will help you not only to deal with customers who are increasingly powerful and assertive but also to strike a better balance between long-term value and short-term results at your business.

LAW TO FOLLOW

Earn and keep the trust of your customers.

***

It's no secret that trust has become a hot topic, with a number of good books and articles written on the subject. This is not just a backlash against the various corporate scandals we've seen over the last few years. Trust may actually be the next big thing in business best practices, and in this chapter we're going to try to explain some of the reasons why.

There are as many definitions of "trust" as there are books and articles written on the subject, but it boils down to this: If you trust me, that means you believe I want what's good for you and that I have the capability to deliver on that goodwill. You trust your doctor not to make you sick just to collect more fees for making you well—even though your doctor certainly could make you sick, and probably without you ever figuring it out. If your child trusts you, he'll more likely tell you the truth, even though it might mean getting into trouble. You trust the bank teller to let you know if there's an extra $20 bill in the pile you just turned over to her for counting.[1]

It really isn't difficult to understand the key role trust plays in customer decision making, especially in a modern, developed economy characterized by an abundance of products and services for sale. Suppose, for instance, you are deciding which of several sellers to buy from. Let's say they all make products of similar quality and, truth be told, you could substitute each vendor's product for any of the others' and be more or less equally satisfied. In fact, there's no difference in price, either. Under these circumstances, which vendor would you choose?[2]

You would select the one you *trust* the most. This might mean the one you've heard of before, or the one you're most familiar with, or the one you've dealt with in the past. Or you might know another customer who has a favorable opinion of the seller. Or you might simply have a better impression of, or be more familiar with, a particular seller's brand. Or, if you have a very good relationship with a particular vendor, you may trust that company to watch out for your own interests and to recommend only things that would truly benefit you—you would trust the vendor to do right by you, and not to take advantage of you, even if they could get away with it.

Consider for a second what customer trust means when it comes to your value proposition with any given customer. You want the customer to create the most possible value for you, considering not just current sales but also any changes in the customer's lifetime value. And, on the whole, it's likely that a customer will create the most possible value for *you* at about the same point that he believes you are creating the most possible value for *him*. But when does this occur? Answer: When the customer *trusts* you the most, that's when.

Customers choose to buy from companies they trust because it is in their own interest to do so—because, in short, they feel they are getting the most value for their money, time, and effort. The highest level of trust—when customers feel certain they are not being "taken" and are confident that the vendor is watching out for their interests—also generates the most loyalty and repeat business.

RECIPROCITY: THE GOLDEN RULE
APPLIED TO CUSTOMERS

If trust means having a commitment to play fair and the capability to carry it out, then to be trustworthy your company must become a kind of advocate for the customer. This doesn't mean that shareholder value takes a backseat. All it means is that you know that customers who trust you are likely to create more shareholder value than customers who don't trust you. They are more likely to prefer to buy from you, both now and in the future. They are more likely to recommend you to their friends and more likely to be honest in their dealings with you. If you want to reap all these benefits, then your customers must trust you, and that means you have to be on their side. You have to take their point of view, and your customer relationships must be characterized by fair play.[3]

A sense of fair play means applying the philosophical "principle of reciprocity" to all customer dealings. Common to all modern religions and humanist philosophies, the principle of reciprocity stipulates that you should treat others the way you would want to be treated yourself. In Christianity, this is known as the Golden Rule. A verse in the Hindu holy book, the Mahabharata, says: "This is the sum of duty; do naught unto others what you would not have them do unto you." Confucius told his followers: "What you do not wish upon yourself, extend not to others." And Mohammed is quoted as saying "None of you truly believes until he loves for his brother what he loves for himself."

Feel free to take this approach out of religious principle, or not, but realize that applying the principle of reciprocity to customers is the easiest, most direct way to maximize the shareholder value your customers are likely to create for you. Either way, to earn and keep the trust of customers, you want your employees constantly to take the customer's point of view. What's it really like to be your customer? What is the day-in, day-out "customer experience" your company is delivering?

- How does it feel to wait on hold on the phone? To open a package and not be certain how to follow the poorly translated instructions? To stand in line, be charged a fee, wait for a service call that was promised two hours ago, come back to an online shopping cart that's no longer there an hour later?
- Or what's it like to be remembered? To receive helpful suggestions? To get everything exactly as it was promised? To be confident that the answers you get are the best ones for *you*?

For a business, reciprocity means operating in a way that constantly looks out for the customer's own interest, putting yourself in the customer's shoes, and seeing things from the customer's own perspective, whether that puts your company and product in a good light or a bad one. Honestly taking the customer's perspective is really at the heart of understanding and managing the customer's experience with your brand or product.[4]

THE MAN WITH THE FOLDING CHAIR

One day a few years ago, a top executive at Siemens AG was on his way to an internal sales meeting at one of the division offices, when he encountered a sales manager carrying a folding chair with him into the meeting. Curiosity aroused, the exec asked what was going on. The manager replied that whenever he brought this chair into a meeting, the whole character of the discussion was different. "Just watch," the manager said, as they both entered the conference room. Several people, including sales reps, were already gathered in the room when the manager brought his chair in, unfolded it, and set it down empty next to his own chair.

"Who are you expecting to join us?" asked several of the sales reps already gathered for the meeting. "Shouldn't we just get some more chairs brought in here?" some others suggested.

"No," the manager replied, "this is my customer's chair. I brought it into the meeting so my customer can sit right here and listen to our discussion." Then, with a nod to the empty chair, the manager said the meeting could begin. But, as the sales manager had predicted, the character of the discussion was indeed quite different from the typical sales gathering. Several times during the meeting, participants found themselves asking whether a particular point would be made in this particular way if the customer were actually sitting there and listening. Would we say this in front of our customer? What would our customer think of our plan for dealing with this issue? How do we think our customer would interpret this new policy? Would our customer agree with us that this is a good idea, or not?

In the corridors of Siemens, based on this and other similar meetings, this sales manager became known as "Der Mann mit dem Klappstuhl," or "the man with the folding chair." There's a lesson in this story for all of us: We should be putting the customer's perspective into every discussion we have and every decision we make. Nothing is more important to the long-term health of our business than the trust and confidence of our customers.

You might even consider carrying a folding chair yourself, just to be sure of capturing your own customer's views and representing his or her interests. Customers don't think about how our systems work, or what our business challenges are, or why we can't manage to get it together to do what works best for them. They just want what they want when they want it, with no hassle, no unnecessary effort. And they want us to play fair. In his book *How Customers Think,* Gerald Zaltman outlines the importance of mapping customers' thoughts about your company and illustrates a customer's thoughts about "a company that has consumer's best interests at heart" as combining dependability, honesty, patronage, moral character, responsiveness, hospitality, and dignity.

USAA, the San Antonio–based direct-writing insurance company with a legendary reputation for customer service, employs a deceptively simple rule for making decisions in all its marketing and customer service actions: "Treat the customer the way you would want to be treated if you were the customer." In other words, when a USAA service rep is making a decision with respect to the best product or service to offer a customer, she might as well visualize the customer as being in the room with her, sitting in the folding chair and listening in on the rep's own thought process.

The result is that USAA customers routinely swap stories of how a service rep saved them money by recommending a less costly option or by selling them a less expensive product than they had been prepared to buy. The firm frequently gives up current fees in order to ensure that a customer's interest is served (and long-term value is preserved or increased).

For a business like USAA, reciprocity means putting yourself in the customer's shoes and seeing things from the customer's own perspective. Of course, this is already an important objective for any company implementing customer relationship programs with newly available technologies. It's called many different things, including customer centricity, CRM (customer relationship management), customer intimacy, customer focus, customer experience management, and one-to-one marketing, but the common thread uniting all these ideas is the belief that a business can compete more effectively by seeing itself through its customers' eyes.

Few businesses are willing to carry reciprocity to its logical conclusion, however, the way USAA does. USAA doesn't give products away at a loss but simply treats customers fairly and openly, acknowledging and dealing with any conflicts between a customer's interests and USAA's. Occasionally this leads to forgoing short-term revenue opportunities. Often, a company can maintain present levels of revenue, but either way, the benefit of this approach is that the customer's long-term value, both as a repeat customer and as a reference for other customers, will be greatly increased.

Want to try an experiment? Find someone who is a USAA customer and ask what they think of the company. Do they trust its recommendations? Do they prefer dealing with it rather than other insurance firms or financial services companies? Would they recommend USAA to a friend or family member? Have they already recommended it at some point? USAA's biggest asset—and it is a huge one—is its reputation for trustworthiness. It is widely known and celebrated as a company that consistently acts in the interest of its customers. With this philosophy of doing business, USAA is building value for the future, balancing this benefit against current revenue rather than always *swapping* future value for short-term gains.

LAW TO FOLLOW

Really taking your customer's point of view means treating each customer with the fairness you would want if you were that customer.

It's a lot easier to take your customer's point of view if you can imagine him sitting right there in the room with you.

Research shows that companies like USAA, with excellent reputations for respecting customers' interests, get a disproportionate amount of additional business from customers. A Forrester survey of 6,000 North American consumers of financial services found USAA at the very top of the list in terms of customer advocacy (defined by Forrester as "the perception by customers that a firm is doing what's best for them and not just for the firm's bottom line"). The research firm maintains that customer advocacy is

> the best indicator of whether financial services companies are able to achieve cross-sell success to a customer base. . . . Firms that score highest on the customer advocacy scale . . . are considered the most for future purchases of products and services.

If you think about it, it's only logical that such companies would be considered more for future business, because when a customer perceives you to be acting in his own interest, then he benefits every time he deals with you.

The opposite of customer advocacy, of course, is what Fred Reichheld, the guru of customer loyalty, calls "extracting maximum value at the expense of the customer." Unfortunately, this is exactly the behavior many companies are driven to when they focus on short-term results rather than on the long-term value of their business as a customer franchise.

DOES YOUR FIRM PRACTICE RECIPROCITY?

It drives customers nuts when a company treats them unfairly. And customers have a very simple definition of "fair play." Fair play is nothing more complicated than reciprocity—applying the same basic principles to yourself and to your company as are applied to the customer. But it's remarkable how many companies fail this simple test.

A friend of ours told us he signed up for Vonage, one of the phone services that allow you to make long-distance calls for free using your computer and an Internet connection. As an Internet-only service, Vonage was extremely easy to sign up for online—just a few clicks and he soon had his monthly account set up. But our friend was not very tech savvy, and after a while he realized he just wasn't getting the value he wanted from the service, so he went online to terminate it, but—guess what? You can subscribe to Vonage with a few online clicks, but you can't terminate your service online. Instead, you have to phone a customer service number that is apparently never answered. Our friend said it took another month (at $30 per month) before he finally connected with the right person and found out how to terminate his service. He had to fax a written letter ending it all! In his letter he requested a refund, but he said he might as well have demanded to see Elvis.

Unfortunately, Vonage is not all that unusual. Most companies' everyday practices routinely violate the rules of fair play. Some examples include:

- You have a complaint for your cable TV company, but you can't call the local office, since no incoming calls are allowed. Nobody's allowed to give you a phone number. But they have your phone number, and they can call you at home any time they like.

- You make a mistake at the bank. Maybe you wrote checks a day early against the deposit you made last week. Your checks start bouncing all over town, incurring "returned-check" notices and overdraft fees. You have to spend time on the phone and at the branch to get it all fixed, and the whole thing costs you a small fortune. A few months later the bank makes a mistake. After you spend time on several phone calls, the bank merely gets it fixed, eventually, and apologizes.

- The telemarketer calls you at your home when she's being paid to handle the call, and you wonder whether you could call *her* back at her home when that's convenient for *you*?

- Have you ever returned something to a shipper or a store because you made a mistake? In many cases, the company will charge you a restocking fee, perhaps as much as 20%, depending on the nature of the purchase. But what if it was the shipper that made the mistake? It may send you a UPS or FedEx label to facilitate your shipping the wrong merchandise back "free," but would the company listen if you said you were imposing your own restocking fee for the trouble the company imposed on *you*?

- You buy a business class ticket on the airline, but the tight connection means there's no more overhead space when you board the plane. Why do the flight attendants, who are being paid, get to find space in the cabin for their roller-boards, even though some paying passengers will end up having to check their luggage?

- You have a problem that's already cost you too much time. Now you're told the reason your problem can't be solved is "company policy." Why would anyone at the company think you would be remotely interested in their "policy," when you don't even work for them? And why should you follow *their* policy, if they won't even consider following *your* policy?

Companies busy with process and today's results will simply not notice how unfair the situation is. These are companies that haven't thought about the customer's point of view since Chaucer wrote books in Middle English. But the customer thinks about it all the time. And he tells his friends. If you don't play fair, don't expect to create a lot of shareholder value.

This is probably why we see more and more businesses assigning "customer advocates" (although we believe that every person on your payroll should really be a customer advocate!) and why more and more CMOs run "The Office of the Customer" rather than the "marketing department."

At Big River Telephone, a locally owned Midwest company offering premium service to some 30,000 customers, CEO Kevin Cantwell gives customers a toll-free number that rings directly into his own home. He began his tenure at Big River by leading an effort to rip out the network of interactive voice response (IVR) units at the company and replace them with live customer service representatives. Over the five years that customers have had his own home number, he said he's received just three calls, which is certainly a testament to Big River's service quality.

If you're worried about how your own customers see you when it comes to making human contact, you might log on to the Web site Gethuman.com, a project by Paul English, the cofounder and chief technology officer of Kayak .com, the travel site. GetHuman.com is a user-generated compendium of more than 500 companies' toll-free numbers, showing the tricks on the phone that are best to reach a live, human operator at each one. Oh, and the users also grade the companies, with marks of A through F, depending on how difficult it is to reach an actual human being at each.

CUSTOMER TRUST IS AN ANTIDOTE TO SHORT-TERMISM

Working to earn the trust of customers is a simple mechanism to help get your business to focus on creating both long- and short-term value rather than simply trying to maximize current-period sales and profit. There is a lot more to the concept of "trust" than we've covered so far, so stay tuned and we'll come back to this topic later, when we talk about using trust both as a basis for a better, more productive corporate culture (Chapter 6), and as a linchpin for creating a more resilient and innovative organization (Chapter 10).

However, for now we can think of customer trust as a simple shortcut to creating real value for your business and extricating yourself from the Crisis of Short-Termism. As we will see, if this is your goal, then concentrating on earning the trust of your customers is a strategy that will be hard to beat.

Great brands tend to inspire the trust of customers, and such trust can come because customers identify personally with a brand, or because they admire and respect it, or simply because they remember it and are more familiar with it. The right advertising can help create a trusted brand, but Amazon, USAA, and Google prove that big-media advertising is not always necessary. And customers understand full well that brand claims asserted in advertising campaigns—even when they're about fairness and trust—are not necessarily the same as the real deal.

In the end, it's your company's reputation that matters, and whether this reputation was created through great advertising, or—more likely—developed as the result of news coverage or customer word of mouth, having a trustworthy reputation is clearly a great asset for a business. According to Reichheld:

> Everyone has a reputation in the marketplace and customers . . .
> ask themselves, "Is this a trustworthy organization that won't take
> advantage of me when I'm vulnerable?"

We concur with Reichheld's argument that "you can't get rich by ignoring the principles that underlie all good relationships: honesty, fairness, integrity, commitment to win/win." Vincent Burks at Amica insurance told us: "Our primary concern is not how we look to Wall Street. We think our policyholders are our primary stakeholders. So we teach our employees 'Just do the right thing.' It's been working for us since 1907." Regardless of how a company comes to have a trustworthy reputation, the very concept of being trustworthy implies that the company will not be acting solely in its own short-term interests. On one level, this might involve simply giving a customer a fairer deal than she otherwise would have known about. Or it could mean providing the information to allow her to compare competitive offers directly—*your* competitors' best offers included. It might mean being completely open with the customer when talking to her about the merits of buying a product or service. (If you're worried about what all this will cost your business in lost revenue, keep reading. You can make your shareholders very happy by treating customers fairly.)

We met a vice president of a large insurance firm, in charge of the southeast region, based in Florida. When he was first assigned to the region, customer satisfaction was very low. Part of the problem he faced was that freezing weather is very unlikely in Florida in any given year, so many construction managers simply don't purchase freeze protection for their projects, confident they'll be able to finish their projects before the thermometer dips below 32°F. But freezes do happen occasionally, and when they do, the pipes burst, damage can be extensive, and customers call the insurance company, looking for relief. Of course, without insurance protection, there can be no payout. Customers are unhappy, and don't really care, at that point, whether it's appropriate to blame the insurance company.

So this VP instituted a new approach. He started by instructing agents to clarify the risk of freezing to customers, more of whom subsequently bought the insurance protection. But he also issued a standing order for his agents to contact every construction customer by voice whenever the weather forecast suggests the possibility of freezing. His agents were instructed to contact *every* customer, whether that customer had purchased freeze insurance or not, and suggest basic tips for how to protect a project from overnight damage, such as leaving water dripping so pipes won't freeze. The result of this new tactic is that the insurance company has less freeze damage to cover from insured customers and much happier and more trusting customers who bought *other* insurance from the company, as well.

Acting in the interests of your customers at all times is an excellent general guide for creating a business with lasting value. And when you look around at how cutting-edge businesses operate today, you'll find more and more examples of companies putting this kind of philosophy into practice.

- If you shop at Amazon and put a book into your shopping cart that you've already bought, before simply accepting your money and shipping you the book, Amazon will remind you that you already bought it.

- Rather than relying on the very lucrative overdraft fees that boost the profitability of many retail banks, Royal Bank of Canada (RBC) offers "courtesy overdraft limits" to nearly all its consumer customers. If you've been a customer at RBC for at least 90 days and you have a low-risk credit score and at least one deposit in the last month, you will have some level of overdraft protection. Not only does this enhance each customer's experience with the bank, but it actually increases the bank's efficiency during the check clearing process, reducing the number of complaint calls to handle and the number of write-offs, and allowing account managers to focus on sales activities. Overall, since 1997 the bank has increased the profitability of its average client by 13%, and increased the number of high-value clients by 20%.

- Progressive Insurance runs television and radio commercials encouraging prospects to shop around and compare prices. In television spots, the firm's agents check the policy premiums of its competitors, and if someone else's fees are lower, the agent lets the customer know.[5]

- E-Loan, the online financial services giant, went against accepted industry practice to provide consumers with access to their own credit scores. It also raised the bar for the entire industry by instituting regular, independent privacy audits, contending that stringent privacy controls were imperative if the industry hoped to gain the trust of would-be consumers.

- Community Financial Services Association of America is an association of 150 member organizations representing more than half the 22,000 locations in the United States where payday advance loans are given. In 2007, the organization ran advertising in *USA Today* suggesting "There are right ways and wrong ways to use payday advances. . . . Payday advances should be used for short-term financial needs only, not as a long-term financial solution. Customers with credit difficulties should seek credit counseling."

- At John Lewis department stores in the United Kingdom, the advertising slogan coined by John Spedan Lewis more than 70 years ago is "Never knowingly undersold." Sales employees of the firm, known as partners, each participate in the company's profits and will monitor other stores' advertising claims to ensure that no patron ever pays more for an item in a John Lewis store. According to competitive retailing executives, the John Lewis group "has become the new measure of trust and honesty."

- Discover Card is launching a new credit card that will rebate interest charges to customers who pay their bills on time. The Motiva Card will reward any customer paying on time six months in a row with a rebate that, over a one-year period, is about equal to a full month's interest.

Unfortunately, for most businesses, these kinds of actions still seem patently absurd. Few self-respecting business executives, responsible for bottom-line results, are going to "give back" to their customers money those same customers might not even know they could have saved. At most businesses, you would have a hard time finding support for a system that always steers customers to the best deal, even when they don't know about it themselves and are perfectly willing to pay a higher price or buy a more expensive service than they need—at least for the time being, before they figure it out and go off and sulk.

Why? Because for most businesses, the Crisis of Short-Termism is so acute that today's results mean more than tomorrow's reputation.

In your own business, if you want a customer to trust you, then start by seeing things from the customer's point of view. Understanding how the customer experiences your product or service—this is the real essence of earning a customer's trust. And in the end it will always come down to having a sense of fair play. As we'll see later, in societies where people are motivated by a sense of fairness, trust tends to be more widespread and commerce tends to move more efficiently.

TREAT EMPLOYEES THE WAY YOU WANT THEM TO TREAT CUSTOMERS

Reichheld says that a prerequisite for earning the trust of customers is earning the trust of employees, and he adds that this is often quite difficult: "Fewer than half the employees in a typical American firm think their company deserves their loyalty, [and] customers must be nuts to put more faith in the company than the employees do." Surveys clearly show that employees have a worrying level of mistrust and cynicism with respect to the companies they work for:

- 49% of employees do not have "trust and confidence" in their company's senior management.
- Only 36% of employees believe their leaders "act with honesty and integrity."
- Fully 76% of employees say that, during a recent one-year period, they have personally observed illegal or unethical behaviors at their companies.

Employee trust is not an easy thing for a company to earn, because hierarchically structured, top-down organizations are just not well designed to encourage trust. Chris Argyris, an academic expert in organizational theory, says that the overwhelming majority of companies have a big problem with what he calls "inauthentic behavior." Part of what gets in the way of honesty, trust, and openness within the ranks at most firms, for instance, is the natural resistance that bosses show to opposition by their subordinates. In a top-down organization, decision making is placed in the hands of higher-ups, an implied recognition of their superior wisdom and leadership character. But people have a natural tendency to try to avoid conflict whenever possible. Bosses would rather not hear about problems and subordinates would rather not have conflicts with their bosses. As a result, as information is passed up the chain in a hierarchical organization, it gets filtered in ways designed to minimize disagreement and trouble (i.e., edited to ensure that the higher-ups are not displeased).

Add to this the fact that, in the vast majority of companies, managers' incentive pay is based not on performance per se but on performance relative to expectations. The performance-versus-plan system can be easily "gamed."

Students of incentives and budgeting processes have pointed out that when you set a target for a manager's performance bonus, you are essentially "paying people to lie," because

> ... two things are sure to happen. First, managers will attempt to set targets that are easily reachable by low-balling their estimates for the year ahead and poor-mouthing their prospects. Second, once the targets are set, they will do everything they can to meet them, including engaging in the kind of accounting gimmickry that boosts this year's results at the expense of the future.

These are the kinds of behaviors that Argyris calls "inauthentic." As inevitable as they may be, they nevertheless undermine people's trust in the whole enterprise. Rewarding people for superior performance is a crucial management tool and an indispensable mechanism for improving a company's overall operation, but don't be deceived: Performance pay, especially when it is earned by individuals rather than by teams, is almost always going to have a corrosive effect on an organization's sense of honesty, openness, and trust. It may well be that the improvement in a firm's operational performance as a result of individual managers trying to achieve their own goals will be worth the cost. But unless it's managed carefully, performance pay can work against a culture of trust.

To earn the trust of customers, a company must first confront the culture of mistrust among its employees. If you want your employees to treat customers the way they would like to be treated themselves, then treat your employees the way you'd like them to treat customers. There's no more direct way to raise the level of customer trust.

LAW TO FOLLOW

To earn your customers' trust, first earn your employees' trust.

This is what Baptist Health Care found a few years ago when it tried to improve its levels of customer satisfaction. A community-owned group of five hospitals in and around Pensacola, Florida, the organization's initiative perfectly illustrates how closely customer satisfaction and employee satisfaction are related, particularly for a service firm. The hospital group had been involved during the early 1990s in nonstop merger negotiations with a number of potential partners. But as 1995 drew to a close, it had become clear that no merger was likely. In the meantime, employee morale and customer satisfaction had sunk to such low levels that the organization was rated in the bottom quintile of healthcare firms, nationwide, in both areas. Moreover, employee trust of top management was almost entirely lacking. As the company's CEO said, "In 1995, before our turnaround began, we were asking our employees to make sick people well, but we were expecting them to do it in an unhealthy culture."

At this point senior management at Baptist Health Care launched a major effort to turn these customer satisfaction figures around, focusing on what they called the "Five Keys" to achieving operational and service excellence:

1. Create and maintain a great culture.
2. Select and retain great employees.
3. Commit to service excellence.
4. Continuously develop great leaders.
5. Hardwire success through systems of accountability.

The secret to the first two keys was to create a work environment that employees would find fulfilling, challenging, and satisfying. It's easy to see that management made an explicit decision to focus on employees first. The "great culture" that became Baptist Health Care's goal was a "culture of ownership," by which they meant that employees should act as if they owned the company themselves. Taking ownership of problems and fixing them, keeping the operation moving efficiently, and ensuring that patients and others being served by the organization were satisfied. There were a large number of practical and detailed initiatives that contributed to the transformation at Baptist Health Care, but one of the most important had to do with restoring the employees' trust in the organization. Among other things, the new policies at the company involved more open and honest communications, sharing bad news as well as good, and involving managers more in day-to-day operations.

The result of all this effort was that within just a few years, Baptist Health Care had risen to the very top of the charts, in terms of both employee satisfaction and customer satisfaction, and it has maintained a position in the top 1% of its category in each measure for several years running.

So the question at this point is: If you finely tune your organization's sense of fair play to earn the trust of customers and improve their experience with your firm, how will it impact the way you create shareholder value? And how will you measure it? These are the issues we'll take up in the next chapter.

5

Increasing the Value of Your Business

Stock analysts, please tell us: If two companies have both met similar quarterly earnings goals, but one company did it by saturating a market with low-priced goods, conditioning its customers in the process to buy only with a discount, while the other company made those numbers but also increased customer trust and future intention to buy and recommend to others, are those companies equally good investments?

When companies focus too heavily on maximizing their current results, they often end up paying a big penalty in terms of future profits. Focusing on current sales and earnings alone is nearly always a recipe for disaster. But when you think not just about short-term profits but about long-term value as well, you'll have a better perspective on maximizing the overall value you create for your shareholders in any given financial period. Wouldn't it help if we could hold managers accountable *today* for how their short-term actions have affected their company's long-term value?

Which begs the question: Just how do we measure the supposed financial benefits generated by earning customer trust and acting in the customer's own interest? The straightforward answer to that question is to consider carefully how profits in the current quarter might affect your profits in future quarters, and then balance the two—because we don't want just long-term profits any more than we want just short-term profits. There is nothing out of the ordinary in this, of course. Any good financial analyst will tell you that when you evaluate a firm's actions, you have to consider how current and future cash flows are each affected.

But this is without a doubt one of the most difficult issues facing business managers. Jack and Suzy Welch, in their *BusinessWeek* column, "The Welch Way," put it very succinctly:

> Balancing the demand for quarterly results with the pressure for a profitable future is what good managers do for a living. . . . Look, anyone can manage for the short term—just keep squeezing the lemon, wringing out costs till there's nothing left but pulp. And anyone can manage for the long term. Just keep telling people, "Be patient. Our strategy will pay off in time." The mark of a leader is someone who has the rigor, vision and courage to do both simultaneously.

But we have a mechanism for helping you think more clearly about the issues involved and for conceiving the policies that actually will result in a better balance of immediate and long-term profits. We are going to suggest you think about the value of your business in terms of the combined values of your customers. You already know that customers are financial assets and that they go up and down in value, individually, as they experience your firm or your brand and their opinions about you change.

EMBROIDER ON YOUR CFO'S PILLOWCASE: CUSTOMER EQUITY

If you were to add up the lifetime values of all your current and future customers, as of today, the result would be "customer equity,"[1] which represents the net present value of all the cash flow that will ever be produced for you by customers. This means customer equity is really equal to the economic value of your business as a going concern, because except for the assets and liabilities you already have on hand, your future cash flows define the value of your business, and these future cash flows will more or less all be generated by your customers and prospects.*

As a business, therefore, you can create new value for your shareholders in two different ways and ideally, in both ways at once:

1. You can generate more earnings today, and
2. You can generate more customer equity today.

How do you increase customer equity? You could do a better job of converting prospects to customers, perhaps. It would help if your current customers recommended you to others. Or you could simply keep your profitable customers for a longer period of time. Or you could reduce the costs of serving your customers, or increase the amount of business your customers do by selling them additional products or services. All in all, these activities can be boiled down into three basic ideas: getting, keeping, or growing customers.

In the short term, of course, all you need to succeed is current earnings. But to continue your success over the long term, you must build your customer equity somehow. Your customers must not only buy things from you today but also have a good enough experience with you today that they will buy more tomorrow, perhaps even telling their friends

---

*Don't spend time now worrying about the practical difficulties of calculating customer equity. It is imminently practical with today's analytics technologies. If you want to know more, start with our book *Return on Customer: Creating Maximum Value from Your Scarcest Resource* (New York: Currency/Doubleday, 2005), p. 7, Chapter 6, and Appendices 2 and 3.

good things about you. In other words, your customers must trust you, and your employees must believe you're a good company for customers to do business with. Trust is the most important ingredient of long-term business growth, but earning the trust of customers and employees requires an investment of time and resources. So how do you convince all the skeptics in your organization?

Ironically, the more successful a business is in the short term, the less willing its executives are likely to be to want to make this investment. The thinking at such companies: "It ain't broke." Using traditional measures, the company is looking pretty darn good and doesn't welcome new metrics that may reveal a spaghetti stain on the blue serge suit. These are the companies that are most vulnerable to their competitors' inroads, customer attrition, and falling off the Dow Jones list the fastest, but it's hard to convince them.

Current-period business success comes in two flavors, and it's critical to know the difference and to manage your business on that basis:

- Good current profitability, and a reputation that enhances long-term shareholder value (have your cake and eat it too), or
- Good current profitability, with a reputation that erodes long-term shareholder value (use up your cake so there's nothing left)[2]

We've been suggesting all along that the Crisis of Short-Termism causes managers to focus almost exclusively on current earnings, while a more balanced approach is actually more beneficial to shareholders. Because customer equity is virtually the same as the going-concern value of your business, you can think of the lifetime values of your customers as a kind of weathervane for your business's value—when your customer equity is increasing, the value of your business is increasing, and vice versa.

You can also visualize customer equity, which is based on your customers' intentions and likely future purchases, as a kind of bank account for earnings. This bank account—your customer equity account—makes quarterly payments to your business in the form of earnings, as your customers follow through on their intentions to buy from you. To build up your customer equity account, you need to add more customers to the franchise, or increase their satisfaction with your firm, or get them to talk about you to their friends, or give them other good reasons to do more business with you over time. Then, as your account grows, it will be able to pay your business higher and higher quarterly earnings. But if your customer equity doesn't grow, or if it begins to shrink, then your business won't be able to sustain its current earnings for very long. Sooner or later, something will have to give.

LAW TO FOLLOW

Regardless of how good your current earnings are, with no customer equity you will have no future earnings.

Ask yourself what would happen if, next quarter, a fund manager or an industry analyst, or your bank, wants to know how much customer equity your firm has and how much that equity has gone up or down since last quarter.

We'll be talking a lot more in this book about methods for increasing your customer equity through innovation, networking, employee engagement, and customer trust, and we modestly refer you to our previous books on building customer relationships, as well. But no matter how you do it, when you raise the value of your customer equity you'll be raising your economic value as an operating business. Over and above whatever profit you earn currently, additional customer equity translates directly to additional shareholder value.

If customers are defecting from the base today, or if the lifetime values of your customers are in decline for some reason, then you are losing customer equity, which means you are destroying shareholder value. You could easily think of this destroyed value as the "cost" of obtaining your current-period results.

Now think: What did it really cost you to make this quarter's numbers?

RATCHETING UP YOUR CUSTOMER EQUITY

Verizon Wireless, a joint venture between Verizon and Vodafone, dramatically increased its customer equity during the four-year period from the end of 2001 through the end of 2005. According to publicly reported figures, the company earned $21 billion in operating income in those four years while growing its customer base from 29.4 million handsets in use to 51.3 million. During the same period, Verizon Wireless reduced its monthly customer churn rate on post-paid retail (contract) customers from 2.6% to 1.1%.

A back-of-the-envelope calculation shows that Verizon Wireless's customer equity grew by around $20 billion during this period. In other words, Verizon Wireless actually created nearly twice as much shareholder value as was reflected in its income statements during these four years. About half the increase in customer equity was attributable to new customers acquired, while the other half came from the increased lifetime values (LTVs) of all customers, due to the dramatic reduction in customer churn during the period.

The truth is, Verizon Wireless's four-year surge in value creation was probably a one-time event for the company, because the more customer churn has been reduced, the harder and costlier it becomes to reduce it further. But other wireless firms throughout the world face opportunities every bit as rich as this, and for the most part they have failed to take advantage of them. In fact, if anything, there is strong evidence that many mobile telecom companies are running in the opposite direction, chipping away at their customer equity as they compete fiercely to acquire new customers at any cost—even when it means acquiring customers with lower and lower LTVs at higher and higher acquisition costs.

As we said earlier, growing your customer equity requires you to get more customers, or to keep them longer, or to grow them bigger, or some combination of these. Get, keep, grow. Unfortunately, the quintessential focus of traditional marketing has always emphasized the getting part, and a robust customer acquisition rate is often trumpeted to shareholders as an indication of a company's steadily increasing shareholder value. Keeping your existing customers longer or growing them into bigger or more profitable customers (i.e., increasing the average lifetime values of your customers) is not as easily measured, nor is it called to investors' attention so often.

Forecasting your customers' future behaviors and estimating the financial impact will never be simple, but with the customer analytics and statistical tools now available, it's no longer rocket science, either. There are some straightforward factors that contribute to increases or decreases in your customer equity, some of which we've already mentioned. Acquire more customers. Acquire customers who are more valuable. Increase your profit per customer. Reduce your servicing costs per customer. Sell customers additional products or services. Increase the propensity of customers to refer other customers. Many of these factors can be measured currently but will affect how your customers buy from you in the future. They are "leading indicators" of LTV change, and based on the type of customer data you have, you may be able to correlate these indicators with the types of customer behavior changes they might suggest.

The conflict between achieving short-term results and preserving or increasing long-term value is one of the most serious difficulties any business faces. If you allow yourself to be seduced by short-term goals, you'll not only penalize good management practices at your firm, but you'll also undermine the trustworthiness and ethics of your managers, in effect encouraging them to "steal" from the future to fund the present. And this lesson will soon permeate the entire organization. Remember the mobile phone company whose service rep refused to budge on a disputed $75 bill sent to an irate $1,000-a-year customer? If you asked the rep whether her action had destroyed value for the company, we bet she would have been dumbfounded by the question. Of course not, she would have said. I *added* value—$75, to be exact. But did she?

By analyzing your business in terms of its customer equity, you'll be able to deal more effectively with the Crisis of Short-Termism. Your financial goal should be to earn a profit today and *also* add to your firm's customer equity. Ideally, you will find a strategy for your business that maximizes the overall combination of (1) current earnings (including profit or loss) and (2) changes in customer equity (including increases or decreases). Have your cake and eat it, too.

WHAT RETURN ARE YOU GETTING ON YOUR CUSTOMERS?

If customers are a scarce productive resource—imposing a constraint on your company's growth—then it would make sense to track how efficiently you use this resource to create value. If you were tracking the efficiency of the money you had to use to create more value, you would use some metric such as return on investment. But for understanding how well you are using customers, Return on Customer^{sm} (ROC^{sm})* is the metric you need. ROC will provide your company with financial bifocals—a single lens through which you can see your earnings from customers clearly, whether these earnings are up close and immediate or in the more distant long term.

To understand the ROC metric, start with a simple analogy. Imagine that last year you bought a stock for $100, and during the year you received a dividend payment of $5, while the stock price climbed to $110 by the end of the year. So your total return on investment for the year was 15%. You put up $100 initially, and the total new value created amounted to 15% of that initial investment. If, however, the stock price had fallen $10 during the year, from $100 down to $90, then your total return on investment would have been a negative 5%, and even though you received a $5 dividend, you would have suffered a net loss overall.

Now apply that thinking to customers. Suppose you began the year with a customer who had an estimated lifetime value of $100, and during the year you made a profit from the customer of $5. And let's say by the end of the year your calculation shows that the customer's LTV had increased to $110. In that case, your ROC was 15%. This measurement of your economic performance that year with respect to this customer captures not just the sales you generated from the customer during the year but also the change, if any, in the customer's value to your business—value that is based on his likely future purchases, recommendations to friends, and so forth, as modeled in your customer database.

---

*Return on Customer^{sm} and ROC^{sm} are registered service marks of Peppers & Rogers Group, a division of Carlson Marketing Worldwide.

To understand why ROC is important, go back to the stock purchase for a minute, and suppose that the only information you have is how much the dividend is. You can't see whether the value of the underlying stock is increasing or not. In that case, even though the actual value of the stock will be going up and down all the time, you really can't say how well your investment is doing. So far as you're concerned, as long as the dividend continues or increases, you seem to be doing just fine, but the truth is that without also knowing how the stock price is changing, it's impossible to say whether you're really creating value or not.

We find that many companies are content to measure, carefully and sometimes maniacally, their current sales from customers, without ever noticing, or measuring, or demanding to know how much the customer equity lying underneath the current numbers has gone up or down. But because customers are a scarce resource for businesses, when a company doesn't try to measure how much of that resource is being used up to create its current numbers, it is getting an incomplete picture of its financial performance.

If you calculate ROC with respect to your company's total customer equity,[3] the result you get is mathematically the same as your total shareholder return (TSR) during the period. Remember that customer equity is virtually the same thing as the value of your firm as an operating business. Therefore, ROC equals TSR.

Return on Customer = Total Shareholder Return

If you try to estimate ROC and use it to begin tunneling a path through the mountain of your company's financial performance, while the accountants try to estimate TSR and begin tunneling toward you on the opposite side, you should meet at roughly the same place in the middle. Because of the ROC = TSR connection, you can be truly happy with your Return on Customer only when it exceeds your cost of capital, because only then are you actually creating value, overall, for your business.

When ROC is less than your cost of capital, leave your money in the bank.

This applies whether you are calculating ROC for the whole company or for some smaller subset of customers and prospects. You know that you don't create value for your business when your TSR is lower than your cost of capital, and this means that ROC must always be higher than your cost of capital, as well. Otherwise, even though you may be generating a current-period profit, you aren't benefiting your shareholders![4]

Many companies that show little growth or hard-fought, tepid earnings are actually not creating net new shareholder value at all but simply harvesting the customer lifetime values they already have "in the bank." If you want your company to continue to grow, then you have to ensure that every sales, service, and marketing initiative will yield a Return on Customer greater than your cost of capital. That way, even as you're realizing earnings in the current period, you'll be building enough new customer equity to support future earnings, as well.

VALUE CREATORS, VALUE HARVESTERS, AND VALUE DESTROYERS

Analyzing your company's ROC at the enterprise level can help clarify your financial prospects in ways that your traditional financial statement isn't likely to reveal. Exhibit 5.1 classifies five different hypothetical companies into three categories, depending on whether each company is creating value, destroying it, or merely harvesting it.

Exhibit 5.1 Are You Creating, Harvesting, or Destroying Value?

	Company 1	Company 2	Company 3	Company 4	Company 5
Customer equity at beginning of year	$1,000	$1,000	$1,000	$1,000	$1,000
Customer equity at end of year	$1,200	$1,200	$1,020	$950	$900
Change in customer equity during year	$200	$200	$20	−$50	−$100
Profit during year	$50	−$50	$30	$50	$50
Total customer value created	$250	$150	$50	$0	−$50
Return on Customer	25%	15%	5%	0%	−5%
	Value Creators		Value Harvesters		Value Destroyer

We are indebted to the insights of Taylor Duersch and other members of Carlson Marketing's Decision Sciences team for helping us to clarify the role that customer equity plays in future earnings.

Companies 1 and 2 in this exhibit are value creators. For these two companies, the combination of short- and long-term value created by their customers is occurring at a rate that is almost certainly higher than their cost of capital. In each case they are ending their year with higher customer equity than they started with, so they can expect to grow their earnings in future years. While it's clear they each are creating net new value for their shareholders, in Company 2's case this net new value is being created despite the fact that the firm's current profits are actually negative.

Companies 3 and 4, however, are value harvesters. They are simply treading the financial water by harvesting customer profits already "put in the bank" in the form of customer equity. Their ROC is not negative, but it is clearly below their cost of capital. While each is earning a current profit, neither one is replenishing its customer equity enough, so it's unlikely that either of these companies will be able to achieve much growth in future years. They may continue to report lukewarm, increasingly difficult profits for the time being, but sooner or later their customer equity will no longer be sufficient to sustain a profit at all. Technically, they may not be destroying shareholder value yet, but if these firms were people they would be living off their savings.

As a value destroyer, Company 5 is in the worst situation of all, with ROC below zero. True, the company has scraped out a profit this year, but this profit was achieved only by stealing even more from the future. One can imagine a car manufacturer offering the deepest-ever discounts in order to prop up this year's numbers, saddling itself in the process with a saturated market and customers trained to wait for discounts, creating a much more difficult problem when it comes to making next year's numbers. Company 5 is on the skids, whether this is revealed in its current financial statements or not. It may be reporting a profit to shareholders. But shareholders who ask whether this company has the

ROC necessary to sustain this level of earnings will see that the answer is no. What this firm is really doing is "eating itself" and reporting the meal as a profit.

From the figures in Exhibit 5.1, it should be clear what kind of company represents the best value for an investor, although to a large extent savvy investors will have already discounted each firm's stock price to reflect its growth prospects. Nevertheless, if a firm succeeds in converting itself from one class to another—say, from value harvester to value creator—this will likely have a major impact on its economic value as an operating business. As investors uncover this information, perhaps by demanding ROC figures, the firm's stock will almost certainly be revalued in a significant way.

The Verizon Wireless case we just discussed somewhat resembles Company 1's situation in the exhibit. The firm produced good earnings while simultaneously accumulating even more customer equity. We calculated Verizon Wireless's ROC in each of those four years, and it averaged a whopping 68% annually. Stated differently, each year during the period we analyzed, Verizon Wireless created enough total new value to equal about two-thirds of its value as an operating company at the beginning of that year.

Yes, such a high ROC for four years running represents a remarkable spurt of value creation, but the way to think about it is that each year Verizon Wireless was revaluing its entire customer base, steadily improving the overall value of its business. Its success in customer retention was building up the company's customer equity account to a level that can support even higher earnings.

GETTING CREDIT FOR EARNING CUSTOMER TRUST

If you concentrate on earning the trust of customers, you'll almost guarantee that they come back to you more often, refer their friends to you, and generally create a great deal of future value for your business. This makes intuitive sense, and it's also what the Forrester survey found (see "The Man with the Folding Chair" in Chapter 4). If customers perceive that you are acting in their interests as well as your own, then they will be more likely to be loyal longer and to buy more products from you. So earning customer trust is a straightforward way to improve your value as a business.

But will the world's stock markets be able to tolerate "doing the right thing" to create long-term value for a company, if it comes at the expense of reduced current-period sales and profits? We think there's hope. In April 2006, for instance, Apple Computer reported somewhat weaker-than-expected retail sales. But one financial analyst saw the slump as a temporary trade-off designed to earn the trust of its customers. AmTech's Shaw Wu noted that his firm was "not too bothered" by Apple's disappointing numbers that quarter, "as we believe most of the weakness was seasonal and from our checks, Apple's sales representatives have been instructed not to push PowerPC Macs [on] customers who want to wait for Intel versions." Wu went on to say that "[i]n this day and age where making numbers is important, we believe Apple is in a rare group of companies willing to sacrifice its near-term revenue opportunity for greater longer-term success by developing customer trust."[5]

Not every company has earned permission from the markets to balance short and long term success, the way Apple has. Apple provides a great example because, for a variety of reasons, Apple's customers are fanatically loyal to the firm. Part of this customer loyalty undoubtedly springs from its clever designs, interesting and "hip" products, and a generally youthful and rebellious brand personality. But part of it also comes from the trust that customers have in the Apple brand. It's impossible to say what part is loyalty and what part is trust, because these are mutually reinforcing qualities—you tend to be loyal to a company or brand you trust, and the more you do business with a company or brand in a way that works for you, the more you trust it.

Based on what the AmTech financial analyst said, you could easily equate Apple with Company 2 in the create-harvest-destroy exhibit on page 90. It was building long-term trust and increasing its customer equity substantially, while paying a short-term price to do so. In effect, it was swapping sales this quarter for even greater sales in the future, simply by acting in its customers' best interests.

So now consider your own business:

- Would you say your firm is creating, harvesting, or destroying value?
- Does your company even think much about its customers' lifetime values? Who is responsible for customer value management?
- What metrics are they using to track customer equity changes, in addition to current earnings?
- What level of customer equity do you think is required to support your multiyear business goals, in terms of profitability and growth?
- How would you go about achieving that level? What type of customers do you need, and what will they need from you?
- Finally, how will you know you're successful—besides a hunch?

The main question you have to answer is, in an increasingly difficult marketing environment, when your customers can leave the franchise with a single click and may be tempted away at any moment by your competitors' promotions, how do you build the kind of management and employee team that can create genuine, additional shareholder value rather than simply harvesting the customer equity you already have in the bank?

As we'll see in the next chapter, in order to earn the trust of your customers and build value for your shareholders, your whole company's culture needs to be set toward that objective.

☙ **6** ☙

Culture Rules

At Baptist Health Care, the first "key" in the service excellence initiative was to create and maintain a great employee culture. This was such an important goal that the bulk of the organization's planning effort was spent trying to think through the kind of corporate culture it needed if it were to become a great service company and then figuring out how to encourage and support that culture.

Every training session at the firm began with an insightful statement: "Culture will drive strategy or culture will drag strategy." We think a version of this is a Law to Follow:

LAW TO FOLLOW

Culture will drive value or culture will drag value.

————————— ☙ —————————

The senior executives at Baptist Health Care focused first on the organization's culture because they knew you can't earn the trust of your customers with a policy statement. You can earn trust only with actions, and these actions are taken by employees. This means the employees not only have to *know* the right thing to do, but actually *want* to do it.

Remember that as far as your customers are concerned, the ordinary, low-level customer-contact employee they meet at the store, talk to on the phone, or interact with during a service transaction of any kind—that employee *is* your company. For a variety of reasons we'll discuss in this chapter, your corporate culture is the most potent tool you have for ensuring that everyone at your firm is pulling in the same direction.

DEFINING AND MANAGING CULTURE

Culture is an elusive yet critical part of a company's nature. Everyone talks about it but no one can really put their finger on it. You could think of a company's culture as something like the DNA of its business operation. It consists of the shared beliefs and values of managers and employees, usually passed on informally from one to another. A company's culture consists of the mostly unwritten rules and unspoken understandings about "the way we do things around here."

As a company matures, shared values and beliefs harden into business practices and processes, until workers and managers find it increasingly difficult to describe their own cultures or to separate culture issues from organizational structure and process issues.

At some organizations, managers take a proactive role in guiding or shaping their own corporate cultures, trying to ensure that the informal beliefs and values of employees and managers support the organization's broader mission. The five-part Toyota Way, Wal-Mart's "Three Basic Beliefs," IKEA's aversion to bureaucracy, and the egalitarian HP Way have all contributed importantly to the long-term success of those firms, and at each of these companies, the managers actively encourage an employee culture based on these value statements.

But regardless of whether you try to manage it or not, every organization—including yours—does have a culture. Difficult or conflicting cultures tend to be the biggest factors accounting for why mergers and strategic alliances fail, why change management efforts don't gain traction at a firm, and why major corporate strategy initiatives fizzle. In our own experience, limitations in culture are one of the biggest impediments to most customer-oriented technology initiatives. In fact, a culture with bad karma impedes virtually every effort you could make toward better and more integrated customer-facing processes.

DO AS I SAY, NOT AS I DO

We're sure we don't have to tell you this, but writing a value statement for your company is not at all the same thing as living it, nor will it have much impact on your real-world culture. We once visited a company that had a written set of official company values, and these values were posted throughout the headquarters, along with the company's official mission statement. You've probably seen stuff like this before (who hasn't?) but to protect the identity of this client, we will paraphrase the mission statement:

Do the right thing for customers and be the world's most admired company.

This certainly seems like the right attitude to take toward customers, and it also gives everyone an ambitious goal to aspire to. Yet when we talked with middle managers at this company about what it really means to do the right thing for customers and to earn their trust, it became clear to us very quickly that these managers were all focused on one thing: Make this quarter's numbers at any cost. The company's official written mission statement was posted for all to see, but it was undermined every day as middle managers desperately tried to accomplish the much stronger unwritten mission—the real mission:

Do whatever it takes to make the numbers.

Now, this "unofficial" mission statement wasn't written down anywhere, so how did it become so important to the firm? Because making the numbers was the most critical task faced by the company's key executives. This was the task that drove compensation, advancement, and power within the firm. Managers who made their numbers got ahead, and everyone else got the message.

"Make the numbers" was the real culture at this company. But, as with most cultures, it was invisible to the managers and employees working there, because they lived and breathed it every day. It was just the way they did things around there, but if you asked them what their "culture" really was (as we did), they would point to the poster on the wall, perhaps commenting wisely on a nuance to it here or there.

This is because culture is propagated the old-fashioned way—by imitation, that marvelously important survival tool. A new employee comes on board and "learns the ropes" by finding out just how things are done around here. When she encounters a new situation, she'll ask someone who's been around for a while. Successful behaviors are those that are rewarded by the organization, so how you provide recognition and incentives is important, but just as important is how the employees already working within your firm tend to socialize the values, processes, and rules when it comes to teaching newbies how to fit in.

The culture at your firm will reflect how you measure success, how you reward people, what tasks you consider to be important, what processes you follow to accomplish those tasks, how quickly and effectively you make decisions, and who approves decisions. Your culture will reflect how friendly or competitive employees are with each other, how trusting they are, how much disagreement is tolerated, how much consensus is required, what privileges go with rank, what information is available to whom, what customers or suppliers are the most valued, and what actions are considered out of bounds.

You can write down the values you aspire to for your firm, but if you want these values to become part of the real culture, then you'd better make sure all your systems, metrics, processes, and HR policies are aligned with them, too.

WELCOME TO THE "CONCEPTUAL AGE"

Importantly, as businesses continue to streamline, automate, and outsource, corporate culture is becoming more important than ever before. There are a number of factors at work in this, including the increased complexity of modern organizations, greater sophistication of the workforce, globalization, and communications technologies that are accelerating the pace of routine business processes.

For all these reasons, controlling and managing organizations the old-fashioned way (i.e., with rules, procedures, and policies) is just not as effective as it once was. So your company's culture is now even more important to your success than it used to be. And it's largely up to you whether the unwritten rules that govern "the way we do things around here" become a long-lasting competitive advantage, difficult for your competitors to duplicate, or a giant albatross with bad breath hung around your corporate neck.

Organizations used to be simpler to control, because most tasks were routine, most problems could be anticipated, and desired outcomes could be spelled out in official policy. An employee's job was to follow that policy. But over the last several years, more and more of these routine tasks have been automated or outsourced, and the resulting organizations are slimmer and more efficiently competitive. What remains at most firms, and will continue to characterize them, are the functions and roles that cannot be automated or outsourced. These are the kinds of jobs that require employees to make decisions that cannot be foreseen or mapped out and therefore aren't spelled out in the standard operating processes. These jobs require *nonroutine decision making.* Many of them involve high-concept roles and other functions that simply can't be covered by a rule book.

In Dan Pink's spellbinding book, *A Whole New Mind,* he persuasively describes this new, postautomation, postoutsourcing "Conceptual Age." It may once have been true that information workers would inherit the world, but today's information workers can live in Ireland or China, and even doctors and lawyers are finding their jobs increasingly threatened by computers and online substitutes. Indian technology schools turn out some 350,000 new engineers a year, and many of them are willing to work for $15,000 salaries.

What type of work can't be outsourced or automated? Pink says the type of work that will characterize successful executives in the future (at least in the United States and other advanced western economies) is work that involves creativity and sensitivity, and requires skills in design, entertainment, storytelling, and empathy. Consider lawyers, for instance: Legal research and paperwork can be outsourced to Ireland or India, but cases have to be argued to juries in the courtroom, in person. Or doctors: X rays can be evaluated remotely and diagnoses rendered, but bedside manner has to happen, well, bedside.

This trend is already showing up in employment figures. At least within the U.S. economy, production and transactional jobs, which recently made up about 60% of the workforce, are being automated rapidly, while the other 40% of jobs, involving nonroutine decision making, have grown two and a half times faster in recent years and pay 55 to 70% more than routine jobs. These nonroutine jobs require workers to deal with ambiguous situations and difficult issues—problems that often have no direct precedent or at least no "correct" solution.

You can automate the contact report that a sales rep has to file, but you can't get a computer to look into a client's eye and judge whether to push for the sale or ask another question first. Jobs like this require judgment, creativity, and initiative on the part of the employee. As a result, according to one study, companies are turning their attention to "making their most talented, highly-paid workers more productive," because this is the surest way to gain competitive advantage.

Companies have spent the last several decades economizing, streamlining, and automating their more routine, core processes, but the cost and efficiency advantages they secured from these activities were short-lived, as the benefits of automation quickly permeated whole industries and their competitors became equally efficient. Efficiency, cost-cutting, running lean and mean—these are just the greens fees required to remain in the game. By contrast, when a company gains an advantage by making its nonroutine decision-making employees more productive and effective, three consultants writing in the *McKinsey Quarterly* suggest that this advantage

may well be more enduring, for their rivals will find these improvements much harder to copy. This kind of work is undertaken, for example, by managers, salespeople, and customer services reps, whose tasks are anything but routine. Such employees interact with other employees, customers, and suppliers and make complex decisions based on knowledge, judgment, experience, and instinct.

If you can figure out how to manage these "conceptual age" employees better, in other words, you'll have an advantage that is hard for a competitor to see or imitate. The secret, however, is not technology and process, because you just can't spell it out like that. After all, if you could document it in advance and define a procedure for it, then why not just automate it, right?

Instead, your company's secret sauce is its *culture*—the unwritten rules and unspoken traditions that define how your employees actually approach their jobs. This is what guides your employees when there is no policy. It's what they do when no one's looking.[1]

GALLOPING DECENTRALIZATION MEANS CULTURE IS MORE IMPORTANT

Further complicating your management task, new technologies now connect your employees to each other very efficiently. In fact, interactive tools connect employees not just to other employees but to vendors and suppliers, to distribution partners, to customers, and others. Many of the jobs your employees need to span a variety of organizational boundaries, some inside your own company and some not. Think of all the ways your own employees—managers, engineers, accountants, writers, supervisors, production managers, sales reps, technicians, and others—come together to solve problems and address issues. Just take a look at the "cc" list on an email string and you'll learn a great deal about the nature of the discussion and problem-solving going on.

In 2002, IBM bought PricewaterhouseCoopers Consulting (PWCC) for $3.5 billion in cash and stock and merged the operation into its own consulting business, which had roughly the same number of professionals. Although the stated values of the two firms seemed very similar, it turned out that their cultures were quite different. One was a culture that favored individual initiative on the part of senior executives, celebrating and rewarding them for bringing in big clients even if sometimes they had to break a few rules or run over a few bodies. The other culture was constantly tuned in to its own efficiencies, so that processes needed to be invented only once and strategies were followed carefully, even when that sometimes meant forgoing lucrative targets of opportunity. The task of blending these two very different organizational cultures together became the subject of a wonderful book on how culture works: *Can Two Rights Make a Wrong?* by Sara J. Moulton Reger.

One thing IBM found, for instance, was that when different cultures are blended together, it rarely makes sense simply to strike compromises, because if employees' internal belief systems aren't changed, the cultures still won't mix. What sometimes happened, for instance, was that decisions would be traded off—we did it your way last time, now this time we'll do it my way, and then next time I'll owe you one. . . . The many problems with this kind of decision making should be obvious, but just as one example, it played havoc with customer relationships, because clients never knew quite what to expect. In the end, the consultants from IBM and PWCC who worked on the transition developed some substantive new tools for assessing and adjusting their corporate cultures, even filing patents for some of them.

But the experience taught the executives involved an important lesson about the role of culture, particularly when the organization's employees are high-end professionals. According to Lou Gerstner:

> Until I came to IBM, I probably would have told you that culture was just one among several important elements in any

organization's makeup and success—along with vision, strategy, marketing, financials, and the like. . . . I came to see, in my time at IBM, that culture isn't just one aspect of the game—it *is* the game.

Obviously, organizations function a lot less like true hierarchies than they used to. The action that takes place in large, global players as well as small- and medium-size firms is increasingly driven by networked groups of employees and partners, communicating frequently and efficiently if not actually in real time, and adding more employees or partners as needed. Individual employees these days are often responsible for more than one job at a time and may participate in several different working groups simultaneously, multitasking across organizational boundaries by using email, intranets, and other tools of electronic collaboration that were just not available a few years ago. Is it possible that doing business at the speed of email requires a qualitatively different type of organization?

Increasingly, companies are recognizing that hierarchical organizations are simply less important than they used to be, and some firms are trying to get the jump on this trend. In October 2006, Hur Jae-Hoon, a strategist at SK Telecom Co. in South Korea and an elite member of the fourth of five rungs of power at the company, found his position changed to "manager," a title that now applied to executives who, the previous week, had been not just managers, but general managers, deputy general managers, assistant managers, and staff. The company dramatically overhauled its strict top-down lines of authority in hopes of spurring more risk-taking and creativity.

New organizational models are being suggested to try to capture the nature of the modern company. Gerard Fairtlough, a retired Shell Oil executive and entrepreneur, suggests that rather than hierarchy, the modern organizational structure should be thought of as one that promotes "responsible autonomy." This is a term specifically designed to characterize how informal, networked groups of employees tend to come together as necessary and collaborate to produce elements of the outcome desired by the broader organization.

Another organizational model being discussed is something Boston Consulting Group's Philip Evans calls a "hyperarchy," defined as a "large-scale, self-organizing community that sets free unusually high degrees of energy and engagement—despite the lack of a clear or direct economic payoff for participants." Evans points out that in 1997, when a fire devastated one of Toyota's tier-one suppliers and threatened to cripple the company's production, this supplier got several tier-two suppliers involved, who ended up mobilizing the tier-three suppliers, as well. Because Toyota had built trusted relationships among these organizations, there was no up-front haggling about how people would be reimbursed. Instead, ad hoc teams spontaneously formed across a number of independent firms to get the job done, sharing blueprints and whatever raw materials had not burned up. The firms simply trusted that Toyota would do right by them in the end—which of course it did.

Instead of formal contracts, hyperarchies use simple rules and transparency to ensure a symmetry of information, which in turn leads to reciprocity, generating a reputation of leadership and trust. This is not just self-organization; it is nested, self-replicating organization, possible only because of the culture of trust Toyota built with and among its suppliers. (We'll talk more about how Toyota's culture works to promote constant innovation in Chapter 10, at the section called "Creativity Cannot Be Commanded.")

There is no doubt that interactive and computer technologies are leading organizations generally to become less centralized, and at the far end of this trend you have completely open systems, such as Wikipedia, or Craigslist, or

Skype, or Linux. One insightful book by Ori Brafman and Rod A. Beckstrom, *The Starfish and the Spider,* suggests that truly decentralized organizations require only a "catalyst" (i.e., a founder) to get them started and infuse them with an initial set of values. Then the catalyst fades away, and the organization—if you can even call it that—continues functioning on the basis of the hundreds, or millions, of independent members making their own independent decisions, but largely in ways that respect these values.

As firms become less and less centrally directed, whether they have fully embraced the principle of the starfish or not, we can expect that culture and values will increasingly come to dominate business performance. As more decisions are made independently of central authority or predefined policies, organizations will become increasingly dependent on the motives and judgments of individual employees. And the principles that guide decisions made by an autonomous group of employees, or by a hyperarchy, or by a decentralized starfish organization, will be the cultural values shared by the group's individual members.

As structure becomes less important, culture becomes more important.

Hold that thought for a minute. Your company is already at the mercy of your culture, but as technologies continue to undermine hierarchies and corporate structures, it is destined to become even more so.

The way your company behaves—toward its customers, toward its employees, toward its own shareholders—derives less from the plans, policies, and rules you've mapped out than from the invisible, unwritten but all-powerful customs that define your corporate culture. Bad culture, bad behavior. Good culture, good behavior.

CREATING A CULTURE
OF CUSTOMER TRUST

For all the competition with others, the political jockeying, sandbagging, overpromising, and nest feathering that goes on among your own employees, the only reason you are still in business at all is that your people also manage to take collective actions that further your company's mission. To encourage this you need to have an employee culture attuned to the "social" goal of your company—that is, accomplishing your company's mission.

And the truth is, most of your employees already want to treat customers fairly, because it's a natural human impulse to want to help others. But before they can act on this desire, they have to know it's a safe thing to do at your firm. By that we mean that your employees must understand and buy in to your company's mission, and they have to trust that the management has employee interests in mind as well as customer interests. They have to believe you have the plain old competence to do what you say you'll do. You can't tell people the mission is earning customer trust but then devote every waking hour to making the numbers at any cost.

Remember Ameriquest? The employees needed their jobs, but they hated working for a company that required them to lie to customers. These employees knew that if Ameriquest would cheat its customers—just use them up and throw them away after the company was done with them—then the company would likely cheat its employees, too, if it could get away with it. It's impossible for employees to trust a company that stoops to generating current earnings at all costs.

Never forget, also, that employees are not only networked with each other, they're networked with the rest of the known universe. In November 2003, Doug Monahan, founder and chairman of tech marketing firm Sunset Direct, sent the following charming message to employees:

> I expect my computers to be used for work only. Should you receive a personal call, keep it short. Should you receive a personal email, I expect the email either not answered, or a brief note telling whoever is sending you emails at work to stop immediately. Should I go through the machines, which I assure you, I will be doing, and I find anything to the contrary, you will be terminated immediately. For those who think I am kidding, and do not get with this program, I promise you that by Christmas Eve 8:00 you will be gone.

Not surprisingly, it's difficult for a company such as AmeriQuest or Sunset Direct to trust employees. And for good reason. In such a setting it's nearly impossible for anyone to feel good about anybody, and whatever culture develops, it certainly won't be based on trust. The employees at Ameriquest sometimes followed their consciences and outright foiled company policy by giving fair advice to disadvantaged civilians. At Sunset Direct, in direct violation of the dictatorial edict, an employee used one of Monahan's computers to post Monahan's message on Internal Memos.com, where it's become a legend. Doug Monahan will now realize immortality on the Web, as Scrooge.

In an organization where employer and employee don't trust each other, they are often at odds over the simple question of what's the right thing to do. In the best-run companies, employees and employers are aligned about what to do, so while there may be discussion and debate about *how* to accomplish the mission, there's not a lot of disagreement about *what* the mission is. But when employer and employee don't trust each other, or when employees don't trust other employees, then you can't rely on culture to help manage the organization, because your culture is toxic.

Remember our friend Fred who spends $5,000 a year on dry cleaning? The manager of the cleaners believed he was doing the right thing to give Fred, easily the firm's most valuable customer, the best deals available without requiring him to jump through bureaucratic hoops. It seemed to be "the right thing to do" to treat this very valuable customer as somebody special and keep all Fred's business at the firm. Imagine what a slap in the face it must have been to this manager when the *owner* disagreed and insisted that Fred had to pay full price unless he abided by the coupon rules. The owner and manager did not see eye-to-eye on how to grow the value of the business, how to treat a valuable customer, how to optimize that customer's value today and tomorrow. Fred left the establishment and found someplace else to put his $5,000 a year. But soon the manager also resigned, realizing it's just not very rewarding to work for a Coupon Nazi when he had other choices where his own point of view would be better aligned with that of his employer.[2]

So, if earning your customers' trust is your mission, then the most effective way to accomplish the mission is to cultivate a corporate culture that celebrates customer trust. Obviously, policies and practices will be involved, but procedures by themselves won't be sufficient. What are the indicators of a culture of customer trust? The single most important indicator will be that the genuine interests of the customer become an important input to every decision employees or managers make. Whenever your employees are solving a problem or undertaking an initiative, at some point they should ask themselves the question: What's in the customer's interest here? This doesn't mean they should give the product away at a loss, but it does mean they should act fairly and reasonably, with openness. Perhaps they should visualize the customer sitting right there in the room with them. In the folding chair.

If being fair to customers sets up a conflict with your company's financial goals, then *your business model is broken*, and you are vulnerable to being overturned by a completely new way of meeting customer needs. In the long run, you will be robbing your shareholders of the value of their investment, possibly without their knowledge, and you will be depriving your employees of their chances for bonuses and promotions, not to mention job satisfaction.

LAW TO FOLLOW

If being fair to customers conflicts with your company's financial goals, then fix your business model or get a new one.

No business can thrive in the long term if its financial success depends on violating the trust and confidence of customers. Just ask Blockbuster.

But when your employees solve problems by taking the customer's perspective, word will get around. Your company reputation will improve and you'll be held in higher regard by customers. Your customers' lifetime values will go up, as they have more satisfying, honest experiences with your firm and they decide to buy more, or to buy more often, or to recommend you to their friends. Your company will build a steady stream of current earnings supported by growth in customer equity and thus future earnings.[3] Remember:

Earning customer trust is a shortcut to creating the most value for your business.

It's an extremely important shortcut, too, because while you might think it would be wonderful if you could automate *all* your processes, both to minimize costs and eliminate mistakes, this ideal is and always will be completely unobtainable. As long as your customers are human beings—or businesses run by human beings—serving them well will require judgment as well as cost-efficiency. It will never be possible to anticipate and automate *everything*.

HEY! THERE'S A PERSON IN THERE!

Abraham Lincoln was once asked the secret of General Ulysses S. Grant's success during a particularly difficult Civil War campaign. Always ready with an anecdote, he told the reporter it reminded him of a story about the great "automaton" chess player that had astonished Europeans nearly a century before. Popularly known as the Mechanical Turk, it had been constructed to resemble a mechanical man, dressed in a costume like a Turk, seated behind a wooden cabinet, and apparently capable of playing chess. It had defeated many human players, but after one celebrated competitor suffered two embarrassing defeats at the hands of the machine, he angrily wrenched off the cabinetry to peer inside and then rose up to exclaim, "Hey! There's a person in there!" That, said Lincoln, was the secret of Grant's success.

It will also be the secret of your company's success when it comes to satisfying customers and ensuring they continue to create value for your business. There has to be a person in there somewhere. At some point, human judgment will always have to be accommodated in your customer-facing processes. It's impossible to serve customers well without it, and generally the more important decisions are the ones that require the most judgment. For a customer, the most vital problem or difficult issue will often involve some type of crisis situation—a situation that is likely to be unusual or at least one that you haven't already anticipated. This means that almost by definition, any issue of utmost importance to a customer is likely to be something that "falls through the cracks" if you operate entirely by predocumented processes and procedures. You won't be able to specify it in advance. You need a person in there, capable of making the right judgment call.

As a result, nowhere is your corporate culture going to play a more important role than in dealing with customers, because this often requires conceptual-age, nonroutine skills such as empathy, creativity, and sensitivity. Many companies try to cut costs by outsourcing and automating their more routine customer service tasks, but most have to find out the hard way that it's a big mistake to outsource judgment calls. Nor is it the best idea to hardwire all your policies and processes into "the system."

Not long ago a friend of ours went online to book family trips on two different airlines for successive weekends. The first trip was on a well-established carrier with a great service reputation, but it is heavily unionized and often hemmed in by its own bureaucracy. It was a complicated itinerary involving coordinating with some other people, so our friend first booked her family's outbound trip, then did some more calling to make sure the return flight was coordinated with others before booking it, too. But guess what? When she booked the return flight, she realized that a round trip would cost less than either of the one-way trips just purchased. So she called the reservations office directly now, having been defeated by the online experience, and— you guessed it—"No, sorry, no can do." Basically, she was told, she had bought the tickets online and a deal was a deal, that's that. Then the agent even said something to the effect that "yes, I know it's unfair, but I am powerless to make the change—the system just won't let me."

Fast forward to the following weekend, and our friend was on the way to a different weekend destination with her family, this time on a new entrant carrier, one of the price competitors. You book your seat, it's a great low price but absolutely nonrefundable. The family ran into a traffic snarl and arrived at the airport way too late for the flight, and our friend found herself thinking that this was going to be a very expensive weekend for not going anywhere at all. But when the family got to the counter, an agent said something like "sorry you missed your flight, but why don't you just take a room at the airport hotel tonight and I'll put you all on the 7:00 AM flight tomorrow morning? Tell you what, I'm also going to waive the $50 rebooking fee, and I'll call your destination hotel, see if they can resell your rooms for tonight, maybe save you some money."

So here are two different companies with two different ways to handle exceptional customer service situations. While it's important to do a competent job using efficient processes, good service cannot spring solely from processes or rules or systems. It is in the exceptions to the rules, the unusual and problematic situations, that a company has to rely on individual people to make wise decisions. If you have the wrong employee culture, for whatever reason, good systems and processes actually might magnify the problem. Instead, particularly if you are in the service sector, you want front-line employees who are not only *empowered* to make decisions and take action (as the first airline's employee was not) but also *motivated* to make those decisions in a way that is in the long-term interest of the firm (i.e., in a way that the customer feels he or she has been treated fairly).

> *Your brand doesn't control your employees.*
> *Your employees control your brand.*

The real key to your brand's success is that your employees have to *want* it to succeed. Employees who are personally motivated to accomplish a mission will remove barriers, overcome obstacles, and take the initiative on their own, provided only that they have the tools and authority to do so.[4] Your primary job, as a manager, is to help them discover the right mission and then give them the tools they need. We're going to plunge more deeply into this issue in Chapter 13, but first let's revisit the role trust plays in a successful business.

~7~

Capitalism Redux: Greed Is Good, But Trust Is Even Better

It might sound a bit utopian to suggest that earning the trust of your customers is a shortcut to creating more long-term value.[1] But one of the reasons we think customer trust may be the next big thing in business competition is because the rise of the Internet has given us all a taste of the genuine benefits of trust. Essentially, rising levels of trust have the effect of reducing the heat and friction generated by economic activity, so businesses can focus more on genuinely value-creating processes and less on paperwork or administrative and security tasks.

This is a critical idea. Technology and rising levels of trust go hand in hand. Trust of others is all the more important in a more networked and interconnected world. But a more interconnected world will tend to produce higher levels of trust, as well.

Throughout history, the capacity for human beings to trust others has expanded, and been expanded by, commerce and trade. In his book *The Wisdom of Crowds,* James Surowiecki argues that the spread of Quaker philosophy hastened the rise of a flourishing trade in England and America in the 1700s and 1800s. The Society of Friends places a strong emphasis on integrity and honesty, which are core tenets of their religious beliefs. Quakers subscribe to a "Testimony of Integrity" based on the belief that people should live their lives so as to be

> true to God, true to oneself, and true to others .... Friends [Quakers] do not believe that one should trick others by making statements that are technically true but misleading.

Quakers prospered as traders largely because they were able to trust each other. Among other innovations, they introduced practices such as public-stated pricing to improve the transparency of their dealings. Over time, the Anglo-American economy as a whole became more transparent and trustworthy, as non-Quakers preferred to trade with an expanding population of Quaker traders in order to be sure they got a fair deal.

It is clearer than ever that fairness and honesty are more likely to characterize developed societies with market economies and free commerce.[2] We might associate capitalism with selfishness and greed ("Greed is good," to quote Gordon Gecko, the hero of the 1987 movie *Wall Street*), but the actual truth is that the success of capitalism owes much more to the fact that our society considers trust and fairness to be important social norms. Trust makes it possible for you to eat prepared food right up until the printed expiration date without fearing sickness, to shake hands with a fellow businessman to cement a deal even before it is written down in precise legal terms, or to write out a piece of paper called a "check," and know you'll be credited with making the payment because of it.

Capitalism and free markets have increased the importance of trust and fairness, but the new technologies that free markets rely on have contributed even further to this importance. As the frictional cost of moving goods and information from one locale to another has declined, the sheer volume and rapidity of interpersonal communication has skyrocketed, so that the importance of a merchant's "reputation" is greater than ever before. Three hundred years ago, perhaps, if you were ripped off by an unscrupulous merchant who didn't live in your own community, you might have told a few friends. But they may not even have been able to recognize and avoid the devious merchant in the future, and in any case this would be as far as the news was likely to travel. In those days, gross generalizations with respect to class or tribe were the most common methods used to enforce fairness. If a merchant from Greece scammed someone in your community with barrels of bad olives, then the whole town would simply shun dealing with Greek merchants in the future. Sounds harsh now, but it worked for townspeople at the time.

Chinese businesses have begun learning this lesson the hard way. Racked by deliberate fraud as well as incompetence, the quality of so many Chinese goods has been called into question—poisoned pet food, lead-tainted toy trains, contaminated toothpaste, faulty tires—that the whole country's export reputation is threatened. One U.S. study found that of all consumer products recalled over the previous year, some 60% originated in China. Recalled products included baby carriers that ejected their babies, exploding air pumps, and circular saws with defective blades. As a result, westerners are becoming leery of doing business with *any* Chinese companies or buying consumer products "made in China." Interestingly, one analyst suggests that the reason so many Chinese goods are defective seems to be that the country is in the grip of its own Crisis of Short-Termism, with a former diplomat suggesting that "anything for a profit" has become China's national ideology.

Before the rise of electronic communications technologies, the best defense against unfair dealing was simply to do business only with people you were related to, people you knew personally, or people who lived in your town and whose children played with your children. As commerce developed and communication became easier, however, people began sharing evaluations of the businesses they dealt with and warning others of unscrupulous vendors. Organizations such as the Better Business Bureau came into existence not just to protect customers from being ripped off but also to protect honest merchants from being tarred by the actions of the unscrupulous.

REPUTATIONS GO ONLINE

These days, computer technology and inexpensive connectivity allow a merchant's reputation, for better or worse, to be shared much more rapidly and widely, in much richer detail than ever before. Any number of detailed, up-to-date evaluations of a seller's reputation can usually be found posted on various online review sites. Thus, people can get the skinny on merchants they've never dealt with before, without even personally knowing anyone who has ever dealt with them. Next time you plan a trip, for instance, if you *really* want to know what the hotel will be like, check out TripAdvisor.com. Or if you want to do a home improvement project, be sure to check your contractors' reputations on Angie's List®. At most of these kinds of sites, other customers have posted their reviews of various products, and the most sophisticated of the review sites allow a consumer to search not just by product category but also by reviewer type—that is, to find reviews that are done by people with similar tastes as the consumer. Epinions.com, for instance, asks readers to rate the reviews they read, which allows the service to get better over time, in two ways. First, overall reviewer quality is tracked, so a user can tell immediately whether a particular review has been posted by someone others have found credible. But second, epinions also tracks the reviewers that an individual consumer has found most helpful in the past, so over time it learns who each user's most trusted reviewers are and is able to connect them more quickly to those particular users.

As this trend has developed, Web sites are springing up to allow individual consumers to share their evaluations, rants, and ratings of their employers (vault.com), healthcare establishments and individual medical doctors (Revolutionhealth.com, healthgrades.com and healthcarecommission.org.uk), universities (theU.com), and individual university professors (ratemyprofessors.com). Entrepreneurs can now share their opinions of the venture capitalists who invest money in them (thefunded.com).

Largely because of cost-efficient interactive technologies, untrustworthiness is now something few businesses can keep secret. Any company that is unscrupulously exploitative of its customers will be quickly and efficiently outed, and its business will suffer. So it's more and more financially risky to take short-term advantage of a customer, even in situations where you think it would be easy to get away with. Once. But then a scorching exposé could easily go online where it could be downloaded by others, for years, and perhaps forever.

One of the very first online word-of-mouth episodes, in fact, is known as the "Yours is a Very Bad Hotel" case, and it is still making the rounds on the Web. It seems that late one night in November 2001, two businessmen were due to check in to a hotel in Houston, but when they arrived all the rooms were already taken. Apparently the hotel's night clerk was so surly and dismissive that these businessmen took the effort to create a hilarious 17-slide presentation about the incident, titling it "Yours is a Very Bad Hotel" and emailing it to the hotel company. Now, years later, you can still find this presentation being passed around on the Web. Bloggers proudly point to the fact that they were officially warned by the hotel's parent company to take its brand name off their Web site,[3] but it is of course way, way too late for that. If you want to see this example of "permanent" word of mouth for yourself, just Google the phrase "Yours is a very bad hotel" and count the entries. That should tell you just how successful any company can be at cleaning up the customer's milk once it has been electronically spilled.

One advertising executive's succinct advice: "You can't un-Google yourself."[4]

TAKING THE FRICTION OUT
OF COMMERCE

Most advanced animal species will exhibit trust when it comes to blood relatives (e.g., a mother will frequently give up her own self-interest to protect her offspring), and in less advanced societies people will trust others in their extended family, their clan, or their tribe. The only nonprimate animal known to exhibit trust when it comes to nonrelatives, however, is, believe it or not, the vampire bat. A mother vampire bat that returns to the cave without enough blood to feed her children can sometimes borrow blood from an unrelated neighbor and is trusted to repay it later. Nearby bats will monitor the transaction, and if the borrower fails to repay the favor, she will be ostracized.

Vampire bats aside, trusting an unrelated stranger enough to place your own vulnerability at risk is not something that can be explained purely in terms of economic self-interest. That is, most economists acknowledge that if people were entirely rational, calculating their every action solely in terms of how it affected their own economic well-being, or "utility," then no one could or would trust anybody. Any display of vulnerability by one would be exploited to another's advantage, because not to do so would be economically irrational.

But of course this is not the way the modern world works. Free markets operate efficiently only because in the end, people do trust complete strangers, whom they will never see again, to perform the services promised or to deliver the product as stated. Trust is essential to commerce, and people tend not to want to buy from a merchant with a reputation for dishonesty, no matter how tightly written the purchase contract might be. As Alan Greenspan once said,

> It is hard to overstate the importance of reputation in a market economy. . . . In virtually all transactions, whether with customers or with colleagues, we rely on the word of those with whom we do business. . . . Even when followed to the letter, rules guide only a small number of the day-to-day decisions required of corporate management. The rest are governed by whatever personal code of values corporate managers bring to the table.

In his book *The Speed of Trust*, Steven M. R. Covey uses a succinct formula to make this same point:

$$\uparrow \text{Trust} = \uparrow \text{Speed} \downarrow \text{Cost}$$

According to Covey's formula, when trust goes up, speed goes up and costs go down. What he means by this is that when two parties to a business transaction trust each other, they can act more quickly, and the frictional costs of the transaction are minimized. It's easy to see why this is so. After all, if I trust you enough to take your word for something, rather than having to verify all the facts myself, then we can act more quickly together. And I don't have to spend as much money on lawyers or contracts or due diligence or audits. Yes, most business transactions require some legal documentation, but generally no amount of careful legalese can cover bad intentions. Covey points out that when Warren Buffett's Berkshire Hathaway acquired McLane Distribution from Wal-Mart, the $23 billion acquisition was sealed over a handshake and completed in less than a month, because both parties knew and trusted each other completely. Normally a deal like this would have required a minimum of six months to do, and perhaps several million dollars of legal and accounting fees.

PLAYING THE ULTIMATUM GAME

There is, of course, a strong logical argument in favor of earning the trust of customers based on the ongoing relationship that a customer might or might not have with you—a relationship that will, if you play your cards right, extend some time into the future and might also influence the opinions of other potential customers. Surely, if you expect to do business with a particular customer again, you should try to earn the customer's trust today. In other words, you should behave fairly to another person because you want to benefit from his goodwill later.

But this explanation of trust is not sufficient to account for how it operates in civilized society, and it's not a good enough rationale for businesses, either. Let's take a simple example. Imagine that you sell to one-time customers only.[5] Actually, such a business is quite rare, but for argument's sake, let's suppose your customers buy once and never ever darken your door another time. Why should you bother to try to treat them scrupulously if you'll never see them again? Our argument is that it will still be in your own economic self-interest, as a business, to treat customers fairly, even if you know you will never see a customer twice. But to understand why, you have to understand the important social role that "fairness" plays in human interactions.

Social scientists have devised a game to demonstrate why trust is motivated by more than simply the fear of some future encounter with a person you may have treated unfairly in the past. Called the "ultimatum game," it involves two participants who have never met and are unlikely to meet again in the future. This is important, because neither participant has anything to gain by "being fair" to the other. Under the rules of the game, some money is produced—say, $20—and one of the two participants is charged with specifying how it should be divided between them. This is the "ultimatum," and the other participant must either take it or leave it. No negotiation is allowed. If the second player accepts the ultimatum, then each player gets to keep her split, as decided by the first player. If, however, the second player rejects the offer for any reason, then all the money is returned to the researcher, and neither player keeps any of it.

What usually happens in this game is that the first participant will offer a split that is uneven but not too lopsided. Awarding the second participant less than around 20% of the total, for instance, is almost guaranteed to provoke a rejection, forfeiting all the money for both of them. But consider the "economic" calculation that must be made by the second player. Literally, even $1 or $2 is better than nothing, so by rejecting a lowball offer, the second participant is actually harming his own economic self-interest in order to express his objection to the unjust split. The ultimatum game clearly shows that people are willing to pay a price—from their own pockets—simply to enforce fairness. When people's sense of justice or fairness is violated, they take satisfaction in punishing the transgressor. Satisfaction they're willing to spend good money on. Or the time and effort to produce a PowerPoint deck.

The success of human commerce depends on the fact that human beings do tend to develop this sense of fairness, which includes a willingness to punish perceived injustice or the unfair actions of others. If I reject your lowball offer in the ultimatum game I am, in effect, paying a price myself in order to have the satisfaction of punishing you. Because you also understand this impulse, you are more likely to make an offer that isn't too unfair or lopsided. You don't want to incur my wrath. Giving me more of the money, therefore, is actually in your own self-interest, because it reduces the chance I'll pull the plug on the whole transaction.

Economists Samuel Bowles and Herbert Gintis have a term for people's willingness to punish injustice in others. They call it "strong reciprocity," which they define as punishing others for unfair or unjust actions and rewarding good actions, even when you yourself receive no economic benefit for doing so. Bowles and Gintis say that strong reciprocity is a "pro-social behavior," because it is the kind of behavior that promotes a social good and goes beyond an individual's more narrow self-interest.

Teaching people to rely on trust in order to facilitate more free commerce is one way development economists promote economic growth in premodern societies. Micro-credit in Kenya, for instance, has sparked 40,000 businesses as its poorest residents borrow from their neighbors.[6] Often the borrowers have only a few pots or perhaps a goat to put up as collateral—goods that many times are worth even less than the small loan needed. So the system has developed a way for these people to put up their *reputations* as collateral. And payback is outstanding. With nothing of value except their good names, repayments are almost universally timely and complete. So are we more like the vampire bats, or are they more like us?

Because trust and fairness are crucial for the success of free markets, wherever free markets operate we also see people who tend to be more trusting of others and more worthy of that trust. Expectations rise, and the willingness to punish unfair behavior rises, too. In other words, the more developed the society, the higher a price a customer is willing to pay to punish injustice. In less developed societies not accustomed to free markets, sociologists have found that people don't exhibit as much pro-social behavior and are not as willing to punish others for perceived injustice. They make, and accept, lower offers in the ultimatum game, not because their living standards are lower and the money is worth more (amounts are adjusted downward when dealing with less affluent societies), but because punishing unfair behavior by others just isn't as important to them culturally.

Robert Axelrod, the game theorist who wrote the classic work *The Evolution of Cooperation* in 1984, argues that the success of commerce requires that individuals must not only be willing to cooperate together, but also have a desire to punish uncooperative behavior, in order to enforce this cooperation more completely. In Axelrod's words, the ideal commercial society would be "nice, forgiving, and retaliatory." The main point here is that the fear of retaliation against injustice deters people from acting unfairly.[7]

TECHNOLOGY FACILITATES RECIPROCITY

This is an extremely important idea for businesses, because new technologies now make retaliation—strong reciprocity—easier than ever. The Internet makes it simple for customers to teach and learn from each other—and virtually impossible for a business to keep bad service or poor quality a secret. Remarkably, however, the fact that businesses must conform more than ever to fairness in their dealings with customers has not put a damper on commerce but has stimulated it. As fairness and trustworthiness have become more transparently visible to buyers, we've witnessed a proliferation of business opportunities opening up.

eBay would not have become the success it did, for instance, except for the fact that buyers can provide feedback on seller transactions for all to see (and vice versa). This allows buyers and sellers, geographically distant strangers all, to trust each other enough to engage in serious commerce.

The electronic trust tools facilitated by eBay have spawned literally millions of new businesses, from mom-and-pop entrepreneurs to substantial Web-based stores.

Prosper.com, one of several peer-to-peer lending sites, was created because founder Chris Larsen wanted "to step back" to an era of "personal accountability in the credit markets." Tapping the collective decision making of its participants, Prosper.com uses a public rating on borrowing and lending to make sure nobody gets stiffed.

LAW TO FOLLOW

Always use technology to create more trust.

The Internet has given a far more expansive role to "strong reciprocity" in our society by empowering customers to communicate more comprehensively and cost-efficiently with each other. Because of the Web, whenever customers feel wronged by an unfair or unjust business, the news spreads faster than a PR hack can type.

But the happy result is that commerce and trade are flourishing in ways that would never have been possible without this kind of technology.

And rather than worry about customer opinions or customer-generated content, you can create substantial benefits for your business by facilitating it. A 2007 survey of e-commerce and online marketing Web sites shows that while less than 30% of them currently offer customer review features on their sites, more than 50% said they were considering them. According to the research, the leading business benefits most Web site operators expected from facilitating reviews and other user-generated content included increased conversion rates, higher customer loyalty and retention, and better search engine optimization.

If yours is one of the many companies considering some kind of corporate blog or online discussion site, now there is reasonably good evidence that trust will play a big part in the success of that venture, as well. A comprehensive study from the University of Missouri–Columbia shows that when an online discussion is moderated, people who read the posts in that discussion are more likely to post their own comments. According to Kevin Wise, the professor who directed the study, this is directly related to the degree to which participants can trust that the discussion won't fall apart on account of bad behavior by some participants:

> This finding might go against the traditional ideal of the Internet as a wide-open frontier in which there are no constraints on communication. On the other hand, it makes sense in light of well-liked online communities that went "feral" due to a lack of moderation. Even a cursory indication that either professionals or peers are moderating an online community might encourage participation by suggesting that the community will not fall apart or be hijacked by troublemakers.

TECHNOLOGY SEEN THROUGH THE WRONG END OF THE TELESCOPE

But let's face it, technology also presents a great temptation to businesses, because of the tremendous amount of customer information it makes available. The urge to use that personal information to sell more things is almost palpable, and you see it every day in the way companies approach their marketing and sales strategies. Rather than starting with the question of how the personal data provided by a customer can be used to improve the customer's life—by making the product more convenient, perhaps, or less costly, or more tailored, or by making the customer reviews more informative, or the blog discussion more interesting—the overwhelming majority of the businesses we've observed have been asking the question the other way around: How can we use this technology and the customer data it throws off to sell more stuff? How do *we* extract the most value from *them?*

The problem is that this is a view of technology through the wrong end of the telescope. The information that technology provides about your customers, and the increasingly cost-efficient tools you have to interact directly with customers and to facilitate them interacting with each other, should be used to build more trust. It really won't matter what your formal privacy protection policy is, or how well you comply with whatever anti-spam regulations are enforced, if you don't see the problem through the right end of the telescope—that is, from the customer's perspective. Fail to take this point of view and you are still going to be undermining your customers' trust.

If you see technology mostly as a way to sell more stuff, then you're probably going to end up destroying value for your business. But if you see technology as a way to improve the customer's life, then you'll probably also sell more stuff.

Technology facilitates customers interacting with other customers, and this magnifies the importance of your company's reputation. Therefore, you have a strong business interest in understanding the nature of customer-to-customer interaction, including the dynamics of how your reputation actually spreads around the customer network. That's the subject we'll cover in the next chapter.

᠊ 8 ᠊

Customers and Honeybees

Because customers now communicate so freely with each other, it is more important than ever to focus your business on earning their trust. Customer "word of mouth" is doubtlessly the oldest medium in the world when it comes to spreading the news about good (or bad) products and services. But with the new technologies powering today's customer-to-customer communications, everyone seems to have simultaneously discovered the possibility that customers might talk about you just among themselves, which of course they do.

Honeybees are social insects, and communicate with each other all the time in order to exploit the food sources that individual bees discover in their explorations. When a foraging honeybee comes across a promising food source, it returns to the hive and does a little "waggle dance" to tell the other bees where to fly in order to find this bonanza. The honeybee's dance has been shown to be sophisticated enough to communicate the direction of the food source from the beehive relative to the sun, its distance from the hive, and its overall attractiveness, as well.

So imagine, for a moment, that you are a food source for honeybees. (This means you are a flower.) With your bright colors and sweet scent, you have no trouble enticing a wandering honeybee to fly over for an on-site inspection.

But when this bee gets back to the hive, it's going to do its dance for all the other bees only if it has judged your nectar good enough to merit the return trip.

Moral of the story: If your customers rarely talk to each other, then advertising rules. Bright colors will get any single bee to zero in and take a look. But if your customers talk to each other, then what really counts is the customer experience. The customer experience will determine whether your honeybees do a dance or stage a sit-in.

Because your customers communicate with other customers, the experience you give them is more important than the message.

Since customers talk to each other, it's important to recognize that a customer can create (or destroy) value for you even if he never joins the checkout line at your store again. Simply by recommending you, or denigrating you, or commenting in any way positively or negatively about you in discussions with other current or potential customers, the customer will create or destroy real value by affecting the lifetime values of other customers and prospects, driving them up or down. In fact, the economic impact, positive or negative, of a commenting customer can often dwarf whatever future business the customer himself might or might not do directly with you.

Customer-to-customer communication clearly changes the dynamic of business, not only enforcing fairness and good behavior but also creating interesting opportunities.

WHO'S ON YOUR SPEED-DIAL?

To explain how word of mouth spreads within a population, the hottest new discipline is probably social networking theory, which can be applied to the study of phone call patterns among terrorists and mobsters as well as to viral marketing campaigns spread over the Internet and designed to create demand for movies, video games, sodas, cars, or superhero school supplies.

In 2006, just eight days apart, two events dramatically demonstrated how the power of social networking has been magnified with modern, interactive technologies. On March 27, 40,000 Los Angeles high school students, mostly Latino, stayed home from school to protest a proposed bill cracking down on illegal immigration. Twice the size of previous Chicano walkouts, this was believed to be the largest such demonstration in the city's history, and during the week many thousands of other Latino students played hooky throughout California, as well as in Texas and Florida. The very next week, on April 4, a 24-year-old aspiring British singer named Sandy Thom signed a five-album deal with RCA/Sony BMG worth £1 million. She had just finished a series of nightly live performances, all "broadcast" from her basement via the Web, building her nightly audience to some 100,000 listeners by the third week.

Each of these events happened because individuals were connected electronically, by social networking Web sites such as MySpace, Facebook, TagWorld, BeBo, and others. Social networks like these are particularly strong among younger consumers—up-and-coming adults as well as teenagers, including L.A.'s Latino students and the world's roots-rock fans. The whole art of conversation and dialogue has been changed by the availability of instant, electronic communications media, and it is the young consumer who is the most eager to use this new technology.

Communicating with others is a deep human need, and just the fact of having a "buddy list" can produce a great deal of comfort and happiness, especially for a young person. Louanne Brizendine, a neuropsychiatrist at University of California (San Francisco) and author of *The Female Brain,* has gone so far as to assert that the satisfaction young women get simply from connecting with others is "a major dopamine and oxytocin rush, the biggest, fattest neurological reward you can get outside of an orgasm." But even though the most novel and interesting uses of interactive technologies seem to be dominated by youth, making connections is something that has deep and universal appeal. More than 30 death-row inmates in Texas have MySpace pages.

It may be the oxytocin rush that drives customers to network with each other, join chat rooms, text friends, share experiences, and make connections, but businesses themselves have a very practical interest in understanding how word of mouth gets passed around. And social networking theory can help explain it.

In 1972, economic sociologist Mark Granovetter published what was to become a truly landmark article in the *American Journal of Sociology* entitled "The Strength of Weak Ties." Granovetter had been struck by the fact that when you get a job through the referrals and contacts of others, it is usually *not* your closest friend who provides the introduction. He began studying why this would be so. And before you begin to suspect your best friend of betraying you, what Granovetter found is that you're more likely to get a lead on a good job by tapping more casual acquaintances simply because you yourself probably already know most of the same contacts your best friends know, while your more distant friends' contacts are more likely to be new and different. In essence, a "weak tie" in your own social network is more likely to have connections with other social networks.

When sociologists and economists map out social networks, they connect "nodes" (i.e., people) by drawing lines that represent "links" (i.e., relationships) between them. What you get when you do this is a diagram (see Exhibit 8.1) that shows small networks joined by links to particular nodes with other networks and systems of networks joined with other systems, and so on.

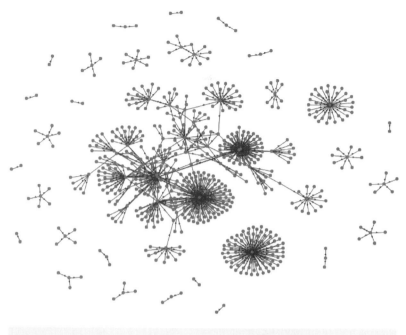

EXHIBIT 8.1 Networks of Networks

DIVERSE CONNECTIONS

Students of social networking point out that the most critical ingredients in these networks are the links between one network and another. It is the fact that networks are connected to other networks that gives them their real power. And it turns out that some people are simply more linked up than others. Author Malcolm Gladwell calls these people "connectors" and suggests that connectors' importance to a social network lies not just in the number of people they know but in the different types of people they know—the diversity of their contacts. Connectors, who form the important hubs of a social network, are the real influencers whom other people in the network tend to rely on.

To see how a network really functions, it's critical to understand how it grows. Social networks don't just pop into existence, fully formed. A social network is continually evolving—accumulating new nodes and connections over time, as people already in the network meet other people, who themselves become part of the network. The way a social network grows follows a rule called "preferential attachment"—which means that each new node is more likely to attach itself to those nodes that already have the most connections. Preferential attachment is a useful way to explain the changing state of many things that can be understood in terms of links and nodes, including the Worldwide Web, snowflake formation, the distribution of wealth, the weather, and the mechanics of evolution.

In a social network, growth by preferential attachment means that the more people who already know you in the network, the faster others will come to know you, too. This gives a great deal of power to the key influencers, who because of their links to other networks may impact thousands, or even tens of millions, of "casual acquaintances" in the online social networks they are connected to. Moreover, the ultimate influence of any single connector has as much to do with the randomness of how the network formed as it does with the expertise or special knowledge of the influencer.

As a result, online networks of consumers and others communicating with each other about business or social issues tend to be driven by a few highly influential people with surprisingly little formal expertise or "credentials" for this influence. In 2007, for example, the *Wall Street Journal* analyzed more than 25,000 user submissions across six of the largest sharing and collaboration Web sites: Netscape, Digg, Del.icio.us, Reddit, Newsvine, and Stumbleupon. What they found was "an obsessive subculture of ordinary but surprisingly influential people who, usually without pay and purely for the thrill of it, are trolling cyberspace for news and ideas to share with their network." For instance:

- At Digg, which has 900,000 registered users, fully a third of the postings popular enough to make it to the home page come from just 30 users.

- On TimeWarner's Netscape site, 13% of the postings rated "most popular" were put there by a single user—a 27-year-old computer programmer from Dayton, Ohio, who goes by the screen name STONERS.
- One of the most influential and widely read users at Reddit, who specializes in newsworthy items about criminal justice and software releases, attracted the interest and favorable reviews of a large number of other Reddit users for his appraisals of the security flaws and price tag of Microsoft's new Vista operating system. His name is Adam Fuhrer, he lives in Toronto, and he is 12 years old. (Remember the old cartoon? On the Internet, nobody knows you're a dog.)

The most widely read reviewers at many of the online customer review sites have accumulated literally millions of page views for the reviews they've written. But because of the way networks evolve, it is impossible to say in advance who these highly influential reviewers will be. The sheer randomness involved in a network's growth means that you cannot predict the key influencers or connectors in advance, no matter how carefully you analyze the initial conditions.

The growth of a social network is "path dependent." The shape and structure of any particular network of acquaintances today depends entirely on how it changed from yesterday—that is, who was added to the network, what additional connections were made, and so forth. But each of these changes has an element of randomness to it, so even though you may be able to infer general trends, you can never actually tell what the network will look like after just a few more iterations. To do so would be like trying to say whether it will rain on May 12 five years from now. No matter how well you catalog and document today's weather, this will remain an impossible task.

Path dependence means it is impossible to reproduce a network from scratch or to predict its shape in advance.

Even if you start with the same initial conditions, the identities of the key influencers would still be different, and while the actual structure of the network might look somewhat similar, the individual connections would be quite different. Every snowflake looks the same but is in fact unique.[1]

CUSTOMER-INSPIRED INNOVATION

Now connected electronically to you and to each other, your customers clearly have become a force to be reckoned with. Their inputs, ideas, comments, complaints, and demands come in a swirling stew of feedback that probably seems hard to make sense of. But if you can plug in to it, your customers actually could produce a steady stream of innovative ideas and suggestions for improving your service, your product, and your business.

Many Web sites and online communities, of course, are based on tapping in to the creative power of customers, sometimes letting products be designed collaboratively for the benefit of everybody. Linux, the open-source operating software continually improved by a network of literally thousands of programmers around the world, may be the poster child for collaborative product design, but it's certainly not the only example. Tripod.com allows customers to create their own blogs and Web sites. Its entry offering is ad supported, and free to users. Thousands of other Web sites have been set up for sharing and collaborating, from Flickr and You Tube to Wikipedia. And some companies blend the "e world" of online collaboration with the "dirt world" of manufacturing, as well. At Threadless, for instance, customers submit designs for T-shirts, vote on each other's designs, and then buy the winning shirts. Jones Soda lets you "personalize your pop" by creating labels for your own home-delivered Jones Soda bottles, with pictures you've uploaded to the site yourself. Then the company lets Web visitors vote for their favorite pictures, selecting the most popular for use in general production.

Procter & Gamble lists thousands of its patents on yet2.com to facilitate connections and funnel new ideas from the outside. Yet2.com is a "global online market-place" that brings buyers and sellers together to stimulate the creation of new intellectual property. Published Procter & Gamble reports credit this kind of approach with over 45% of its new product introductions over the last several years, contributing to a doubling in its innovation success rate. And National Semiconductor's business customers use the company's online design platform to create their own proprietary product designs, generating a staggering 20,000 or more ideas per month.

Online customer research firm Hotspex provides a service dubbed "Ideaspex." Users submit product develop-ment ideas into an ongoing contest for approval by their peers. Ideas rated highly by other users bubble up to the top of the list, providing submitters with notoriety as well as reward incentives. Sponsoring corporate marketers can take the highest-potential ideas into their own product develop-ment process. As a form of consumer research, interactive technologies are capable of eliciting more realistic feedback than traditional focus groups or surveys do. "You don't nec-essarily reach a different customer, but you do get a different response from a customer at 3:00 AM in his underwear than you would if he were in a room with eight other people," according to Shane Skillen, president of Hotspex. Results so far have been impressive. One Ideaspex client in pack-aged goods managed to get over 9,000 peer-rated names for a new product package within 24 hours of posting the product's image and description and putting out a call for input, Skillen says.

This type of customer-driven creativity and innova-tion goes by a number of interesting names, including "co-creation," "open-source innovation," "crowdsourc-ing," and "customer collaboration." Trendwatching.com calls it the "Customer-Made" movement, defined as: "The phenomenon of corporations creating goods, services and experiences in close cooperation with experienced and cre-ative consumers, tapping in to their intellectual capital, and in exchange giving them a direct say in (and rewarding them for) what actually gets produced, manufactured, de-veloped, designed, serviced, or processed." We are talking about something here that goes far beyond customer feed-back. Customers are actually participating, up front, in the design, development, and delivery of products and services.

Customers are increasingly empowered by interactive technologies to exert their influence over the configuration of the products and services they consume. In the United Kingdom the Topfield TF5800 is a digital video recorder that owners can program with a variety of simple software tools shared among an online community of users, who reg-ularly swap applications and improvements to the "Toppy," as the device is popularly known. Some Toppy users write code, others suggest ideas for new features, and others serve as beta testers at the online site. Users themselves discovered, for instance, how to hook the Toppy into the Internet and download program guides, upload and download whole TV programs, and program their recorders using remote PCs or even mobile phones.

On October 14, 2005, these Toppy machines suddenly all began failing, with frequent crashes and reboots. It was soon discovered that the BBC had introduced new interac-tive software that day and that this software was incompat-ible with the Toppy. What is interesting, however, is how quickly the Toppy user group dealt with the problem. Some users devised temporary patches and shared these with the community. Some users got the Korean manufacturer in-volved, and it started to work on a firmware upgrade. Then the user community persuaded the BBC to pull their new software release until after the firmware upgrade was available from Korea. And all this happened in 24 hours.

In August 2007, HSBC had to reverse course in response to a student rebellion organized on Facebook. The bank's policy had been to offer interest-free overdrafts to university students, but that summer it changed the policy, imposing an interest charge on overdrafts between terms. A number of students organized a protest of this policy by relying on the social networking site Facebook, and the bank soon rescinded the policy.

Regardless of what you call it, this phenomenon allows enthusiasts and naysayers alike to interact with your company and with each other. Tapping in to this kind of customer interactivity not only allows you to avoid some costly business mistakes but also to produce a steady stream of fresh, innovative ideas from the creative minds of thousands of your customers—perhaps millions of them—rather than only from those folks with high IQs and pocket protectors back at the R&D lab. The sheer diversity of inputs to your innovation process is likely to produce more useful and profitable ideas. (We'll talk much more about the importance of diversity in Chapter 12, "The Wisdom of Dissent").

And customers enjoy giving this input, too. According to Reinier Evers, Trendwatching.com's founder, "Consumers have always been eager to give feedback, but companies rarely listened. Then came the Web, and consumers could publish their feedback for all to read. So the long expected conversation was finally possible, but it became a conversation mainly between consumers. Now organizations are finally joining in." Evers notes that when feedback takes this next step, it could open a Pandora's box if not managed correctly by the enterprise. "Once they become accustomed to Customer-Made being an option, consumers will take even less kindly to corporations who don't communicate, who don't respond to feedback, who don't use open source, who don't act upon suggestions, who keep throwing new stuff over the wall, hoping some-one will like it. It's time to open up."

In entertainment, consumer co-creation and innovation seem to be driving the industry. One of the newest and most innovative forms of music, for instance, is probably the "mashup," which results from creatively remixing and altering existing artists' works. Music and video can be distributed very efficiently online, and one result is that consumers are sampling, cutting, copying, switching, altering, and pasting entertainment files together at an astonishing rate. That these files often consist of copyrighted material, making many types of reuse illegal, seems to have had very little effect on the overall pace of innovation in the field. The sheer popularity of the process can be deduced from the many different names applied to this kind of creative product, which include not just mashups, but smashups, bootlegs, boots, bastard pop, blends, cutups, powermixing, and probably others, as well.[3] In their book, *Wikinomics,* Don Tapscott and Anthony Williams call the process "prosumption," building on Alvin Toffler's term "prosumer"—meaning individuals who both consume and produce. And the Pew Internet and American Life Project estimates that more than half of all online teenagers (57%) can be defined as "content creators."

Online collaboration among large numbers of people promises tremendous benefits. There is, of course, the famous SETI (Search for Extra-Terrestrial Intelligence) project, involving more than 3 million volunteers lending their own personal computers' processing power to help crank through radio signals from outer space. Narrow-bandwidth signals are not known to occur naturally (and therefore probably would indicate intelligent life), but finding a narrow-bandwidth needle in a data haystack the size of the known universe requires massive amounts of computing power, so volunteers download special software that lets their personal computers participate in the effort when they aren't otherwise occupied. And when the aviator Steve Fossett went missing in 2007, thousands of volunteers joined the search by combing through satellite imagery provided by GeoEye and DigitalGlobe, two companies that supply photos to Google Earth. Interestingly, the coordinator of this search is a division of Amazon called "Mechanical Turk," named after the same machine that figured in Lincoln's anecdote we related in Chapter 6 ("Hey! There's a Person in There!"). This Amazon unit manages a number of similar online human-computer collaborative efforts to accomplish tasks that can't be done easily by computer alone, such as assigning labels to images or transcribing speech.

If you want to participate in this bonanza of customer-driven creativity, then you need to make it easy, interesting, and rewarding for your customers, because it's your customers who will drive the train. Your role is to make it simple for them to connect with each other (what *they* usually want most) and to engage with you (what *you* want most). O'Reilly Media's Tim O'Reilly says you should concentrate on improving your "architecture of participation." Self-help Web sites, customer blogs for posting product reviews, and third-party forums where designers and user groups can connect directly online are a few examples. By taking an active role in the innovation cycle, customers can create the rewarding experiences they're looking for. In the process, provided you have a robust architecture of participation, your customers can be relied on to pump innovative ideas into your organization.

WORD OF MOUTH: BUSINESS OPPORTUNITY?

What customers really want is not to collaborate or co-create with *you* but to talk and interact with *each other*— with their own friends. Peer-to-peer communication is the real driver of Web and Internet usage these days, which sometimes manifests itself as customer-to-customer inter-action. You're not a natural part of this collaboration. You have to make a role for yourself, and you have to do it on your customers' terms. Still, when your customers do in-teract with each other, even though you're not participating in the conversation directly, you might occasionally be the subject of it.

Planning a strategy for generating positive word of mouth about your product does not require that your cus-tomers interact with each other electronically, of course. If you have a high-quality product or service, a person will tell friends about it in the everyday course of conversation, just doing the friend a favor. Heard about Chipotle's yet? This Mexican fast-food chain decided to promote itself with-out the luxury of traditional big-budget brand building. Its *annual* advertising expenditure is equal to what former par-ent McDonald's Corporation spends in 48 hours. Chipotle's budgeted $35,000 for the opening of the Manhattan store, and rather than spend the whole wad on a couple of ads in the newspaper or a few cable TV spots, the company posted flyers announcing the opening and then gave away 6,000 burritos, knowing that the firm's customers (what founder and CEO M. Steven Ells calls their "all-volunteer army") would spread the word fast. Seems to be working so far, too. Chipotle stock has doubled in value between its IPO and the time this book headed for press, a year later.[4]

Entrepreneur Steve Wynn didn't get to be the Las Vegas mogul he is without understanding something about how word-of-mouth recommendations spread in that town. He knows he needs big signage and other traditional marketing to attract visitors to his Mirage, Bellagio, and The Wynn hotels and casinos, but guess what Wynn considers to be his most important audience? Taxi drivers. Because visitors often ask cab drivers where the best places are, and highly value their opinions, Wynn has set up special bathrooms and vending areas just for taxi drivers at a number of his properties.

But marketers are not blind to the implications of technology when it comes to customer word of mouth. Increasingly, when consumers want to know something about a potential product purchase or service, they go online to discover what other consumers know. eMarketer estimates that businesses will spend about $900 million on social network advertising in 2007 and are likely to spend around $2.5 billion on it in 2011, all in an effort to become the next viral marketing sensation. Which is why word-of-mouth marketing has become such a buzzword (pardon the pun) in the corridors of marketing departments around the world, spawning all sorts of articles, conferences, and even books on the subject.

While all the books about word-of-mouth marketing emphasize the power of technology-facilitated customer-to-customer interactions, in the end they tend to reach the same basic conclusion as would have been reached more than 20 (or 200) years ago: that to generate positive word of mouth and avoid negative word of mouth, you have to concentrate on the customer experience itself—the nectar, not the flower. Andy Sernowitz, president of WOMMA, the Word of Mouth Marketing Association, defines word-of-mouth marketing, very practically, as "giving people a reason to talk about your stuff and making it easier for that conversation to take place." He suggests four simple ways to generate positive word of mouth:

1. Be interesting.
2. Make people happy.
3. Earn trust and respect.
4. Make it easy.

In an attempt to produce more word-of-mouth referrals from existing customers, you might be tempted to reward them for talking to friends. But be careful here. Be very, very careful. As Sernowitz says, "mixing love and money is usually a bad idea." Despite the long and proud tradition of member-get-a-member rewards programs in loyalty schemes and more or less throughout the entire direct marketing industry, the truth is that when you tell customers you're willing to pay them for their referrals, you risk communicating that your value proposition isn't very strong. Naturally, if your product or service were great on its own, then a customer would like nothing better than to suggest it to a friend, because it would be doing a good turn for the friend.

It's not impossible to design a member-get-a-member program that is successful and also builds trust in your brand, but it's difficult to strike that balance. MCI's original Friends & Family is one promotion that seemed to strike the right balance. (Sernowitz calls Friends & Family the best word-of-mouth marketing program ever.) The program involved recruiting the friends and relatives you called most frequently to join your "circle" on the MCI system, and then every circle member who signed up would receive a 10% discount on calls to other members of the circle. The mutuality of the benefit among friends made the program not only attractive but also inoffensive, as well.

But this is a precarious balance to achieve, and even the most well-meaning efforts to turn customers into advocates can backfire if you cross the line. In 2007, the office-supplies chain Staples launched a word-of-mouth marketing initiative it called "Speak Easy," trying to encourage its most loyal customers to talk up the benefits of various products. The company began sending a monthly supply of free product samples to a select group of its frequent-shopper club members who signed up for the program. The company includes in its shipment a write-up of talking points touting the benefits of each product. Other than the free samples, no additional compensation or benefit is given, and members of the program aren't monitored for whether they actually do talk the products up or not. But this program, along with other, similar ones, has nevertheless become the subject of some controversy in the press and on various customer blog sites.

Different people will see manufactured word-of-mouth programs in different ways, but many consumers are likely to see them as something vaguely manipulative or seedy. You might be able to dispel part of this feeling by encouraging your brand advocates to disclose to their friends up front their relationship to your company, but even then, we think it will always be risky to be seen tainting relationships with friends with the somewhat unpleasant odor of crass commercialism.

It bears repeating that some of the most valuable word of mouth you can generate will come simply from having a reputation for being completely open, fair, and trustworthy. So it would be deeply ironic if you tried to design a manufactured word-of-mouth program to stimulate referrals in the most ethical manner possible, only to have it negatively affect your reputation for trustworthiness.

The simple truth is, you can't really *buy* authentic word of mouth, because if it's not spontaneous, it's not really authentic.

Authentic word of mouth just happens—or it doesn't happen. And because of the nature of social networks, most of what does happen involves a great deal of randomness. So you have to face a very unsettling fact about customer word of mouth: You simply cannot control or predict what customers will decide, of their own volition, to say about you.

Word of mouth cannot be managed. All you can do is set up conditions for the best word of mouth while preparing for the worst.

JupiterResearch reports that five out of six viral marketing efforts fail to generate any positive word of mouth at all, even though two-thirds of the viral marketers surveyed claim their efforts do lead to some increased brand awareness.

With respect to harnessing "buzz," in other words, your best hope is to lay the groundwork for more positive than negative word of mouth. But one tactic for doing this is to identify and try to anticipate the needs of the key connectors—the influencers or "hubs" within your network of customers.

DoubleClick, the dominant player in Web advertising, did a quantitative study of influencers within networks of online customers in 2006, finding that there are indeed some identifiable traits and characteristics setting them apart. From an initial survey of 6,000 respondents, the company identified just over 1,000 influencers, distinguishing them by how they rated such statements as "I am an expert in certain areas . . . " and "People often ask my advice about . . . " The study revealed that influencers tend to use the Web more than twice as much as noninfluencers when researching a new product prior to buying. Importantly, while influencers were more likely than noninfluencers to pay attention to Web advertising and to want more personally relevant ads, they were also more likely to delete or clear their cookies regularly and to fast forward through the commercials on their digital video recorders.

In essence, the picture painted by DoubleClick's study of connectors and influencers is one of proactive information seekers—curious, inquisitive people who want to *know* but don't want to be *sold to*. Influencers—the key nodes in your network of customers who have the most links with other nodes—are less likely to be swayed by sales pitches but more likely to want to find out for themselves what's what.

Connectors and influencers are curious, inquisitive people who want to know but don't want to be sold to.

Honesty, trust, and straight facts are the most valuable currency of communication with this kind of customer—the kind of customer who is likely to influence the opinions of other customers—provided that the quality of your product and service is good. If your quality is not so good—well, then we suggest you try to make it better before reaching out to these influencers, because the kind of word of mouth you're likely to get might be just what you don't want.

Anyone who has followed Reichheld's work on customer loyalty knows that one of his latest ideas is the Net Promoter Score, a compact metric designed to quantify the strength of your word-of-mouth reputation among existing customers. Reichheld suggests surveying customers to see how willing they would be to recommend you to a friend or colleague, on a scale of 1 to 10. Then he says to subtract the percentage of customers who rate the likelihood anywhere from 1 to 6 (the detractors) from those who rate it 9 or 10 (the promoters). With research from Bain and Satmetrix, Reichheld claims the resulting metric is positively correlated not only with customer loyalty but with a company's growth prospects and its general financial performance.

There is some controversy about just how good Net Promoter Score really is when it comes to predicting a company's growth or customer loyalty, and whether it's actually superior to *all* other metrics,[5] but we still like it for its simplicity and practicality. Significantly, the Net Promoter Score requires you to subtract the detractors from the promoters, which is critical, because customer dissatisfaction is a much better predictor of defection than customer satisfaction is of loyalty. Despite this, most companies that do track their customer satisfaction scores don't bother trying to track dissatisfaction scores. We think this is a big mistake, because when customers talk about you with other customers, it isn't always positive. And negative word of mouth can be an insidious, destructive force all by itself, with a real effect on the financial value of the firm.

If for no other reason than the inherent randomness involved in how social networks form, negative customer word of mouth is still going to happen occasionally, even to the very best, most customer-respecting and trustworthy companies. So as people continue to get ever more efficiently connected, it would be highly useful to know the best ways to recover from occasional word-of-mouth disasters. And that's exactly what we'll take up in our next chapter.

~ 9 ~

Oops! Mistakes Happen:
Recovering Lost Trust

On Wednesday, February 14, 2007, just prior to the Presidents Day holiday weekend, a snow and ice storm hit New York City, crippling operations at several airlines. The degree to which it incapacitated JetBlue, however, was of a different order of magnitude altogether. A low-fare new entrant that had previously earned high marks among passengers for efficient service and friendly, capable employees, JetBlue had to cancel more than 1,000 flights over the course of a few days. Angry mobs formed at several of its gates. Passengers were stuck on one plane for a full ten hours without taking off (and then interviewed about their experience on every network news program). In the aftermath of the crisis, previously loyal customers publicly bemoaned what an awful company JetBlue had suddenly become, and congressmen began beating the drum about customers' rights. This nightmare would be enough to make the average CEO want to curl up and hide.

Instead, JetBlue's founder and then-CEO David Neeleman responded quickly and with sincere atonement, hitting every media outlet he could, taking responsibility for the problem, discussing its causes openly and honestly, and issuing apologies not just to all the inconvenienced flyers but to his airline's own crew members, as well. He sent apology emails to every customer affected, and also to the members of the airline's True Blue loyalty program who weren't even flying that weekend. The company posted Neeleman's video apology on its Web site, and the video was soon circulated and posted at different sites all over the Web.

In addition, the airline announced a Customer Bill of Rights, promising specific compensation payments for delayed and inconvenienced customers in the future, including travel vouchers worth at least $25 for passengers experiencing a ground delay of more than 30 minutes once they arrive at their destination airports (ranging up to full round-trip refund vouchers for arrival ground delays of more than three hours) and vouchers worth at least $100 if ground delays of more than three hours occur on departure.

In media interviews, Neeleman said the airline would make the Bill of Rights retroactive, sending the appropriate travel vouchers to all passengers already inconvenienced by the previous weekend's operational catastrophe. He estimated that this could cost the company $30 million or more, counting about $10 million for refunding tickets for canceled flights, $16 million for issuing travel vouchers, and $4 million for internal process costs, such as hiring overtime crews. But this short-term pain was just part of Neeleman's long-term vision of success for his airline. "I'm not focused on the first quarter," he said during a conference call. "I'm focused on the second, third, and fourth quarter and rebuilding our reputation in the eyes of our customers and crew members." He added, "If there's a silver lining, it is the fact that our airline is going to be stronger and even better prepared to serve our customers."

When bad things happen to your business, the most serious damage will be the erosion of customer trust, and recovering that trust is the most important step you can take to resume the task of making a profit and building shareholder value. In JetBlue's case, even after Neeleman's extensive apologies and new policies, many customers continued to rail against the airline in a blogosphere thick with customer outrage. Blogs like Church of the Customer seethed with resentment at JetBlue for this unmitigated service disaster.

But just when it looked as though no one, anywhere, would step up to Jet Blue's defense, someone did. Who? The company's most frequent flyers. These were the folks who, month in and month out, had been treated decently in the past by JetBlue—actually, a good deal more decently than the other airlines were treating them. These customers knew that JetBlue's intentions were good, and they trusted in the airline's ability to make it better next time.[1] They believed the company's apology, applauded the remedial steps, and came to the blogs to defend the airline's reputation.

In their book *Authenticity,* Jim Gilmore and Joe Pine suggest that JetBlue was able to recapture its reputation with its Customer Bill of Rights primarily because a Bill of Rights like that fit authentically into the character of the JetBlue brand. It was, in fact, exactly the kind of thing you would expect from an airline like JetBlue, which had built its reputation on being fair, open, and honest with customers. Its "authentic" reputation was already one of trustworthiness.

The customers who trust you most will be first to come to your defense.

Your customers' trust is the most effective elixir for rising from the flames of a service or quality disaster. It's not easy to find a trustworthy business to buy from, so if you can prove yours is one, then your customers are much more likely to give you a second chance or even come to your defense. In view of the rising power of customer opinion and the unpredictability of word-of-mouth messaging, having an army of supporters is probably the best insurance policy you can have.

COMPETENCE ALSO REQUIRED

More than 2,000 years ago, Aristotle observed:

> Men acquire a particular quality by constantly acting in a particular way. . . you become just by performing just actions, temperate by performing temperate actions, brave by performing brave actions.

He could have added that you become trustworthy by performing trustworthy actions. No matter how you define "trust," earning it requires action, not just good intentions. Wonderful if you can put the principle of reciprocity into practice at your company, but to be trustworthy, as Jet-Blue found, it's not enough just to have your heart in the right place. You also have to have the competence to follow through on your good intentions with effective actions.

In *The Speed of Trust,* Stephen M.R. Covey suggests that trust requires not just character but at least some level of competence, as well. He said one way to understand the interplay between actions and intent in establishing trust is to imagine that you are an expert witness at a trial, and your attorney is trying to establish your credibility. In that case, the attorney will probably try to show that you (1) are a person of integrity, (2) have good intentions, (3) have credentials, and (4) can get results, perhaps as evidenced by your track record. In Covey's opinion, character is a universal prerequisite, because you can't be trustworthy if you lack character. *Competence,* however, is more situational—that is, the level of competence you have to display to be trustworthy depends on the situation you face.

The point is that you can't hope to earn or recover your customers' trust with good intentions by themselves. You have to have the capability and competence to deliver on your honorable motive. Even if a customer feels you have taken her interest to heart, if she thinks you lack the sheer competence to do what you promise, then she still can't trust you.[2]

In early 2005, ChoicePoint—which proclaims itself the "leading provider of identification and credential verification services"—discovered that it had sold the personal data of 145,000 people to a number of shady recipients, including an identity-theft ring in Los Angeles. As recompense, the company offered the consumer victims a free credit report. No one thought seriously that ChoicePoint had *intended* to sell personal data to people engaged in identity theft, just to make a short-term profit. The company's intentions were never in question, although its competence and its actions certainly were. Either way, however, the trust it had once enjoyed was tarnished.

Then, astoundingly, ChoicePoint charged these wronged customers full price to see the more detailed information the company had already provided to the criminals! This final insult was probably just the result of profit-oriented "standard operating procedures" running full speed ahead in an organization that apparently up to that point hadn't valued privacy protection enough to have given it much thought. The overall fiasco created a firestorm of public condemnation and ignited a government investigation. This, despite the fact that up to then, ChoicePoint was by all appearances a "good" company, conforming carefully to all the regulatory requirements that surrounded its business, which by its very nature dealt with highly sensitive financial, health, and other personal information. Customer trust often is eroded when product defects or security breaches call into question the reliability of a firm, as happened with ChoicePoint, and sometimes the companies themselves make matters worse (as ChoicePoint did) simply through incompetence.

RECOVERING LOST TRUST

Research has shown that both your perceived concern for others (i.e., your intentions) and your past behavior (i.e., your actions) are major factors in the degree to which others trust you. Academicians studying trust to learn what conditions promote it or discourage it, how it is broken, and how it can be restored, have found:

- One way to help restore trust, when it has been lost through untrustworthy behavior, is simply to apologize. Customers can forgive incompetence if you recognize and acknowledge your own boneheaded behavior as such and if you state clearly how you are cleaning up your processes to make sure it doesn't happen again. Hint: If you do apologize, just do it, without excuses. Don't say "But you have to understand . . . " or "It wasn't our fault entirely." Just say "We goofed, we're sorry, won't happen again." Include a gift, if appropriate, as JetBlue did, in order to drive home the sincerity of your apology.[3]

- Good behavior is the single most effective way to restore trust after an episode of bad or untrustworthy behavior. Even though a stated promise of better behavior does accelerate the growth of trust, trustworthy actions alone are every bit as effective in the long term. ChoicePoint's problem, following the security breach, was that it needed time to demonstrate the competence of its future behavior.

- Although trust lost through bad behavior can generally be restored after a period of good behavior, when trust is violated with both bad behavior *and* deceptive statements, it never fully recovers. Incompetence can be forgiven, in other words, but bad character is a fatal flaw. This is one of the biggest problems plaguing most firms, because the first officials on the scene of a service disaster are usually the PR folks, and no matter how good it is, spin is the opposite of straight talk.

• Interestingly, research has also shown that using a binding contract probably erodes the trust of a customer or business partner. People who use binding contracts make situational judgments, rather than personal judgments, when assessing how trustworthy the other party is.*

This list covers the things that academicians say you need to consider when figuring out how to recover a customer's broken trust, and for the most part they are a mixture of good intent followed up with competent behaviors. But what's interesting about the whole problem is that if you already have gone to the trouble of creating a company based on earning the trust of customers, you will be more than halfway there.

LAW TO FOLLOW

Customers may forgive honest mistakes but will never forgive dishonesty.

_____ ⌇⌇⌇ _____

In ChoicePoint's case, the effort to recover consumer trust began with actions immediately following the security breach. The firm significantly curtailed the access certain

---

*It's ironic that contracts are antithetical to building trust. We think they're still important, mostly because they force everybody to articulate and clarify exactly what everyone means. Nevertheless, no amount of legal verbiage will protect you from genuine ill will. Note that the Customer Bill of Rights from JetBlue is not really a contract, because a contract spells out requirements for both sides, while in its Bill of Rights, JetBlue made all the promises and demanded nothing in return from customers.

clients had to the most sensitive personal information in the firm's database (Social Security and drivers' license numbers, for instance), in effect cutting off certain types of clients altogether, such as private investigators and other similar small businesses. This definitely harmed Choice-Point's short-term profits, depriving it of some $15 to $20 million of revenue annually. (The firm's competitors remain more than happy to provide this kind of data, but Choice-Point no longer does so.) The company also overhauled its privacy and security policies, bolstering procedures that cover everything from physical- and remote-access security to incident response to data destruction. Most stringent is the third-party service provider policy. Fearing that individuals who enter ChoicePoint facilities could be exposed to sensitive personal information, the firm now asks vendors to fill out a 24-question self-assessment questionnaire. Vendors that don't give privacy and security training to employees who potentially could come into contact with ChoicePoint information, for example, no longer make the cut.

The architect of many of these new policies was Carol DiBattiste, who joined ChoicePoint in April 2005 as chief credentialing, compliance and privacy officer, rising soon to general counsel/chief privacy officer. Charged with taking a thorough and comprehensive look at all the company's security and privacy-related business practices, DiBattiste brought in Ernst & Young's privacy team and invited input from other ChoicePoint business units. She strengthened the firm's credentialing process for would-be clients, creating a centralized credentialing team at the company's Alpharetta, Georgia, headquarters. (Previously, people within the geographically diverse business units had handled the task independently.) She reinvigorated the company's audit and compliance processes and moved to better educate the company's employees, introducing mandatory privacy, information security, and code-of-conduct training programs.

The result of all this activity? Within just 18 months of receiving a "Lifetime Menace Award" from Privacy International because of the privacy breach and the firm's self-serving efforts at damage control, ChoicePoint is now celebrated as one of the business world's most vigilant privacy and security practitioners, and its business practices in these areas are almost universally acclaimed by its former critics.

In January 2002, Eli Lilly settled with the Federal Trade Commission (FTC), which had charged that the company's privacy policy was "deceptive" because of what amounted to incompetence. According to the FTC, Lilly had failed to provide enough training to sensitize employees with respect to the importance of privacy protection, failed to oversee inexperienced employees who had access to sensitive information, and violated its own internal written security procedures. In early 2001, through its prozac.com Web site, Lilly offered a "Medi-Messenger" service for consumers who signed up, to remind them by private email when it was time to take or refill their medications. In June 2001, however, a Lilly employee wrote a computer program to announce the termination of the service by email, failed to run preliminary tests on the program, and ended up outing everyone who had subscribed to the prozac service. If you were one of the 669 subscribers, you saw everyone's email addresses in the "To" line of the message, including your own! Again, there was no question about Lilly's good and honorable intentions. But incompetence is no defense when customer trust is shattered.[4]

COMPETITIVE SUCCESS CAN HARM TRUST

Sometimes a lack of trust on the part of customers might arise simply because a company is highly successful financially or extremely competitive and aggressive in its business. Globally successful companies are easy targets for popular resentment and mistrust. You don't need to have sinned as badly as Ameriquest, either. Any large, successful company—particularly one that has grown rapidly, or a company with a great deal of market power—will incur suspicions.

Consider Wal-Mart, for instance, a firm that has now grown so large that, if it were a country, it would be China's eighth largest trading partner! Wal-Mart revolutionized the retail distribution system in the United States with a set of processes making it 40% more productive than its competitors during the 1980s and early 1990s, bringing low prices to the entire U.S. population. A McKinsey study from 2002 estimated that innovation in the retail sector, driven largely by Wal-Mart and its computerized systems, accounted for nearly a quarter of the country's phenomenal productivity growth during the period.[5] Nevertheless, it's still easy to arouse populist sentiment against Wal-Mart. And any good local politician with a reporter's ear can jump on the bandwagon.

Popular mistrust of other globally successful firms, such as McDonald's, ExxonMobil, or Microsoft, is also easy to arouse. The only good defense against this vulnerability, especially if you are a large multinational company, is to constantly look for ways to act in the interests of your customers.

In November 2005, Chris Atkinson, VP Sales & Marketing for Microsoft Asia, was considering how to improve the level of trust that corporate customers had in the firm. It was the classic short-term versus long-term trade-off. Could Microsoft convince enterprise customers that it would act in their interests even when this sometimes conflicted with Microsoft's own short-term interests?

Elsewhere in his organization, the sales and marketing people were wrestling with their own issue: unredeemed training vouchers. Microsoft's customers come in many different sizes, from large enterprises down to small- and medium-size businesses and individuals. Larger-volume customers have specially negotiated rates for licenses, as well as other value-added services. When selling software or SQL server installations to enterprise customers, it was the firm's practice to provide, free of charge, a number of vouchers allowing the customer to send key personnel to special Microsoft training courses, conducted through the firm's network of certified partners. Training is one of Microsoft's most important value-added services, because it is designed to appeal especially to the kind of enterprise customer more likely to want a collaborative, long-term commercial relationship.

The problem was, fewer than 20% of these vouchers were actually being redeemed. Apparently, four out of five vouchers simply languished in customers' bottom drawers, never to be used. The marketing people had mixed emotions about the low redemption rate, however. While they acknowledged that training was a great service that could help cement the company's relationships with large enterprise customers, high levels of voucher breakage were good for the marketing budget. Every voucher *not* redeemed represented marketing money that could fund other activities.

In the end, Atkinson and his staff decided that customers who were not redeeming their training vouchers were just not getting the most benefit from Microsoft's products, and even though it cost money to do so, they began sending out reminders to those customers. There were absolutely no strings to these reminders, which were simply notices to customers that they should be sure to take maximum advantage of the training vouchers they had been provided and not yet redeemed. This program immediately doubled the redemption rate in the Southeast Asia region and caught the attention of Microsoft corporate product marketing in Redmond, as well, with the result that it is now standard practice around the world to send out reminders to enterprise customers who have unredeemed training vouchers. As of this writing, the highest redemption rate in any region is about 60%, and Atkinson is shooting for a 70% to 80% redemption rate in Asia.

This is completely consistent with Microsoft corporate vice president Jon Roskill's view that Microsoft should be focused on building long-term relationships with customers and not just "selling seats." Roskill believes that Microsoft succeeds when his customers' businesses succeed and when they look forward to hearing from Microsoft.

In a similar move in its consumer business, Microsoft announced in July 2007 that the Xbox 360 warranty would be retroactively extended to three years from date of purchase, since some Xbox owners had experienced a general system failure users referred to as a "red ring of death." Covering both shipping and repair costs required a $1 billion pre-tax charge on Microsoft's earnings in the Entertainment & Devices division for the fourth quarter, but Microsoft's goal was to ensure peace of mind for all Xbox owners, according to Peter Moore, corporate VP of the E&D division.

It is at least partly because of customer-oriented initiatives like this that Microsoft has recently become one of the world's most trusted brands. That's right. The software behemoth that critics have sometimes called the "evil empire" has, over just the last few years, made a very significant move toward earning the trust of its customers and other constituencies. At the 2006 World Economic Forum in Davos, Switzerland, for instance, Richard Edelman, CEO of the public relations firm that bears his name, released his company's latest "Trust Barometer" and reported that Microsoft had become the globe's single most trusted brand. Other brands were stronger in their home countries—Toyota in Japan, Siemens in Germany, and so forth—but across the entire world, no brand is more trusted than Microsoft. Other surveys also tend to show rising customer trust in the company, due to a variety of factors. It has now settled most of the lawsuits against it, it has placated many of its more outspoken critics, it has become one of the most open and transparently managed companies, and it probably also enjoys a "halo" effect from Bill and Melinda Gates's very significant philanthropic activities.

TRUST, COMPETENCE, AND YOU

If Microsoft can do it, you can, too. But before you get too comfortable in your own chair, think about all the ways your company undermines customer trust, simply by fumbling the ball with respect to routine operations. Usually this happens whenever you haven't thought through the way a customer experiences your operation. After all, if you're hell-bent on making the numbers this quarter, why would you take the time to explore something that has such long-term implications?

For instance, do any of these things happen at your own company?

- New solicitations get mailed out to current customers. Often.
- A customer calls in and is asked by the recorded voice to enter his account number, but then when he is finally connected to a live operator, the first thing he is asked is: Account number, please?
- A customer makes a mistake on the Web site order entry page, goes back to correct it, and finds that all the fields have been reset. Or he leaves a shopping cart in progress while he's called away for 30 minutes and returns to find his effort wasted, as the shopping cart was "emptied due to inactivity."
- Notice-required-by-law gets written in legalese, printed in 6-point font, and sent out to all customers with

no plain-English decoder ring included. (That'll fix the feds with all their stupid regulations!)

Customer trust can be destroyed all at once by a major service problem, or it can be undermined one day at a time, with a thousand small demonstrations of incompetence. Either way is effective.

We think ChoicePoint's comprehensive approach to policy change, coupled with its willingness to forgo some earnings from sources posing more of a threat to the interests of consumers, represents an excellent lesson for everyone. When you face a situation in which the trust of your customers has been called into question, you have to take it seriously, which means not just reviewing your standard operating procedures but also being willing to put your money where your mouth is.

We also think that JetBlue's novel Customer Bill of Rights might have lessons for many businesses outside the airline industry. You may want to consider a formal policy of compensating customers for the mistakes you make. This would codify your commitment to acting in the customer's interest, and it would provide impetus to your internal efforts to improve your own processes, as well. In JetBlue's case the policy change was precipitated by a customer service disaster, but it's likely to have a long-term beneficial effect on the way the airline's people treat customers in a variety of situations, and a similar approach could have a similar impact on your own business. It reminds customers—and employees—that customers have rights, too.

Always point out your own mistakes before your customers have to do it for you.

When Southwest Airlines makes a boo-boo, it apologizes with free flights. On a daily basis, Southwest assumes that if you need to change your reservation, you need to, and if the airline has room on a different plane, it will accommodate you, no extra charges or fees. Spending now to make more money later. Spending now to make customers more valuable later. Same thing. Southwest has a higher market cap than all the other U.S. airlines combined. Coincidence?

So, what are we left with? Cut through all the academic studies, the guidelines, and the interesting tactics, and once again a single very important principle stands perfectly clear: Having the trust of customers is paramount. If your customer trusts you, he will be more likely to give you the benefit of the doubt, he'll accept your apology, he'll give you a second chance, and you can both go back to business as usual. Disaster averted, and you keep doing what you like to do, which is providing value to customers while earning a profit for yourself in the process.

～ 10 ～

Innovate or Die

In 2006, the oldest known animal in the world, a turtle named Harriett, died in an Australian zoo. Originally taken from the Galapagos Islands by Charles Darwin, she was thought to have been at least 175 years old. (Burdened by Darwin's own false assumption, it wasn't until 1960 that the poor turtle was renamed "Harriett" instead of "Harry.") As Darwin was reported to have said, in summarizing his radically new theory of evolution, "It is not the strongest of the species that survives, nor the most intelligent, but the one most responsive to change."[1]

RESPONDING TO CHANGE

In his marvelous book *The Origin of Wealth,* Eric Beinhocker gives us a sweeping, comprehensive review of how the thinking in economics has changed over the last two centuries, and he makes a compelling case for the idea that economic progress and development should be seen as a process of evolution. This is quite different from traditional, classical economics, which is based on perfect markets and all-knowing, perfectly rational investors. Traditional economics thinking is based on the constant equilibrium of supply and demand. But Beinhocker's argument is that in just the last couple of decades, there has been a tectonic shift in thinking, as economists have increasingly glommed on to the fact that "equilibrium" is not a realistic way to describe how the economy works.

In reality, the economy is never in a state of equilibrium. Economic activity is driven by change—by a constant flow of new products and services created by self-interested but not entirely rational people seeking a profit. As new products and services are produced, old ones fail and disappear. New companies come into existence constantly, replacing old ones that sink into business oblivion.

Increasingly, economists are coming to think of the economy as a different kind of evolutionary system. Under this theory, it is progress, creativity, and innovation that are the real drivers propelling economic activity. People create new things and devise new technologies in order to make a profit by meeting some need. The innovations that make the most profit are the most "fit" for survival, so they are likely to have a larger impact on overall progress as the economy continues to evolve into higher and higher technological states.

Changing technology and constant innovation make it extremely difficult for companies to survive and prosper over any substantial period of time. One comprehensive study examined thousands of firms in 40 industries over a 25-year period in order to understand how long the most profitable ones could maintain their superior economic performances—which the researchers defined in terms of a statistically significant difference relative to their peers. The study revealed that the periods during which any single company can consistently maintain above-average results are decreasing, regardless of industry, size of firm, or geography. Using a series of rolling five-year periods for their analysis, the researchers found that just 5% of companies are able to string together ten or more years of superior performance, and less than a half percent of their sample (only 32 firms out of the 6,772 analyzed) performed above their peers for 20 years or more.

The truly outstanding performers in this study were those able to string together a series of short-term competitive advantages rather than maintaining a long-term advantage. You can gain a short-term advantage with a differentiated product or service, but to survive the evolutionary process you need the ability to respond to change and string a number of these advantages together. In Beinhocker's words, the truly successful firms are those that "rise into the top ranks of performance, get knocked down, but like a tough boxer, get back up to fight and win again." This is certainly how Apple could be portrayed. And 3M. And GE. It remains to be seen whether that once-great competitor Dell will have the resilience and resourcefulness to "get back up to fight and win again."

But note carefully: If this evolutionary view of economic progress is correct, then there really is no such thing as a "sustainable" competitive advantage for a business. Instead, success in business, as in the natural world, comes to those "most responsive to change."

This is not Lake Wobegon, folks, where all the children are above average. Here on Earth half of all businesses are below average, and because of the increasing pace of change, it takes less time than ever to slip below the line.

TECHNOLOGY, PROGRESS, AND CHANGE

Economist Paul Romer suggests one way to understand the role that innovation and new ideas play in an economy is to think of an idea as a kind of product. In contrast to a physical product, however, every newly created idea-product becomes virtually free for anyone to use (not just its creator). Even when patents are plentiful and well written, this is still true. Consider the flurry of accessories businesses that support iPods and all the non-eBay people getting rich from eBay—all without violating a single patent but using someone else's very good idea. Because every new idea has the potential to lead to additional ideas, the more there are, the faster they come. This means the business of creating ideas is subject to increasing returns to scale, in sharp contrast to the diminishing returns that characterize traditional economics.[2]

However, while the possibility of increasing returns might lead you to conclude that creating a new idea should be a very profitable activity, don't forget that if anyone can use your new idea, then it may be difficult for you to make much money from it yourself, even after going to all the trouble and expense of having come up with it in the first place. True profits can be generated only during the time periods that lie between when a new idea is devised and when it is duplicated by competition. And as the pace of change and innovation continues to accelerate, these time periods are getting shorter and shorter.

But here's the real point: Instead of counting on making money from every new idea, you have to be able to *produce more new ideas*, constantly. Innovation, creativity, and adaptability are traits that are more important than ever, precisely because they're more common than ever. Your most successful competitors have these traits. Business conditions change with every new innovation, and you will survive as a business only if you can adapt (i.e., innovate). While technology has always marched steadily forward, the pace of this march seems to have accelerated in recent years to such an extent that the actual *character* of business competition has undergone a qualitative shift. You may not make an elevator go faster by jabbing at the call button, but neither can you stop the process of its arrival once you've called it.

To understand how innovation actually creates value for a business, think back to the long- versus short-term argument we made with respect to the customer's memory and experience. Give a customer a good experience today, and the customer will remember it and be more likely to buy from you in the future. The increased likelihood of future business from the customer, which translates directly into an increase in the customer's lifetime value, is in fact a form of value created today, with the customer's experience, even though you may not realize the cash effect until later.

You can think of "innovation" as a way to help customers create that longer-term value. Because you want to generate value from customers tomorrow, you have to develop better products and improved services today. But it's not the selling of the product tomorrow that creates value for your business. Rather, it's today's act of innovation that created the product in the first place. Selling the product is just how you realize the cash effect of the innovation.

It's also important to execute well, of course, but the original innovation is what generates the opportunity to make any kind of profit from great execution.

LAW TO FOLLOW

Success requires constant innovation.

———————— ∽ ————————

Simply stated, if your company isn't able to come up with new ideas, create new products, launch new services, and execute well, you will soon find yourself in what GE CEO Jeffrey Immelt once characterized as "commodity hell." Increasingly, innovation and creativity are essential not just for your company's success but for its very survival.[3]

Note carefully, however, that innovation's role is to help *customers* create value. Innovation, by itself, has no value.

It can even be destructive. There is already a great deal of hype surrounding innovation, but to create real value for your business, your innovation has to involve more than just coming up with cool new ideas for their own sake. That's the kind of "innovation" that brings you a remote device for your home theater system that can't be decoded without a geek license. Innovation that isn't wanted or valued by customers is just self-indulgence, and some of the most "innovative" technology companies in the world are guilty of it.

To overcome the hype and to focus on *profitable* innovation, you have to keep the customer's future behavior firmly fixed in your mind. But if your whole organization isn't already tuned to the customer's wavelength, this just isn't likely to happen.

CREATING A CLIMATE
OF INNOVATION

Economist Romer suggests that if a government wants to promote economic growth, then it should create what he calls a "climate of innovation." It could do this by, for instance, enforcing legal protections for intellectual property rights, improving education, subsidizing research, and bringing in new ideas from other societies and geographies.[4]

But trying to create a climate of innovation is good advice for a business, as well. In order to grow your business—or even just to make sure your business survives—you need to be able to innovate. How can you get better at coming up with new ideas and innovations and then putting them into production or operation? How can you turn your employees into more flexible, adaptable, and creative people? And how would you architect your firm, if your goal is to be adaptable, inventive, and responsive to change?

When asked how to coach innovation, Intuit's Bill Campbell equates firm durability and lasting value with "operating values that cherish ability to keep up the good work," done by people who have a sense of mission and want to do something great. He points out that innovation will look different at different companies. Google innovates by letting a thousand flowers bloom, for instance, while Apple innovates by applying technology.[5]

Apple, regarded as one of the world's most trusted brands, also has a reputation as one of the world's most creative and inventive firms, consistently ranking first in polls of the world's most innovative companies. According to one assessment, four factors drive Apple's inventiveness. First, it relies on "network innovation," regularly involving outsiders in its creative process, from technical partners to customers and others, rather than simply locking engineers away in the R&D department. Second, it is ruthless about designing new products around customer needs with as much simplicity as possible. Third, it understands that customers don't know what they don't know—that is, breakthrough innovations will often fly in the face of what "the market" is saying. The iPod, for instance, was originally ridiculed when it was launched in 2001. And finally, Apple has learned that one secret for constant innovation is to "fail wisely." The iPhone rose from the ashes of the company's original music phone, designed with Motorola. And the Macintosh sprang from the original Lisa computer, which failed.

Failing wisely. That's an important clue for setting up a climate of innovation, because every new idea has a high probability of failure, but without making the attempt, the small proportion of successes will never be discovered, either. James Dyson, the British vacuum cleaner magnate, claims he built 5,127 prototypes of his revolutionary new vacuum before one of his designs made him a billionaire. The Wright brothers tested some 200 different wing designs and crashed 7 of them before successfully lifting off at Kitty Hawk. And WD-40 is called "WD-40" because the first 39 "water displacement" formulas tested by the Rocket Chemical Company in 1953 failed.

If you want to keep the CFO in your company from going apoplectic at the thought of supporting a froth of "creative destruction" and intrepreneurship, then you might try classifying your business failures into two different categories:

1. *Fiasco failures* are the result of stupid mistakes, lack of homework, laziness, misguided decisions, general incompetence, and mindlessly following the old Rules to Break.

2. *Wise failures* are the result of well-executed smart ideas, based on carefully considered risks.

Jim McCann, founder of 1-800-Flowers (and a business philosopher in his spare time), feels that innovation requires a company to celebrate its failures. He's convinced that if your best people never fail, then you're not getting the most from them. In 2006, Neville Isdell, the famed CEO of Coca-Cola who has stated publicly that it doesn't do any good to make this quarter's numbers if the company isn't also building for the future, announced that he wants Coke to "take bigger risks," and to do that, he knows he needs to "convince employees and shareholders that he will tolerate the failures that will inevitably result." At your own company you may want to consider rewarding both successes and (wise) failures, while trying to discourage *inaction*. After all, if the evolutionary model of economics is correct, then progress occurs by a process of trial and error. But without error there can be no trial.

As hockey superstar Wayne Gretzky once said, "I never made a shot I didn't take."

The central question you face when trying to grow your business—even just trying to make sure your business survives—is how to foster your own company's "climate of innovation." Can you live with, and even celebrate, failures? Is it possible to turn your employees into more flexible, adaptable, and creative people?

SUPPORTING THE LUNATIC FRINGE

One of the obvious first steps, if you want to encourage innovation, is to staff your company with more creative people, either by hiring more creative people in the first place or by teaching your people to be more creative, if that's even possible.

The problem is that no one really knows what creativity is or how it happens. Don't let anyone tell you otherwise. Just think about it: If you could define creativity and map out exactly how it occurs, it wouldn't really be "creative," would it? Instead, to paraphrase what Supreme Court Justice Potter Stewart once said about obscenity, you may not be able to define creativity, but you'll know it when you see it.

Nevertheless, anyone who thinks or writes much on the subject will tell you that one secret to creativity seems to be crossing boundaries, cross-pollinating or combining different concepts, and taking new perspectives on old issues. A creative idea is usually the result of a single human brain making a connection between two previously unrelated concepts and having some blinding insight as a result—often an insight that appears to have nothing at all to do with the original concepts. Or maybe it isn't a blinding insight, but just a glimmer of understanding, or even a suspicion of something sort of interesting. This is certainly one reason why economist Romer says the rate of innovation and change is accelerating in the world—because the more new ideas there are, the more combining and cross-pollinating can take place.[6]

However they arise, creative ideas seem to come more frequently to people when they are attempting to reconcile or compare unlike things or to make connections between diverse ideas. Hungarian economist Mihalyi Csikszentmihalyi produced an extremely interesting statistical study showing that androgynous people—meaning effeminate men and masculine women—tend to be relatively more creative, probably because they spend their lives having to reconcile diverse perspectives. And in Walter Isaacson's richly documented biography, he catalogs a number of factors behind Albert Einstein's extraordinary creativity, including that he was naturally rebellious and anti-authoritarian, that he was well read not just in physics but in philosophy, psychology, and other disciplines, that he drew constant analogies between physics concepts previously thought to be unrelated (acceleration and gravity, for instance) and, to top it off, that he was a German Jew claimed by his home country as a celebrity and shunned by it at the same time.

By most accounts, highly creative people tend to be intelligent and intellectually curious, as well as flexible and open to new information. But they are also prone to be intense, motivated, mentally restless, anti-authoritarian, unorthodox, and often (as in Einstein's case) a bit rebellious. For business, a productively creative person must also be extremely goal-oriented, able to recognize and define problems clearly, and capable of putting information together in many different ways to reach solutions.

Goal-directed creativity is the essential first ingredient of business innovation, but you shouldn't forget the fun part, either, because a highly creative person tends to have a finely developed sense of humor. Intuit's Bill Campbell calls these creative people the "crazies with quality assurance," adding that the role of an organization's leadership sometimes is to support the lunatic fringe.

Dartmouth Tuck Management School professor Chris Trimble told us: "You must display a willingness to be a bit bizarre to get the juices flowing. Companies that are good at this, like Microsoft, Apple, and MLB.com (Major League Baseball's interactive group), create unusual interactions for their employees. They have offsite meetings. They mix people up. One company I worked with mixed their executives with customers from Third World countries just to find out if there were any ideas they might be missing out on."

CREATIVITY CANNOT BE COMMANDED

Intuit itself, of course, has an innovative track record, and Bill Campbell knows full well that you can't simply command people to "innovate." It doesn't work that way. All you can do is create an environment in which innovation is encouraged to flourish—a climate of innovation. You may decide to organize somewhat differently, and you should encourage creativity with your policies in addition to hiring people who are more likely to be original thinkers. But in the end your firm's creativity cannot be commanded. It must spring up from the culture.

Uh-oh. There's that word again. But hey, guess what?

The same corporate culture that will help you earn customer trust will also help your company remain adaptive, resilient, and innovative.

Harvard Business School professor Clayton Christensen (of "disruptive innovation" fame) suggests that your company's ability to innovate and adapt depends on how you define your capabilities, and that a company defines these capabilities differently as it goes through its life cycle. For a young firm, the *resources* it has available—things like people, technologies, expertise, or cash—represent its capabilities. During a company's growth phase, these capabilities begin to morph into well-defined and understood *processes*— including processes for product development, manufacturing, budgeting, and so forth. Then, when a company matures into a larger firm, its capabilities will be defined by its *values*—including things like the limitations it places on its own business, the margins it needs before considering an investment, and its corporate culture. According to Christensen, the reason younger companies are more flexible, adaptable, and innovative is that "resources" are simply more adaptable to change than are "processes" or "values," which, by their very nature, are designed to turn repetitive activities into routines and to minimize variation.

In Christensen's hierarchy it is clear that he regards a company's values and culture as the most hardened of capabilities, and we certainly agree with that. Nothing is quite so difficult to change as a company's culture, and once "the way we do things around here" becomes "the way we've always done things around here," your company already has one foot in the grave. But this argument implies that a company cannot become large without losing its innovativeness.

However, what if the culture that hardens into a company as it becomes mature is a culture that celebrates change, creativity, and innovation applied to the business? What if the repetitive activities and routines that a firm's culture enshrines have to do with a constant exploration for innovations and improvements? Some established, mature companies really do seem to have cultures that allow them to innovate and adapt more effectively while adhering to efficient business practices. Apple is not the only large firm with a track record of constant invention. GE, Disney, 3M, and Toyota also come to mind.

Despite the fact that it has 52 non-Japanese manufacturing companies marketing vehicles in some 170 countries, Toyota is surely one of the most innovative and creative companies in the world, and the secret behind its success seems to be the type of employee culture it maintains. The five-part "Toyota Way" pretty much sums it up, and is clearly designed to encourage creativity, initiative, and innovation among the firm's employees, right down to the rank-and-file factory workers:

1. *Kaizen* is the well-known Japanese process of continuous improvement. More a frame of mind than a business process, *kaizen* means Toyota employees come to work each day determined to become a little better at whatever it is they are doing than they were the day before.

2. *Genchi genbutsu* (GG) roughly translates into "go to the source." Employees are urged to find the facts of an issue, because it is easier to build consensus around well-supported arguments. In contrast to practice at many western companies, GG means Toyota employees spend time and effort carefully defining whatever business problem they are facing, before they leap to a solution.

3. *Challenge.* Reminiscent of the Chinese curse "May you live in interesting times," the idea of challenge encourages Toyota employees to see problems not as undesirable difficulties but as opportunities to improve their performance further.

4. *Teamwork.* Putting the company's interests before those of the individual is essential to good teamwork. Employees are expected to share knowledge with others in the team. Working well together is an acquired skill, so Toyota devotes a lot of time and money to on-the-job training.

5. *Respect for other people.* Everyone is encouraged to respect others not just as people but also for their skills and the special knowledge that derives from their particular position in the company. Different opinions are encouraged, but disagreement must be handled in a respectful way.

Toyota's culture allows its managers to network and team together in ways that enable the firm to devise and implement breakthrough innovations. The company's just-in-time inventorying system is based partly on letting factory workers themselves control the flow of the supplies they need. In many respects, Toyota's approach to addressing this and other manufacturing issues resembles the way diverse groups of software engineers network together to attack an open-source software issue.

Takis Athanasopoulos, who heads the company's European operations, says Japanese employees who know the culture well reach a point of "emotional fortitude," when their behavior is entirely consistent with the company's own culture and beliefs. In the West, he says, where individuals tend to put their own interests before those of any group, it is more difficult for employees to reach this state. One of the most important keys to Toyota's enormous success, however, is that its employee culture is explicitly designed to encourage trust and collaboration among employees, in order to seek constant improvements and innovations.

In fairness to Christensen's argument, it remains to be seen how Toyota might respond to some truly disruptive innovation within the automotive industry. We can only speculate what such an innovation might look like, but perhaps it would involve cars capable of remarkably high mileage using a mix of gasoline and electric technologies (whoops! like the Toyota Prius?), or cars that can be highly customized to individual taste and still delivered at low cost, high margin, and within days (like the Toyota Scion?). Neither of these new ideas may qualify as a truly "disruptive" innovation per se, but it's still out of line to argue that Toyota is too big to be innovative. Even as a mature company that prizes efficiencies and cost containment, Toyota continues to demonstrate a remarkable capacity for new thinking.

~ 11 ~

Order and Chaos

A psychological study of professional football players once revealed some interesting differences between defensive and offensive players. Apparently, offensive players' lockers were found to be neater and more orderly than those of defensive players, as a rule. Now, there may be many reasons for this, but the most obvious inference is probably right: Offensive players get ahead by following well-crafted plans, executed flawlessly. Timing, position, and order are everything to them. Defensive players, in contrast, get ahead by wreaking havoc with others' plans. They are simply more at home with disorder, chaos, and unpredictability.

A similar dichotomy plagues business when it comes to managing both execution and creativity. Efficient execution requires order, routine, and invariability. Creativity and innovation involve disorder, randomness, experimentation, and failure. Few companies have resolved this inherent conflict successfully. But there are some, just like there are a few pro ball players who can star on either side of the line. As the pace of change continues to accelerate, however, it will be increasingly important to navigate frequently between the close-ordered drill of production and the chaotic experimentation of innovation.

Your company is an organization made up of individual employees and managers who interact with each other and, while pursuing their own individual objectives, produce a collective outcome. Academics call this a "complex adaptive system." The beehive we considered in Chapter 8 is a complex adaptive system, too. The behavior that emerges from such a system is often different from what you'd expect if you observe the actions of any single member of the system. You could watch a honeybee's actions all day, for instance, and still not know the shape, texture, or social structure of the hive.

Your business makes a profit or incurs a loss in the current period, and you build or destroy customer equity. These events are the collective result of the individual actions of all the employees who make up your company. Like honeybees, your employees are each pursuing their own objectives, but the overall outcome of all the employees working together is the short- and long-term value that your firm creates for shareholders. And this outcome itself becomes additional feedback driving future employee behavior.

Sometimes a system's behavior can appear irrational. For example, if managers and employees can get ahead by achieving immediate, short-term results in their own particular areas, then the firm's overall behavior may be characterized by a lack of coordination among various silos of the organization, coupled with frequent abuses of customers, perhaps in direct violation of the company's written mission statement to "act in the customer's interest at all times." Even though no single manager thinks she is undermining the trust customers have in the firm, the overall behavior of the company still has that effect.

The success of a complex system—beehives and businesses included—depends on its being able to strike the right balance between exploiting known food sources and exploring for additional sources. We've already talked about what great exploiters honeybees are, doing dances for the other bees in order to direct them to any new food source.

But in addition to exploiting known food sources, bees are constantly exploring for new food, even when they already have more than they need. And they are excellent at it. Scientists have shown that bees will find virtually any viable new food source within about two kilometers of their hive with great efficiency, regardless of the current nectar resources available.

The analogy with business is clear. When a business is exploiting its known sources of income, it is living in the short term. Long-term success requires exploration, as well. But one of the biggest problems with most businesses is that they just don't do as good a job as honeybees do when it comes to constantly exploring for additional income sources. The way businesses are organized, financially measured, and rewarded simply makes most of them better at exploiting than exploring.

EFFICIENCY OFTEN UNDERMINES INNOVATION

Not giving enough priority or attention to the "exploration" side of the business is the biggest strategic mistake most companies make. Dell had a marvelously large food source in the form of its novel business model: direct to consumer computer sales, generating revenue even before incurring inventory costs. But by concentrating solely on exploiting this food source as efficiently as possible in order to meet Wall Street's quarterly expectations, Dell eventually put its entire business at risk. *BusinessWeek* headlined its article about Dell's fall from grace with the observation: "In a too-common mistake, it clung narrowly to its founding strategy instead of developing future sources of growth." For most firms, the tension between exploration and exploitation is complicated by two things: (1) the ruthlessly short-term dynamic introduced by the expectations of the world's financial markets, and (2) the fact that the financial metrics used by most companies are plainly inadequate when it comes to tracking the daily up-and-down changes in the long-term value of a business.

Suppose, in an experiment, we could alter the DNA of a hive of bees, genetically programming them to focus exclusively on exploitation rather than exploration. Then we put that hive of bees down in the middle of a large field of flowers. What would happen? Over the short term the hive would grow much more rapidly than the surrounding hives, because every available bee would be put to the task of exploiting the field. But what happens next? Once the field is fully exploited, the growth in nectar supplies would tail off, and soon the hive would have to fire its CEO, get in a new management team, and try to move the whole operation into a different field somewhere, that's what.

To balance exploitation and exploration, you must be willing to devote resources to both activities. Google maintains its innovative edge by encouraging employees to dedicate one day per week to exploring innovative or creative initiatives of their own choosing. If you think about it, that's an investment equivalent to 20% of the company's overall personnel budget. Emerson Electric has a strategic investment program that allocates as much as $20 million a year as seed capital for employees' various unproven but potentially lucrative concepts. Traditionally, 3M's researchers have been encouraged to spend 15% of their time on unstructured projects of their own choosing.

No matter how you define it—exploitation versus exploration, production versus innovation, or selling more today versus selling more tomorrow—it ought to be clear that a business will always experience some tension between short-term profit and long-term value creation. We've already talked extensively about how important it is for a company to balance short-term results and long-term value, optimizing the blend of current sales and changes in customer equity.

But the Crisis of Short-Termism derives from another conflict, as well, one that has been identified in a wide variety of both popular and academic business books.[1] This is the conflict that arises when managers must choose how much to concentrate on operating a business for the present versus innovating for the future. Operating a business as flawlessly and efficiently as possible requires setting up fixed routines and repeatable processes, while innovation requires you to encourage the nonroutine. To operate efficiently you want to eliminate variances, but innovation thrives on variances, at least insofar as they lead to more creative thinking.

This conflict has been sharpened immensely by the radical improvements in information technology we've seen over the last 20 years or so. These technologies have fueled a global rush of efficiency-improvement and cost-reduction initiatives, as processes are more easily automated, routines are codified, and the everyday frictions of ordinary commerce melt away. The result is that while companies were always better at exploiting than exploring, technology has now made them even *better* at exploiting.

Exacerbating this problem is the fact that while efficiency-improvement programs, such as Total Quality Management, ISO 9000, or Six Sigma, can significantly improve a company's operational execution and streamline its cost structure, they may also tend to limit a company's ability to think outside the box, reducing or eliminating altogether the chance a firm will be able to bring to market a truly breakthrough idea. According to Vijay Govindarajan, of Dartmouth, "The more you hardwire a company on total quality management, [the more] it is going to hurt breakthrough innovation. . . . The mindset that is needed, the capabilities that are needed, the metrics that are needed, the whole culture that is needed for discontinuous innovation, are fundamentally different." The problem, according to one IT industry analyst, is that innovative ideas can easily meet a roadblock when up against a "long-running, moderately successful Six Sigma quality effort led by fanatics."

Thus, as more and more companies have used technology to streamline and accelerate their operations, they have become either less capable or less willing to consider game-changing innovations, which means the innovations most firms do come up with today tend to be more incremental and short term in nature. These types of innovations involve less risk and are more likely to return a profit in the short term, of course, but they also have much less upside. The truth is, tiny or incremental improvements in a product barely qualify as real "innovation," but that seems to be the type of innovation preferred more and more.

One academic study, for instance, found that the proportion of truly new-to-the-world innovations under consideration has declined precipitously in recent years, shrinking from 20% of all innovations in 1990 to just 11.5% in 2004. Another study, focused specifically on the types of patents issued in the paint and photography industry over a 20-year period, showed that after a company completed a quality improvement initiative, the proportion of patents based on prior work (i.e., incremental innovation rather than breakthrough innovation) went up dramatically. Still another study found that 85 to 90% of the innovation projects in a typical company's pipeline today represent purely incremental improvements rather than creative breakthroughs.

3M LOSES ITS INNOVATIVE MOJO, THEN GETS ITS GROOVE BACK

Revered for decades as one of the world's most innovative companies, 3M may have lost its innovative mojo in the wake of a significant effort to upgrade its operational efficiency. In 2000, the 3M board brought in a new CEO to try to gain some needed control over the company's runaway costs. James McNerney, a Jack Welch protégé from GE, immediately introduced the Six Sigma discipline at 3M, eliminating more than 10% of the workforce, streamlining work processes, and earning praise from Wall Street.

Created at Motorola in the 1980s, Six Sigma involves the careful, statistical measurement of business processes, seeking to improve quality and consistency by steadily driving the error rate down. The name "Six Sigma" stands for six standard deviations from the mean, which on a bell curve would represent an error rate of 3.4 defects per million, a gigantic improvement over the 2,700 defects per million generated by the "average" organization. Defects are thought to cost the average firm between 20 and 30% of its revenue, compared to just 1% for a Six Sigma organization. Key to the success of a Six Sigma improvement is eliminating the variances that lead to quality problems.

At GE, the Six Sigma discipline became a legendary profitability tool, and is now one of the most widely admired and accepted programs for controlling costs and improving the quality of a business's production. So as soon as he arrived at 3M, McNerney began putting thousands of employees through training to become Six Sigma "black belts"—the company's internal consultants in the discipline. And soon 3M's finances did indeed improve, with profitability growing and operating margins increasing from 17% in 2001 to 23% by 2005.

But McNerney was considerably less successful when it came to applying the Six Sigma discipline to 3M's research and development processes, and many blame the effort for a general fall-off in the number of innovative products developed by the company over the last several years. Remember that many breakthrough innovations come by happy, unanticipated accident rather than by plan, but Six Sigma is all about planning, documenting, adjusting, and improving. Applied to R&D, Six Sigma attempts to turn the innovation process into a repeatable routine, which ends up favoring incremental improvements over breakthroughs. According to Steven Boyd, who had been a 3M researcher at the company for 32 years, "You're supposed to be developing something that was going to be producing a profit, if not next quarter, it better be the quarter after that."

Many of the researchers and scientists at 3M bridled at the requirement to fill out constant reports and justifications for doing the kind of "tinkering around with things" that usually led to the more important creative ideas. According to one participant in the process, after a briefing on how the Six Sigma program was to be applied to R&D, "we all came to the conclusion that there was no way in the world that anything like a Post-it note would ever emerge from this new system." And Art Fry, the 3M scientist (now retired) who invented the Post-it note, contends that 3M's recent sluggishness in innovation is directly attributable to the Six Sigma method. In the innovation process, Fry says, "you have to go through 5,000 to 6,000 raw ideas to find one successful business," but the Six Sigma discipline implies you should just focus on the one right idea in the beginning and not waste time on all the nonstarters.

In July 2005, McNerney left to become CEO of Boeing, and within a few months, 3M appointed George Buckley, a seasoned international executive with an engineering background, to be the new CEO. Buckley has tried to preserve the benefits of the cost-cutting and efficiency-improvement efforts while simultaneously restimulating the creative and innovative juices at 3M. His solution was in part to exempt a lot of the research process from the more formal Six Sigma forms and reports. According to Buckley, "Invention is by its very nature a disorderly process. . . . You can't put a Six Sigma process into that area and say, well, I'm getting behind on invention, so I'm going to schedule myself for three good ideas on Wednesday and two on Friday. That's not how creativity works."

Invention is indeed a disorderly process—a process of experiment and failure, accident and coincidence, bad luck and good fortune. Success often comes simply from being in the right place at the right time, but when your company is always trying new things, your odds greatly improve that one combination of things or another will in fact be a success. So how does a leader cope with this kind of less ordered, less structured, less predictable organization? Probably not by directing but by facilitating. 3M's Buckley, like Intuit's Bill Campbell and 1-800-Flowers' Jim McCann, knows full well that the innovative leader's role is to hire the right managers, provide the proper tools, create the right environment, and then *get out of the way* of this very disorderly process.

Everyone wants more innovation. But the one thing that ought to be clear at this point is that you can't *make* innovation happen no matter how hard you try or how many resources you put on it. Your most effective strategy will be to create a climate of innovation and *let* it happen.

HAVING IT BOTH WAYS

Is it possible to be both efficient and innovative, both disciplined and creative? Can the order of execution coexist with the chaos of creation? This problem has always plagued businesses but has been brought into sharp relief by new technologies, which can automate and streamline operations in ways that were just not possible before. There's hardly a management book written in the last several decades that doesn't make at least a passing reference to this problem, whether it's *Creative Destruction*, suggesting that there is a tension between operating and innovating, or *In Search of Excellence*, advocating that businesses need to be both "tight" and "loose," or *Winning Through Innovation*, arguing that a company must be "ambidextrous" to be successful both as an operator and an innovator.

But probably the best overall description of the organizational traits more likely to succeed both in operating their current business and in innovating for the future can be found in Jim Collins and Jerry Porras's classic 1994 best-seller, *Built to Last*. Collins and Porras identified a number of companies that have been consistently more successful than others in their competitive set not just for a few years but for decades. Then they directly compared the philosophies, policies, and characteristics of these long-lasting companies with other, not-so-successful firms, in order to uncover the secrets of long-term corporate success. What they found was an incredibly resilient ability to hold on to a core set of values while simultaneously tinkering, exploring, and experimenting with new ideas.

Above all, companies that prosper over the long term will almost inevitably have an extremely strong corporate culture. At most of the durably successful companies Collins and Porras studied, including HP, Wal-Mart, Nordstrom, GE, Walt Disney, Johnson & Johnson, 3M, and Marriott, among others, the culture is something almost tangible. It is a quality that infuses the employees at these companies with a sense of purpose, a mission that goes well beyond simply making a profit or building shareholder value. The cultures at these long-lasting companies are "almost cult-like"—so strong that a new employee either fits in well or is "rejected like a virus."

This is the kind of "core ideology" that was threatened by increasing process regimentation and efficiency at 3M. According to Art Fry, "What's remarkable is how fast a culture can be torn apart. . . . [McNerney] didn't kill it, because he wasn't here long enough. But if he had been here much longer, I think he could have."

While respecting their core ideologies, long-lasting companies constantly experiment with new ideas and innovations, failing frequently but keeping what works. R. W. Johnson, founder of Johnson & Johnson, famously claimed that "failure is our most important product." Motorola's founder Paul Galvin encouraged dissent, disagreement, and discussion at the company, in order to give individuals "the latitude to show what they could do largely on their own."

Experimentation, trial and error, and accidental innovation play a big role at most of the built-to-last companies studied by Collins and Porras. This pattern of random-but-successful innovations is the unmistakable hallmark of a growth process based on an evolutionary model. "If we mapped 3M's portfolio of business units on a strategic planning matrix, we could easily see *why* the company is so successful ("Look at all those cash cows and strategic stars!"), but the matrix would utterly fail to capture *how* this portfolio came to be in the first place." In other words, 3M's innovative success is yet another example of how a path-dependent network of innovations grows over time. Its current set of businesses and products was not carefully planned in advance and then developed in an orderly way. Rather, 3M (and most other long-lasting, constantly innovative companies) arrived at its present state as the result of constant tinkering and experimentation, with the best, most desirable innovations claiming more and more of the firm's resources over time.

Collins and Porras suggest that another important trait of long-lasting companies is that they often are simply not willing to make trade-offs between goals that might seem to be conflicting. What they found in their study was that such companies rarely pursued some single, all-important objective; instead they pursued multiple objectives that were sometimes at variance with each other—change and stability, conservative and bold, creative autonomy and consistency. They simply refused to choose between building shareholder value, for instance, and making people healthier, or designing better engineered electronics. In *Blue Ocean Strategy*, authors Kim and Mauborgne emphasize that often a truly innovative firm will end up reinventing its category by refusing to make trade-offs. For instance, while business strategists often suggest that an effective strategy is one that makes a clear choice between differentiation and low cost, a "blue ocean" strategy sometimes can be based on pursuing differentiation and low cost simultaneously.

One study of long-lasting European companies suggests that truly durable firms tend to be extremely good "exploiters," placing a strong emphasis on getting the most possible leverage out of their existing assets or advantages before exploring for new things. This trait, however, is paired with a high emphasis on careful diversification—not just because of the scale benefits of conglomeration, but in order to have resilience and flexibility.

YOUR CUSTOMERS CAN HELP YOU STRIKE THE RIGHT BALANCE

No matter how closely you look at the issue, it's clear that if you want your company to prosper over the long term, you have to strike the right balance between exploring for new sources of revenue and exploiting your current assets for what value you can create from them. Just where that balance lies is a matter of judgment, but the penalty for ignoring the future is becoming more severe as the pace of change accelerates.

On the "exploitation" side of your business, if you treat products and technologies as the assets to be exploited for all the value they can yield, as most companies do, then finding this balance will be difficult. One problem is that in the product-centric business model, money is the scarcest resource, and every dollar spent on exploiting will be one dollar less spent on exploration. So, as technological progress continues to undermine your product's advantages, exploiting it to create value will soak up more and more of your budget—for more frequent incremental product improvements, more aggressive marketing campaigns, deeper price discounts, cost reductions, and so forth.

And don't kid yourself: Acquiring new customers is not really "exploring" for new sources of revenue. Customer acquisition is just another way to exploit your current business proposition. For product-centric businesses, it is almost always the primary goal of "marketing." But inevitably, your activities will be centered more and more on the short-term actions that can drive immediate revenue, and the more successful you become at this, the more exploitation will come to dominate your company. Then sooner or later you'll wake up one morning, as Dell did, or 3M, or Blockbuster, and realize that your whole business has become vulnerable because you've already driven costs as low as they can go, you've already saturated the market with your best prices and most attractive offers, and you have nothing to replace your exploitation engine once technology leaves it behind for good.

However, if you think of *customers* as the asset to be "exploited" for all the value they can yield (in the sociological sense of the word), then you'll find it much easier to achieve the right balance between exploitation and exploration, for at least three reasons:

1. Customer equity is inherently more long term in nature than any product advantage could ever be, so if one of your current-period business objectives is to preserve or increase customer equity, then you'll see destructive short-term revenue fixes and discounts for what they are. You'll also quickly see that one of

the most important ways to increase your customer equity is to have more products and services that are relevant to meeting customer needs. This means exploring for product and service innovations—finding products for customers, not just finding customers for products.

2. In the customer-centric business model, it will be easier to allocate investments between exploitation and exploration, because you'll be treating your customers themselves as the actual scarce resource. Doing a better job exploiting means getting the most possible value out of every available customer or prospect (including not just current-period revenue but customer equity, as well)—by providing the greatest value *to* customers who can trust you. Therefore, you should be allocating your capital to both exploitation and exploration in whatever way best maximizes your overall Return on Customer.

3. And finally, when you build your employee culture around treating customers with fairness, it will be that much easier to generate a climate of innovation at your company, because trustworthiness itself provides a great platform for taking risks and encouraging creativity.

DOES TRUST ENCOURAGE INNOVATION?

People in an innovative organization won't always agree, nor should they, but they must disagree respectfully. Handling disagreement in a respectful way holds a lot of implications for the type of workplace that best facilitates a climate of innovation. It means the boss shouldn't just squash conversation by issuing edicts. It means setting up a "zing-free" workplace, where it's not okay to make snide comments about coworkers, either in their presence or behind their backs. It means assuming the people who work with you deserve explanation and clarity about what's going on behind the scenes. It means rewarding people who work with others and serve as catalysts for group action, and not just the lone rangers who succeed because they trounce everyone else. It means you don't pull the rug out from under people. It means, in other words, that a climate of innovation starts with an environment of trust.

In Chapter 4, we learned that you can create the most value for your firm by earning the trust of your customers, which means practicing the principle of reciprocity with them. But you have to apply that principle to employees, as well, because if you want your company to behave in a trustworthy way toward customers, then your employees have to trust the company, too. Then in Chapter 6, we discussed the important role that a company's culture (i.e., its values, unwritten rules and customs) play in determining its behavior. We suggested that to overcome the Crisis of Short-Termism and orient your firm toward creating lasting value in addition to current earnings, you should try to cultivate a culture of customer trust among your employees.

Creating a culture of customer trust at your firm will provide an important advantage when it comes to building a long-lasting, valuable business. But this kind of culture will also have a broader effect on your company—an effect that actually will translate to more than mere economic success. Stop for a minute and think about the kind of organization you would have if everyone knew that the mission was to treat customers the way you'd like to be treated yourself as a customer. Imagine that your employees are trained to do this, and that as a policy your company treats employees with the same respect and reciprocity that you want them to show toward customers.

Now think about how difficult it would be in this kind of environment to hatch a massive fraud or deception. You can never completely eliminate corruption, but if your employees all buy in to the reciprocity principle, then your company will have antibodies against corruption and deception and cheating, whether the deception is perpetrated on clueless customers or hapless shareholders.

Earning the trust of customers is not just a shortcut for creating value.
It is a shortcut for creating a better company.

In the Enron trial, one of the most telling clues that the company wasn't just rotten at the top but rotten at the core was the poisonously cynical attitude that Enron's rank-and-file employees had toward the firm's own customers. Enron had a strongly innovative culture, but it was built on deception and guile and short-term profits obtained at any cost rather than on customer trust and long-term value. For instance, introduced at the trial were transcripts of the recorded conversations of Enron's gas traders as they openly mocked the stupidity and gullibility of the customers they were trading for, while the California energy crisis continued to wreak tremendous economic damage on the state. As we all found out in the end, however, it is a very short step from deceiving customers to deceiving shareholders. And of course now "the smartest guys in the room" have become "the smartest guys in prison."[2]

Trustworthiness is not an elastic concept. It doesn't stretch. No one ever has just "some" integrity.[3] You either have integrity or you don't. You are either trustworthy or you are not trustworthy. And if earning the trust of customers is the central mission at your firm—the primary way to create value and grow the business—then it is highly likely you will also enjoy the trust of suppliers, vendors, channel partners, investors, stakeholders, and other employees (and perhaps even politicians, reporters, and consumer advocates, as well).

This is extremely important when you think about your company's climate of innovation, because new ideas tend to come from mixing up existing ideas, crossing boundaries, and taking new perspectives. Such activities inevitably generate disagreement, dissent, and argument as well as discussion, so your company has to be able to deal effectively with conflict if you want to reap the rewards of your employees' and partners' diverse points of view. When your workers trust each other, your organization will be more capable of dealing with the widely different perspectives necessary to stimulate creative ideas. Remember that one linchpin of Toyota's highly innovative culture is "respectful disagreement." And Apple is successfully inventive at least partly because it knows how to "fail wisely."

If the most useful way to understand how an economy works is indeed by thinking of it as an evolutionary system, one in which each new innovation is built on top of successful previous innovations, linked to other technologies in an increasingly complex web of change, design, experimentation, failure, and success, then a truly successful business will be one that continually adapts to the changing demands of this system. Beinhocker suggests that for a firm to have a greater chance of success in an evolutionary system, it must have cultural values and norms that allow it to adapt, innovate, and respond to constantly changing conditions. Among the norms he proposes are honesty, mutual trust, reciprocity, shared purpose, and openness.

The point is, if at least a few large firms can remain innovative over longer periods, then there must be things any company, including yours, can do to encourage innovation, change, adaptability and resilience. Creating a climate of innovation is not just another quixotic "leadership" task. A corporate culture that creates a climate of innovation is probably the single most valuable asset your company can have. Especially since it has many of the same qualities as a culture of customer trust.

≈ 12 ≈

The Wisdom of Dissent

Successful innovation requires synthesizing a great deal of information about complex existing technologies and processes and then taking a different or unusual perspective. If you think about your own experience, you probably already know that your best new ideas often come simply by crossing a boundary into a discipline you don't know so much about. Creative innovation, in other words, tends to be more a function of perspective than expertise, which is why technology guru Nicholas Negroponte asserts that the toughest engineering problems are frequently solved by nonengineers. And most firms find that the best innovations don't actually come from their R&D departments. A 2005 IBM survey asked 750 global CEOs where their companies' innovative ideas came from, and just 14% said traditional R&D. One 1997 study of 30 Global 500 firms found almost no correlation between increased R&D spending and improved profitability. Even in the consumer healthcare category, where product innovation is absolutely the lifeblood of almost every company, a Booz-Allen study found that "innovation effectiveness does not correlate well with company size or with the scale of R&D investment."

One of the reasons breakthrough innovations are so important to a company's success is that the marketplace has become so product-saturated. By one estimate, if you consider all the different types of products and services available for purchase in the modern world economy, it would be on the order of 10^{10} items. That's roughly ten *billion* different things-you-can-buy, from antibiotics to zoom lenses, from accounting services to zodiac readings.

The problem companies face is that innovation itself has become a must-have for financial success and growth, primarily because the pace of innovation and change has picked up so substantially. To be successful on a continuing basis, you have to keep the innovation engine firing on all cylinders, continually. One academic article summed it up well:

> In times of relative stability, a given stock of knowledge can create value indefinitely.... During times of accelerating change, by contrast, the lifetime value of knowledge shrinks rapidly because it becomes obsolete more quickly. Now the game is using it to connect more rapidly and effectively with others in the creation of new knowledge.

Usually, of course, the most interesting connections happen by accident, producing the biggest innovations in the process. 3M's Post-It Notes, for instance, were created after Art Fry's experiment to produce a stronger adhesive failed, accidentally yielding a very weak adhesive that turned out to be just what people wanted. Alexander Fleming famously discovered the infection-curing effects of penicillin when a bacterial culture he had been observing was accidentally contaminated with a species of Penicillium mold, inhibiting the growth of the bacteria. Arno Penzias won a Nobel Prize for discovering background radiation providing the first evidence confirming the Big Bang theory, but he originally thought the annoying hiss coming through his radio telescope was caused by bird poop on the antenna. A small sample of modern conveniences and products resulting from accidental innovation would include anesthesia, cellophane, cholesterol-lowering drugs, dynamite, the ice cream soda,

Ivory soap, NutraSweet®, nylon, photography, rayon, PVC, the smallpox vaccine, stainless steel, Teflon, and Viagra®.

Connecting knowledge with other knowledge, in order to create new knowledge. That is what creativity and innovation are all about, boiled down to their essence. Whether it involves connecting distant synapses in your own brain to hatch an interesting new idea, or connecting disparate points of view within your customer base to come up with a product improvement, the key to innovation is to combine diverse points of view, jumble them around a bit, and make some interesting connections. The overwhelming majority of these interesting connections will be completely useless, but then, by accident, you'll discover that microwave energy can melt a candy bar, or that the drug you originally designed to reduce hypertension actually increases male sexual potency, or that stale wheat berries forced through rollers would not produce the desired long sheet of dough but instead would unintentionally become "corn flakes."

DIVERSITY AND VARIETY

When you consider creativity and innovation at your company, of course, you're no longer thinking just about the creative ideas a single human brain can produce. Your goal is to harness your firm's collective intelligence. You want the creativity and innovativeness that can be found in many different brains, working together. And, as with individual creativity, it turns out that the most interesting, creative, and useful ideas produced by a collective group of people come when the people themselves bring a variety of backgrounds and perspectives to connect to the problem.

For instance, even when considering a complex technical problem, groups composed partly of experts and partly of nonexpert "laymen" tend to make better, more accurate

decisions than groups composed entirely of experts. Organizational theorist James G. March demonstrated that a
group composed entirely of experts (as would usually be the
case with senior managers making all the major decisions in
a hierarchical organization) tends not to make the best decisions because, generally speaking, this kind of group is less
inclined to investigate alternatives. But whenever a group
incorporates new members with different perspectives and
points of view, its decisions get better—even when the new
members are less experienced, less knowledgeable, and of
lower organizational rank than the existing members. Diverse people bring diverse viewpoints, and the connections
people draw between previously unrelated ideas often result
in new levels of understanding for many group members,
including the experts.

The truth about innovation and creativity is that great minds
think . . . differently.

Nassim Nicholas Taleb, in his thought-provoking book
The Black Swan, suggests that "the problem with 'experts'
is that they do not know what they do not know." This
is complicated by the fact that people in general are prone
to overestimate their own competence in any given area.
Ninety-four percent of Swedish drivers, for instance, think
that their driving skills put them in the top half of all
Swedish drivers, and a full 84% of Frenchmen believe their
lovemaking abilities would put them in the top half of all
Frenchmen. Experts and senior business executives are no
exception to this human trait: They will regularly overestimate their own level of expertise and competence. Ninety
percent of managers think they're among the top 10% of
performers in their workplace, according to one poll, for
instance. The only defense is to ensure that the groups of
people making decisions and coming up with new ideas or
solutions to problems at your company are a mixed lot.

LAW TO FOLLOW

Dissent and diversity drive creativity and innovation.

———————————— ⟐ ————————————

Highly successful firms recognize the power of diverse inputs to group decisions. Jack Welch attempted to describe what made GE so successful:

> What sets GE apart is a culture that uses diversity as a limitless source of learning opportunities, a storehouse of ideas whose breadth and richness is unmatched in world business. At the heart of this culture is an understanding that an organization's ability to learn, and translate that learning into action rapidly, is the ultimate competitive business advantage.

Employees at most companies—particularly information workers—are already networked together fairly efficiently by new technologies. And your employees are paid to operate as a group, taking collective action toward a collective goal. The trick is to incorporate the most diverse possible viewpoints while having a fairly robust and objective way to resolve conflicts and agree on outcomes.

A market mechanism, for instance, is a nearly perfect way to evaluate objectively a group's collective decision. We all know that markets are sometimes prone to fads or bubbles, but it's still hard to find a more powerful mechanism to prove the case that group intelligence is potentially the most insightful of all. When it comes to predicting Florida weather, for instance, orange-crop markets do a better job than meteorologists. And presidential "decision markets" do a better job predicting election outcomes than even the best, most comprehensive polls.

Perhaps the most famous example of market wisdom, however, involved the stock market's reaction to the explosion of the space shuttle *Challenger* on January 28, 1986.

Within minutes of the disaster, investors punished the stocks of the four main shuttle contractors: Lockheed, Rockwell, Martin Marietta, and Morton-Thiokol. But while news commentators, engineers, ex-astronauts, and other shuttle experts puzzled over the disaster and debated on television the merits of various theories to explain the explosion, Thiokol's share price was hit hardest from the very beginning. By the end of the trading day on January 28, while the stocks of the other three contractors had begun a gradual upward movement, Thiokol's shares had doubled their initial slide, losing 12% of their value. It would be several weeks before engineers figured out the culprit was frozen O-rings and Thiokol's ruptured fuel tank, but somehow the *market* already knew.

Using a market mechanism to capture important innovative ideas at your firm might not be a bad thing to consider, particularly if you can get a large enough number of diverse employees energized and involved in the project. It could be a morale booster, too. In January 2005, Rite-Solutions, a software firm specializing in law enforcement and security applications, set up its own make-believe internal stock market called the "Mutual Fun." The goal was to solicit and evaluate innovative ideas by inviting employees to participate. Each of the 55 stocks initially listed on the exchange was set at a starting price of $10 and had a detailed description attached to it, which Rite-Solutions dubbed an "expect-us" (get it?). Employees received $10,000 of "opinion money" to buy up the stocks of ideas or products they thought would be the most likely to succeed, and they could even volunteer to work on a project to help boost this likelihood. Then, if the stock later became a real product and produced profit or savings for the company, the volunteers received a share. Turns out that one of the first stock hits on the Mutual Fun has already paid off big for Rite-Solutions. It was an idea to use video game–like 3D technology to help simulate emergency situations faced by security personnel. Even though it was originally rejected by the company's executive decision-making process, this Rite-View product soon accounted for some 30% of the firm's sales.

SIZE DOES MATTER

Another way to ensure that innovative initiatives receive the kind of group attention and objective vetting required for success is to break your formal organization into smaller groups of collegial employees—teams of employees who know each other personally. There is a limit on how big such an organization can be, however, because no one can know everyone. Most people can maintain genuine social connections only with around 150 people at a time. Lots of reasons have been suggested for this, from the types of societies we evolved in to the size of a human being's neo-cortex, but regardless of the reason, whenever a close-knit organization grows larger than around 150 or 200 people, it tends to become a lot less close knit. So if you want to create a company in which everyone knows everyone else, and teams of interactive employees collaboratively tackle problems, then you need to respect this organizational size as you set up divisions and teams.

One highly innovative company that may have cracked the code on this kind of collaborative culture is W.L. Gore. Known primarily for its Gore-Tex® brand of high-performance fabrics, privately held Gore employs some 7,000 people generating about $2 billion in sales and has a number of innovative successes besides Gore-Tex, including electrical, industrial, and medical products. Gore employs an extremely flat, team-centered environment to encourage innovation. Its employees have no formal job titles, other than "Associate," and salaries are even decided collectively. According to author Malcolm Gladwell, at Gore "people don't have bosses, they have sponsors—mentors— who watch out for their interests. There are no organization charts, no budgets, no elaborate strategic plans." In its own press materials, Gore notes that it has cultivated this unique employee culture for more than 50 years now and that Gore is "one of only four companies included in every edition of *Fortune* Magazine's '100 Best Companies to Work For' since the list began in 1984."

Gore's unique culture almost certainly helps the firm maintain its innovative edge, but its organizational structure is what facilitates collaboration and collective creativity. The company's plants and research facilities are all organized into compact teams, so that sales and manufacturing and product development people tend to know each other personally. When one team becomes so successful that it must grow beyond around 150 people, or when it becomes unwieldy as a team, Gore splits off the function and forms two teams, each of which will operate more efficiently than a larger organization would. As one Gore associate related, "The pressure that comes to bear if we are not efficient at a plant, if we are not creating good earnings for the company, the peer pressure is unbelievable. This is what you get when you have small teams, where everybody knows everybody." Just as customers are more influenced by other customers than by ads, peer pressure, according to this associate, is many times more powerful than a boss when it comes to performance.

AVOIDING BAD GROUP DECISION MAKING

As important as it is to connect your employees together into collaborative teams in order to get the benefit of every-one's individual talent, groups of people making collective decisions do not always perform better than individuals. Sometimes a group can do even worse than an individual. The biggest problem in any kind of group decision making occurs when the group concentrates more on *con*sent than *dis*sent, especially in the initial stages. When a group doesn't look for different avenues to explore but solely for areas of common agreement, the decision they make is likely to be flawed. Concentrating only on harmony means that the group won't be exposed to the richness of the diverse opinions available to it, and its decisions will end up being no better than those that an average group member could have made by herself. Often, in fact, they can be worse.

In contrast to the stock market's quick and accurate evaluation of the *Challenger* explosion, James Surowiecki says the NASA task force set up to deal with the Shuttle *Columbia* situation in January 2003 made poor decisions. He points out that the task force held many discussions but apparently never took a single actual vote, making all its decisions by unanimous consent or even by acclamation. This decision-making process may have proved fatal for the astronauts. While the *Columbia* was in orbit, everyone knew that foam had pulled off the launch vehicle and crashed into the underside heat-shield tiles, but no one really knew the extent of the damage. One of the first conclusions reached by the task force, however, was that if there were in fact a safety problem, nothing could be done, because there was no viable option for returning the astronauts to Earth except via the shuttle they'd gone up in. Because of this early decision, any exploration of other possibilities was essentially curtailed, and the opinions of the several engineers who felt there was a safety hazard became less relevant. Had the group ever taken an actual, honest vote—maybe by secret ballot—the dissenting opinions of some of the engineers might have been exposed, and it could have led the whole group to explore additional options. As it turns out, some time after the tragedy NASA engineers were indeed able to identify two different methods by which they could have returned the crew safely to Earth, even though the *Columbia* itself would not have been able to make the trip.

Many other studies of group decision making have shown that in the absence of diverse perspectives and good discussion, groups of people can easily succumb to "groupthink"[1] or veer off the tracks and make decisions that, in retrospect, seem stupid or ill considered. Importantly, the NASA organization in charge during the *Columbia* disaster was relatively uniform in its makeup, as opposed to the NASA that successfully brought *Apollo 13* back to Earth. That earlier NASA organization was populated almost entirely by scientists and engineers who had spent a great deal of their professional lives outside the space business and would by definition have a great deal more diverse and different opinions. It's also interesting that NASA's comprehensive evaluation of the 2007 gash in the shuttle *Endeavor*'s heat shield, prior to its successful return to Earth, differed significantly from the process they followed for *Columbia*, incorporating many different points of view and ensuring that all engineers' opinions were aired openly.

If you want creative and innovative decisions, then your team should look less like a blue-ribbon panel and more like a patchwork quilt.

To put it simply: If the group making decisions at your company is basically all the same and they agree on everything, then you won't get any advantage from taking up the time of a bunch of people. You get better decisions when members of the group bring different realms of knowledge, and viewpoints, to the buffet table. This of course implies that there will be disagreement. But if you've managed your corporate culture well—if you've been smart about creating a true climate of innovation and trust—then it will be respectful disagreement. Toyota's innovative employee culture is based on the idea that respectful disagreements among employees lead to productive, genuine progress. If two employees always agree about everything, goes the car company's philosophy, then one of them is redundant.

There's one other important benefit of innovation. Innovation, creativity, and—yes—change are what make your company an exciting, attractive place to work. If your employee culture celebrates innovation and creativity, the way Toyota's does, you'll probably retain your employees longer and keep them happier, too. Hal Sirkin, a senior vice president at Boston Consulting, suggests that innovative cultures "create more opportunities for people, both because of the growth and also because of the environment that inherently comes with innovation. . . . Everybody wants to help their customers do better. It's just part of who we are as human beings. And so by doing that, you create more value for your people too. It's a win-win."

~ 13 ~

Engaged and Enabled

Your employees are already connected to each other more efficiently and constantly than ever before. Don Tapscott and Anthony Williams say this kind of ubiquitous electronic connectivity is changing the very nature of work, making it "more cognitively complex, more team-based and collaborative, more dependent on social skills, more time pressured, more reliant on technological competence, more mobile, and less dependent on geography." Because of this, they say, firms are decentralizing their decision making, relying more and more on individual initiative and responsibility. And people are going to get even more connected in the future. New Web-based tools promote collaboration and networking among employees in ways never before possible. Whether we talk about blogs, chat rooms, peer-to-peer networks, or virtual-reality meeting areas such as Second Life, what is clear is that technology is now facilitating people working together in ways that change the qualitative nature of what it means to "operate" a business.

One of the most important implications for corporate connectivity is that, if it is handled correctly, it actually can facilitate a network effect among employees, allowing companies to leverage their employee resources in ways that weren't possible before. For example, many of the world's largest firms are actually growing *at a faster rate* than other, less enormous firms, because they are harnessing their employee cultures and the power of networking among diverse employee and partner groups. Rather than simply exploiting their size to extract more favorable prices for supplies and services, global firms are benefiting from larger, better-connected pools of professional talent while using technology to deal with the complexity of their operations and harnessing "unique intangibles," such as their own base of technical knowledge, or their relationships with customers and partners, to forge a competitive advantage.

Toyota is certainly one good example, but we could also point to ExxonMobil, a company so large that if it were a country, it would have a GDP the size of Taiwan's. With 86,000 employees working in ten separate operating companies in 150 countries, ExxonMobil succeeds by executing its core processes well, including capital allocation and R&D, but also by tapping its enormous talent pool in a well-networked, collaborative culture.

There's that word yet again. It is this aspect of the company's organization—its culture—that allows it to use these new technologies to operate in a flatter, less hierarchical way, with more autonomy given to individual business unit managers. It's worth noting that fewer than 400 people work at global headquarters of ExxonMobil.

Interactive communications technology has liberated businesses to tap in to their global talent pools in unique and very innovative ways, but only to the extent that they can rely on their employee cultures to make autonomous decisions and take actions that will further the corporate mission.

The latest innovation at Emerson Electric, for example, is known as swarm engineering. It uses engineering talent from low-cost areas, such as India, China, and the Philippines, to speed the development of new products and other engineering innovations. According to CEO Chuck Knight, the cost of engineering talent is so low in these countries that "we employ more high-quality engineers there at a constant level of spending. ...That's what swarm engineering does: It lets us assign large teams of engineers to swarm to a project and break it into steps that can be done in parallel rather than in sequence." According to Knight, a big, complex development that might require 50 engineers working sequentially five years to complete can now be attacked by a swarm of 90 lower-cost engineers who, because they work in parallel on some of the components, complete the project in 30% less time. Moreover, he says, "with component costs coming down, say five percent a year, with swarm we could actually redevelop the product twice in a five-year period for the same cost as the traditional method. That's a huge competitive advantage."

Much of the current success of these very large companies can be attributed to what amounts to the "network effect" of mobilized professional talent. If you link your employees together with efficient technologies, and if your employees are engaged in their jobs and enthusiastic about the mission, then the more talent you plug into the network, the more efficiently your overall network will perform. It is a classic increasing-returns scenario.

The truth of the argument is shown in measures of profit per employee for today's most successful firms. From 1970 to 1990, the average profit per employee at most large firms remained fairly constant, but with new technologies this changed dramatically. In the decade from 1995 to 2005, one quantitative analysis of the 30 largest companies in terms of market capitalization showed that profits per employee more than doubled—from $35,000 per employee to $83,000, on average. Coupled with an increase in the number of employees for these companies, the result was that the median market cap increased by almost 500%, from $34 billion to $168 billion.

THE POWER OF THE NETWORK

Because of technology, in other words, business success is increasingly attributable to employees' working and interacting smoothly together, collaborating across business units and geographic boundaries, and making decisions with a degree of autonomy that would have been unimaginable just a decade or two ago.

Writers Lowell Bryan and Claudia Joyce suggest what will drive growth in twenty-first-century firms is

> large-scale collaboration, across the entire enterprise, enabled by digital technology.... [Y]ou must create a sense of mutual self-interest by holding talented, ambitious employees accountable not just for their own work but also for their performance in helping others within the organization.

They argue that just as in basketball, where a talented player is rewarded not just for the points he scores himself but for the "assists" he delivers to others, companies should use digital technologies to track not just individual accomplishments but also employees' contributions to the efforts of others. The goal should be to "help self-directed people work more effectively with one another, outside the company's hierarchical structures, from a sense of mutual self-interest."

The informal communications networks of employees that form within an organization, but outside of the hierarchical structure, play a big role in defining the organization's culture. And, because employee networks form by the rule of "preferential attachment" in the same way customer networks form (see "Diverse Connections" in Chapter 8), the structure of any individual company's network of connected employees is not predictable and cannot be directed. Instead, you have to understand it first, and then tap it for its power as a creative or managerial tool.

An employee network operates like other social networks, including networks of customers. The influence and role that individual employees have within such a network is a function of how numerous or diverse their connections are to other employees, at other levels within the hierarchy, or in other departments, functions, or regions. Rob Cross, of the University of Virginia's McIntire School of Commerce, classifies the members of an employee network based on the nature of their connections, for example:

- "Central connectors" are the kinds of employees who tend to know everyone within a particular function or department. They are critical players when it comes to change management, and can represent either genuine sources of expertise or bottlenecks in the organization.
- "Brokers" are the employees with the most connections between departments, regions, or functions in an organization and the ones most likely to facilitate cross-departmental cooperation.
- "Peripheral players" tend to be on the outskirts of the network, loosely connected to just one or a few others. According to Cross, these types of employees often represent new sources of expertise or perspective.

Using employee questionnaires and other techniques, it is possible to paint a picture of the informal connections employees have with each other, and this can be a tool for understanding the hidden culture within your organization. In one celebrated story of change management, for instance, Bell Canada's executives administered surveys and scoured the performance reviews of its 50,000 employees, in order to identify the most influential people who shared the values the executives felt were important for the firm as it emerged from its protected monopoly status, including commitment, passion, and competitiveness. The result was a list of some 14 low-level and mid-level managers, who recommended another 40 like-minded associates. By relying on this team of "Pride Builders," the company was able to seed the changes it needed throughout the organization, raising customer satisfaction measures by percentages that ranged from 35% to as much as 245% and improving employee satisfaction by as much as 71%. And in June 2007, Bell Canada's parent company was able to go private in a $33 billion transaction, the largest in Canadian history.

EMPLOYEE ENGAGEMENT

Employers have long recognized that there is more to creating value for employees than mere compensation. In the middle of the last century, large firms began using surveys to focus on employee morale and general job satisfaction. It became obvious that, in addition to salary, bonus, fringe benefits, and other forms of extrinsic motivators, worker satisfaction depended on a variety of more intrinsic motivators, as well. These motivators include pride in their work and accomplishments, a sense of belonging and the support of colleagues and fellow workers, an opportunity to grow and contribute, responsibility and authority for their own functions, a clear mission or sense of purpose, and recognition for achieving goals or meeting objectives. Many believe that teams should be rewarded intrinsically for the most part, while individuals will need both intrinsic and extrinsic rewards.

The term "employee engagement" is now widely used to describe employees who are well motivated and committed to their work. By most definitions, engaged employees are those who show an enthusiasm for their jobs that goes above and beyond their specific work requirements or duties. These are the employees who eat, sleep, breathe, and bleed their jobs, always trying to do things better, faster, or less expensively, and exhibiting what amounts to a kind of "owner mentality" at work. While adequate compensation and other extrinsic motivators are a necessary precondition, engaged employees apply a self-directed energy to their work that can only derive from a healthy dose of intrinsic motivation, as well.

Hay Group, the global human resources consulting firm, maintains that employee engagement is more important than ever, because in the fast-changing world of modern business, organizations need employees who will actively seek out solutions to previously unanticipated problems and issues, and those solutions should be based on the organization's own core values, objectives, and culture. To do a better job engaging your employees, according to Hay, you should:

- Provide clear and promising direction, with goals that are achievable and will be seen by employees as promising long-term success for your company.

- Promote collaboration and collegiality, because the support and friendliness of coworkers is a key element of every engaged employee's job satisfaction.

- Inspire confidence in your company's leadership, so employees know that their own careers are in capable hands.

- Ensure that employees see clear development opportunities, allowing them to grow in their jobs, improve their skills, and advance their careers.[1]

The truth is, because you had the energy and initiative to pick up this book and read this far through it, you're probably an engaged employee yourself, and it ought not to be too hard for you to understand how an engaged employee operates. Just think about what it feels like when you really get into the flow of your own work. How happy are you when you lose yourself in the job? What was the last thing you did that made you feel a true sense of accomplishment? Have you ever realized that sometimes, you can't tell where work ends and leisure begins?

Engagement is not a mystery. The *Gallup Management Journal* conducted a survey to compile a picture of how engaged employees view their jobs compared to unengaged employees. Of the 1,000 full-time employee respondents, Gallup classified 29% of them as engaged, 56% as not engaged, and 15% as "actively disengaged." Gallup concluded that engaged employees "drive innovation and move the organization forward" and that "engaged employees are more productive, profitable, safer, create stronger customer relationships, and stay longer with their company than less engaged employees."[2]

The survey also showed that engaged employees are more innovative in general—with the majority of engaged employees (almost 60% of them) reporting that their job brings out their most creative ideas, and a similar number saying that they feed off the creativity of their fellow employees or that they have a friend at work with whom they share creative ideas. In contrast to these figures, only about 20% of the not-engaged employees and considerably less than 10% of the actively disengaged ones report similar feelings.

On one hand, this research probably shows that an employee's likelihood of becoming engaged with work is at least partly a function of his own preexisting creative inclinations. If creative people are more likely to become engaged with their jobs, then hiring more original thinkers will give you not only more creative ideas but more engaged employees, as well. Clare Hart, the CEO of Factiva, the news and business information provider, would certainly concur with this. She suggests that CEOs in her industry ought really to be hiring more young people, in order to stimulate new thinking, because "part of innovation is linked to lack of experience—like the child who will find 14 ways to get downtown versus an adult who will find three. We have to bring in new people–Gen X-ers and Gen Ys–who don't have preconceived views." They don't *know* "the way we've always done things," and as a result, they may find a better way.

But the research probably also shows that the act of creating, all by itself, tends to engage workers, as well. So ensuring a creative environment within a culture of trust is more likely to result in more engaged employees. Again, respectful disagreement is called for. You want employees who love their work and are highly innovative? Try throwing young workers in with the, um, less-young. Men and women. Different cultural and educational backgrounds. We're not talking about political correctness here. We're talking about building a stronger company.

One quality that engaged employees have in common— and something more and more actively sought by HR recruiters—is "positivity," or a generally positive and optimistic attitude about life and work. In addition, increasing numbers of companies are evaluating "character." When it comes to some companies' hiring, character is now more important than credentials. What matters most in predicting the effectiveness of a new executive, says one commentator, is "how they behave, the values they hold dear, and what it's actually like to work with them, side by side, day after day."

What matters to your company is having effective, capable, motivated employees. But what matters to the employee is having a fulfilling, happy life. And recent research has shown fairly conclusively that money really can't buy happiness. People living in poverty will tend to be less happy, but once a person's basic needs are met, additional money doesn't buy additional happiness. Studies of major lottery winners, paraplegics, and the wealthy have repeatedly documented the fact that a person's happiness seems to be much more the result of innate attitude and predisposition than external situation.

Carlson Marketing's Jennifer Rosenzweig coined the term "positive engagement," based on the principles of the modern "positive psychology" movement, to describe employees who are not just happy as employees but happy generally: people with a positive outlook, balance, and fulfillment in their lives. According to Rosenzweig, the elements of positive engagement include wellness and good health, connections with others, and appreciation and gratitude for what they have. Such employees are also open to new ideas and innovative, they are curious and seek to improve their skills constantly, and they are self-directed. In a nutshell, they are not just happy employees. They are happy *people*.

This would certainly not be news to Baptist Health Care. One of the goals of the cultural transformation there was not just to create an organization that benefited from more innovative and engaged employees, but to ensure that the employees themselves truly benefited. According to CEO Al Stubblefield,

> I am convinced that employees who are satisfied, even delighted, with their jobs make better spouses, better parents, better t-ball coaches, better Girl Scout leaders.

The Gallup survey also shows that there is a *type of company* more capable of attracting positive and creative people and engaging them with their jobs in the first place. For example, the majority of engaged employees agree with the statement that "My company encourages new ideas that defy conventional wisdom," compared to just 4% of the actively disengaged, and three out of four engaged workers agree that "At work, we give our customers new ideas," compared to just one in eight actively disengaged.

EMPLOYEES WITH A SENSE OF MISSION

Gallup found that engaged employees "work with passion and feel a profound connection to their company." In other words, they have a sense of mission, or a purpose, that seems to transcend the day-to-day responsibilities of their jobs. When employees have a sense of mission, they will break down barriers and overcome obstacles to achieve the mission, often going above and beyond the formal job description, whatever that is. But it can't be just any mission. Values matter. Your employees must recognize and strive for values that will benefit your company and contribute to its success, not just in the sense of short-term profits but also in terms of creating lasting value. And they must see the justice and fairness in these values themselves. Are your employees proud of their jobs when they describe where they work to family and friends? Do they sometimes find so much fulfillment in their work that they can't always tell when work ends and life begins?

It would be hard to conceive of a more effective mission than one centered on earning and keeping the trust of customers. When a sales rep, for instance, is tasked with achieving the most customer benefit—as opposed to the largest and most immediate product sales—he is much more likely to enjoy his job and remain enthusiastic about it. Solving customer problems, making the customer's life better, delivering a product or service at a fair profit that is faster, cheaper, better fitted to the needs of the customer—these are the kinds of tasks that can infuse employees with enthusiasm. Of course, the effectiveness of this approach assumes

you have been able to build a business model in which
"what's good for the client is also good for the firm"[3] and
that you can document your progress in some way. Pay attention, in other words, to the kind of financial issues and
metrics we discussed in Chapters 2, 3 and 5.

A healthy employee culture based on earning the trust of
customers is simply more likely to provide the kind of environment in which employees can become truly engaged
in their jobs. Gallup's research revealed a strong relationship
between the level of employee engagement and a company's attitude toward its customers, finding that engaged
employees tend to connect innovation with solving customer problems or bringing customers better products or
services.

Service organizations, in particular, tend to rely on
their strong cultures to ensure employee engagement. Brian
Grubb, corporate director of learning and content delivery
for The Ritz-Carlton Hotel Company, says, "Why do people want to work at the Ritz-Carlton? For excellence." And,
it seems, excellence is why people want to keep working at
Ritz-Carlton, as well. "We believe that it's that one interaction with one customer every day; one on one on one," he
said, suggesting that great service at his hotel chain is a blend
of "random acts of kindness and resolving defects." Echoing
Lou Gerstner's comment about the importance of culture
at IBM, Grubb explains: "We don't believe that culture is
part of the game; it *is* the game."

Employee engagement is explicitly linked to customer
trust, according to the Gallup survey, with more than half of
engaged employees agreeing that "At work, my coworkers
always do what is right for our customers," compared to
just one in ten disengaged employees. Other research has
shown that 50% of disengaged employees admit they have
personally acted unethically with customers.

Moreover, at most companies, employee engagement
must come before genuine customer satisfaction, and this

is particularly true of service organizations. At Wells Fargo, Chairman Richard Kovacevich has explained his bank's effort to transform the corporate culture this way:

> If you pay more attention to your people they, in turn, will take care of the customers, and if they do that, shareholders will prosper. . . . A lot of people have it backwards. They start with the shareholder.

Wells Fargo is a large, publicly held firm. The CEO is not saying that shareholders are not important. Far from it. He is saying that in order to benefit shareholders properly, you have to take good care of customers, and in order to do that, you first have to have committed, engaged employees.

This sentiment is echoed not just by Baptist Health Care managers, but by nearly every forward-thinking service company. Costco founder and CEO Jim Sinegal, when he was asked whether balancing the needs of customers, employees, and shareholders meant that shareholders seem to come third in that equation, responded, "That's not the case. We want to obey the law, take care of our customers, take care of our people and respect our suppliers. And we think if we do those four things, pretty much in that order, that we're going to reward shareholders. By the way, we sell for a pretty rich multiple. We're not getting penalized by Wall Street."

GIVING YOUR EMPLOYEES THE TOOLS AND THE POWER THEY NEED TO CREATE VALUE

To have a more innovative and adaptive company, it's vital that your employees be engaged in their jobs, which will mean they are more productive, creative, mission-oriented, and trustworthy. But in the same way that earning a customer's trust requires not just good intent but also competence, having employees who *want* to do the right thing for the business is only half the battle. Employees must also be *able* to do the right thing. So in addition to *engaging* them, you have to *enable* them to accomplish the mission.

A highly motivated employee who doesn't have the capability, training, tools, or authority to act will simply end up frustrated, while an employee who does have capability and authority but isn't properly engaged and motivated is less likely to make the right decisions. Hay Group maintains that properly enabling employees requires effective performance management; authority and empowerment (i.e., giving employees more autonomy, discretion, and independence); access to supplies, information tools, and other resources (what Microsoft ads call "people-ready"); and training. To analyze the importance of enabling employees, the company considered the case of a financial services firm, where it had done cluster analysis to group employees into categories based on the degree to which they were either engaged or enabled or both. In reviewing the performance reports for these different types of employees, Hay Group was able to show that the number of engaged-and-enabled employees with performances exceeding expectations was 50% higher, even when compared to other employees considered engaged but not enabled.

The point is that for employees to be effective and happy themselves, they need not only to be thoroughly engaged with their jobs but also to have the tools, training, and authority necessary to act on their decisions. If they do, then not only will their attitudes improve, but it's also likely that the quality of their decisions will actually improve. One interesting psychological study demonstrating this point involved tasking two similar groups of people with solving some puzzles while random, distracting noises were sounding loudly in the background. One of the groups was given a button to push if they wanted to eliminate the sounds, while the other was not. The group with the button was several times more effective at solving the problems than the one without the button–despite the fact that the button was never actually used. The mere fact that they had the power to control their own environment had a salutary effect on the effectiveness of their decision making.

So when a Stena Ferry Lines employee is given the authority to commit up to £1,000 of the company's money on her own initiative to redress a customer complaint, or when a Ritz-Carlton bellboy knows he can spend up to $2,000 without a supervisor's approval if he deems it necessary to fix a customer problem,[4] the quality of the employee's own judgment and decision making will almost certainly improve, as well.

Empowered and enabled employees are exactly what customers are demanding, also, as their expectations of better service continue to rise. Customers want the people they deal with at the companies they buy from to be capable of helping them, whether this involves fixing a problem, or selling an additional product, or making an exception to corporate policy because the customer's circumstances are exceptional. This means customers expect employees to have not just the authority but also the tools, the information, and the training necessary to deal with whatever the issue is. One survey found that customers' desire for marketers to empower their employees was second only to their desire for product improvements. And Gartner's Ed Thompson maintains that "through 2010, empowering employees will be the quickest route to improving the customer experience."[5]

What would your company actually look like if it were primed for creativity and constant innovation? A customer-oriented, constantly innovative company operating in a networked and information-rich world would have several characteristics:

- Employees would be both engaged in their jobs and enabled to act. They would have a sense of mission that transcends their specific roles or positions.

- The corporate culture would place a high value on acting in the customer's interest at all times, in order to earn and keep customer trust.

- Employees would make an assumption of goodwill, deliberately trusting management and each other, and actively networking and collaborating to accomplish the mission. They would be self-initiating and require relatively little top-down direction.

- Diverse and dissenting opinions would be solicited constantly and evaluated in a respectful way, and decision making would be objective, unbiased, and relatively nonhierarchical.

But above all, perhaps, this would not just be a company with a brighter financial future and a better reputation. It would be a better company, period.

～14～

Leaders Needed.
Inquire Within

Face it. This is not going to be easy.

The whole business community is hardwired for short-term results. It's built in to the market. Ingrained. You haven't even started yet, and the system is already rigged against you.

To extricate yourself from the mess of short-term management and penny-wise-but-pound-foolish financial expectations, you need a new mental model to define what "success" actually means for your business. This is what we tried to provide in our book, and as our argument progressed we highlighted 12 Laws to Follow if you want to beat the Crisis of Short-Termism. Follow these laws and you can be a master rather than a victim of the new technologies now revolutionizing how businesses operate.

The Laws to Follow pretty much summarize our whole argument.

Create the Most Possible Value from the Customers and Prospects Available to You

Customers are the only source of organic growth for a company, and they are a scarce productive resource, like capital or labor. But in contrast to capital, customers truly are limited in number. You can't borrow them from a bank, and your business growth is probably more constrained by lack of customers than by lack of capital. Your financial budget is an *artificial* scarcity of money, an imposed constraint on your activities, but your "customer budget" is an *actual* scarcity of customers. The limited availability of customers is a genuine constraint on how much shareholder value your company actually can create. Therefore, you have to generate the most possible value per customer used, rather than focusing on how much value can be generated per dollar used.

But doing this means entirely rethinking how your employees and managers are recognized and compensated, and even how your business is structured. Someone, somewhere in your company, must be responsible for ensuring that each customer creates as much value for your firm as possible. At present, probably no one is.

Earn and Keep the Trust of Your Customers

Customers prefer to deal with companies they trust, so if you want to sell more, to more customers, then you have to increase the level of trust your customers have in you. It's really that simple. It would be hard to name any management task more important than simply building and protecting your reputation among customers and prospective customers, so that they continue to keep you in business.

There are many gradations of trust, but to ensure your customers create the most possible value for you, show them that you are always trying to act in their interests and that you have the capability and competence needed to deliver on those good intentions. Doing this means practicing the principle of reciprocity and putting yourself in the customer's shoes at all times. But this, too, is a revolutionary thought, because companies, industries, and whole business models often are based on making money by withholding information from customers, or by taking advantage of customer mistakes, or just by selling a customer something he's prepared to buy even when you know he doesn't need it.

Every time your company stoops to this kind of tactic, you ought to feel a little whoosh of air leaving the room. That would be the sound of customer trust being deflated.

To Earn Your Customers' Trust, First Earn Your Employees' Trust

You can't expect your employees to take your customers' interests to heart unless they themselves feel they can trust your company, and the sad truth is that most employees don't really trust the companies they work for. Partly this is because the hierarchical structure of any company naturally erodes the trust of its members. It can't be avoided; that's just the nature of hierarchies, and hierarchies are necessary. But it's also a fact that employees are the ones who see customer trust being violated on the front lines. Many companies, even very honest and reputable ones, offer products or services to customers that employees themselves are reluctant to buy. Why? Do you think these employees might know something that customers don't?

Customer trust and employee trust are inextricably linked. To earn the trust of employees, it's vital to ensure that they have a sense of mission that goes beyond mere profit or shareholder value. Your employees have to be genuinely *engaged* in their jobs—motivated to accomplish the mission and energetic enough to take the initiative. Provided your employees are engaged in their work, then what they need from you most is for you to *enable* them by providing the tools, training, and authority to take the actions necessary to accomplish the mission.

Employees who trust the company they work for are more likely to become engaged, productive workers in the first place, and the more engaged employees become in their work, the more likely they are to believe that their companies and coworkers always do what is right for customers.

The reverse is also true. Employees who *don't* trust their employers are much more likely to violate a customer's trust and to undertake activities that are unethical or even illegal.

Customers May Forgive Honest Mistakes but Will Never Forgive Dishonesty

More than just good intentions are required to earn a customer's trust (or anyone else's, for that matter). In addition to having the right "heart," you also have to show that you are reasonably competent to carry out your intentions. Both good intent and competence are required to enjoy the trust of customers and to benefit from their patronage in the future. This means execution counts. Having a well-disciplined operation makes a difference. Regular, routine attention to detail will improve your ability to earn your customers' future business and the business of their friends and colleagues.

But you can't stop mistakes from happening, either. That's why they're called "mistakes." The real problem, of course, usually occurs in the aftermath of a mistake. The cover-up is almost always worse than the crime. So when you screw up, apologize. Honestly.

Most of all, adopt a philosophy and build a culture in which dishonesty toward customers, vendors, shareholders, and other employees is unthinkable.

Always Use Technology to Create More Trust

You can't hold it back. New technologies are pushing everyone into closer and closer electronic proximity. We are all virtual next-door neighbors now. Customers talking with other customers, employees networking with other employees, and with suppliers and channel partners and customers, too. Everyone is using technology to connect with everyone else, and as your business continues to be buffeted by the arrival of new technologies, more and more decisions will be required of you. But these decisions will be less about what type of server to buy or what kind of phone system to use, and more about what type of information to make available, under what conditions, to what customers, employees, or other businesses.

Anytime you see a new use for technology, check the way you're implementing it, and be sure you are generating a net increase in trust: the trust of your customers, your employees, your shareholders, your channel partners, your suppliers. Whether you are considering how your privacy policy should be applied, or how easily to allow customers to unsubscribe to your service, or how best to put out a corporate blog, the safest, surest way to make certain your technology creates lasting value for your business, rather than just cutting a few costs, is to ask yourself whether it creates more trust. *Is this in the customer's interest? If your customer were sitting right there in that folding chair watching and listening, is this how you'd talk about your plans – and how you'd do things?*

Success Requires Constant Innovation

It's a rat race out there, and the other rats seem to run faster and faster. Because the pace of technological innovation is actually accelerating, business innovation has to accelerate, as well. Used to be if you had a great product or service, you could pretty much rely on it to provide for your retirement, but no longer. Instead, you have to design your business to come up with a steady stream of new products, new services, new ways to do things, constantly.

Success in the short term is straightforward. All you need is a decent value proposition: good product, customers willing to buy, reasonable cost structure. But if you want your business to live to see tomorrow, then you have to equip it to generate constant new ideas. This means encouraging creativity, celebrating trial *and* error, and refusing to settle for what already works while continuing to hold firm to your core values. When it comes to creating a climate of innovation for your company, your culture will make all the difference.

Culture Will Drive Value or Culture Will Drag Value

Every company has a culture, consisting of the unwritten rules about "how things get done around here," but it's hard to define, harder to manage, and harder still to change. Because technology connects employees more and more seamlessly, however, organizational structures and hierarchical rules no longer work as well as they used to, and they are likely to become less and less effective as technology continues to improve, which makes your company's culture way more important than it was before.

If you want to earn your customers' trust, in order to create a business that is not just profitable in the current period but sustainable in the long term, then your corporate culture must be oriented around acting in customers' interests at all times. Whenever two or more employees or managers get together to solve a problem or discuss an initiative, the first question they should consider is: What's in the customer's interest?

Ultimately, your company's culture will be the result of thousands of decisions made by executives and employees every day. To have any kind of sustainable competitive advantage, your policies and practices, rules, reporting structures, compensation, metrics, recruiting, and training must all focus on the importance of fairness and trustworthiness. A culture of trust will earn more current profit *and* long-term value from your customers because it will encourage customer-centricity, reciprocity, and taking the customer's perspective in every decision. But it will also support a more innovative and creative organization, as well—an organization that encourages a diversity of viewpoints and the kind of respectful disagreement required to produce the best decisions.

Dissent and Diversity Drive Creativity and Innovation

The best way to generate new ideas is crossing boundaries, getting different perspectives, and cross-pollinating old ideas. These are probably the biggest factors determining how creativity works in the human brain, and it is also the way creativity works in an organized group of brains. If you have a strong culture with values that celebrate trust, vigorous but respectful disagreement, and a diversity of intellectual inputs, then not only are your employees likely to be more innovative, but they're also likely to make better decisions in general.

They're also likely to be more engaged in their jobs, more motivated to make your company a success, and more attuned to the genuine needs of customers.

Dissent, diversity, respectful disagreement, and trust. These are the vitamins you need to beat the Crisis of Short-Termism.

Really Taking Your Customers' Point of View Means Treating Each Customer with the Fairness You Would Want if You Were the Customer

Treating customers as genuine financial assets and trying to create as much value from each of these assets as possible doesn't mean taking advantage of them. What it does mean is stewarding a customer's relationship in order to generate value in the long term as well as in the short term. And to do that you have to take the customer's perspective. You have to try to see your business through the customer's own eyes.

Taking the customer's point of view is one of the most frequently advocated ideas in business. It's not only the secret to good customer service, but the very definition of "customer-centricity" or managing the "customer experience." At many businesses, however, the true implications of taking the customer's perspective are never fully realized.

You can't see your own company and its products and services through your customer's eyes if you don't expose yourself to the customer's own mind. So any effort to view your business from the outside in rather than from the inside out inherently requires putting yourself in the customer's place and demanding for him or her the same things you would want if you were that customer. And who would *not* want to be treated with fairness and honesty?

Being fair to a customer is the first step in taking the customer's point of view.

If Being Fair to Customers Conflicts with Your Company's Financial Goals, Then Fix Your Business Model or Get A New One

Are you hamstrung by the need to generate earnings today? Do you find yourself thinking that you'd really like your company to act more in your customers' interests, but if you did so it would simply be too costly? Maybe acting in your customers' interest would mean proactively reducing a price (and giving up perfectly good current earnings), or showing a customer how to use less of your product or service (giving up more earnings), or *not* selling a product to a customer who's already prepared to buy it, because it's just not the right thing for that customer right now (giving up earnings again). Or maybe it would require none of these things, but would instead require the creativity to overhaul a business model that seems at present the only logical possibility.

Whenever financial considerations cause a chronic annoyance among customers and employees or prevent you from being completely open and honest with customers, you have a business-model problem. And even though your company's survival may not be threatened by this problem right now, sooner or later someone who has less invested in your business model than you do will figure out how to make money by serving your customers more fairly and openly, paying closer attention to their interests. Technology's rushing advance is producing entirely new business models at a blistering pace, so if you just can't afford to act in the customer's interest today, you probably won't have long to wait before a competitor you never imagined figures out how to do it and undermines your core business.

You'll know when it happens, because you'll be trying not to get trampled by customers as they stampede for the exits. *Then* you'll figure out how to change, after losing a slew of your best customers.

Regardless of How Good Your Current Earnings Are, with No Customer Equity You Will Have No Future Earnings

You can generate great current results—terrific numbers—but unless you also continue to replenish or build up your customer equity, you will have nothing in the bank to support your earnings goals in the future. Can you answer these questions: *Will our ROC support our ROI goals? Are we creating, rather than harvesting or destroying, value? We have to meet our current numbers; do we know whether we are making our current numbers while building for the future, or while eating up our future value?*

As a business, your customers are probably the most important financial assets you have. When you allow these assets to decline in value, no matter how important it is to make the numbers today, you are destroying shareholder value just as surely as if you were depleting a current bank account.

Long-term Value Is as Important as Current Sales and Profit

Your job as a business manager is plainly twofold:

1. Generating current value for your shareholders in the form of earnings
2. Stewarding the underlying assets of your company, preserving or increasing them so that value can also be created in the future

The reality is that when it comes to producing both current and future value, your most "productive" assets are probably intangible, customer-oriented things like brand preference and customer trust—assets that require a great deal of stewarding. These are the assets that are likely to be damaged when a company takes drastic measures to shore up current-period sales or earnings, even though traditional accounting principles have been plainly inadequate when it comes to tallying such damage.[1]

The traditional argument that intangible assets like these are too economically squishy to value accurately is a product of twentieth-century thinking. With the kind of computer analysis and statistical modeling available today, customer lifetime values can be estimated and managed at many companies in a variety of industries, and not just at high-volume consumer marketing firms. Where this kind of measurement isn't happening, it's not because of the impracticality of the task but because no one is being held accountable for stewarding a company's most important asset—the value of its customers—over the long term.

The fact remains that generating current results is just not adequate as a business goal. It isn't balanced. No business should measure its success entirely in terms of sales and profit in the current period, and with the analytics tools available today you don't have to. Your company is a collection of small financial assets with memories, called customers. It is because customers have memories, and because they communicate with other customers, that the experience any particular customer has with you today impacts not just your current results but your future cash flows from that customer and others, as well. Just by tracking the factors that tend to increase or decrease customer lifetime values, you can zero in on the changes in your company's long-term value caused by today's actions.

You need a new mental model for how your business works, in both the short term and the long term, and you can start right here.

Notes

CHAPTER 1 FALSE ASSUMPTIONS

1. On March 8, 1886, Daimler took a stagecoach (made by Wilhelm Wafter) and adapted it to hold his engine, thereby designing the world's first four-wheeled automobile. In 1888, Karl Friedrich Benz started to advertise his three-wheeler, but the public refused to buy it. It was after his family (his wife and two sons) stole the car one night and drove it from Mannheim to Pforzheim (approximately 65 miles) that the public became fascinated by it and the Benz started to sell. After 1893, Benz changed his vehicle to a four-wheeled design (the Benz Viktoria). Gottlieb Daimler helped to start a company called DMG, which sold its first car in 1892. Although Daimler died in 1900, the company joined forces with Karl Benz in 1924 and combined to form Daimler-Benz. (Wikipedia, "Gottlieb Daimler," September 2007.)

CHAPTER 2 "VALUE" IS THE NEW "PROFIT"

1. Romer suggests that commercial activities consist either of discovering new rules and instructions for how to create value, or following instructions for creating value. In 1900 at U.S. Steel, employees were heavily engaged in following instructions: instructions for mining and shipping ore, operating blast furnaces, and making steel. In 2000 at Merck, the pharmaceutical company, workers were more heavily engaged in trying to discover new instructions—instructions that will permit them to manufacture new and different drugs. In his seminal 1990 article on technology's role in economic growth, appearing in the *Journal of Political Economy,* Romer proposed that ideas and new instructions (1) are "non-rival," meaning that unlike products, everyone can use the same idea, (2) have increasing returns to scale, instead of decreasing returns, and (3) are difficult to protect and make money from, without regulatory intervention. See "The Growth of Growth Theory," *Economist,* May 18, 2006. Also see Michael J. Mauboussin, *What You Don't Know: Finding Financial Wisdom in Unconventional Places* (2006), pp. 99–100.

2. In his book *More Than You Know: Finding Financial Wisdom in Unconventional Places* (New York: Columbia University Press, 2006), Michael Mauboussin talks about fund turnover rate and short-termism on pp. 62–63. Also see "Growing the Private Club," in which Orit Gadiesh and Hugh MacArthur astutely point out that although many people see "private equity" as a way to put performance pressure on a company, the private investors tend to think about results in three to five years rather than *this quarter*. No wonder so many companies are asking themselves these days: "What would we do differently if we were to go private?" We think it may also be useful to ask what it means to your company if you already have, or may see, competitors who are private.

3. Yet an additional theory to help explain the short-term orientation of investors is what some analysts call myopic loss aversion (MLA). Essentially, because of MLA, investors try to avoid losses roughly twice as much as they seek to achieve gains. While stocks go up more than down over the long term, they are volatile in the short term, and it takes nearly a year before an individual stock with average volatility is twice as likely to show a gain as a loss. But this is too far beyond the equity fund manager's 90-day cycle. See Don Peppers and Martha Rogers, "Beware the Siren Call of Short-Term Results," *1to1 Magazine* (October 2006).

4. For five years running, Dell was the only major PC maker that was profitable, with profit margins 10 points higher than rivals, but "rather than use that cushion to develop fresh capabilities, Dell gave its admirers on Wall Street and the media what they want: the highest possible earnings." All short term. No long term. The company assumed short-term success would last forever. Nanette Byrnes and Peter Burrows, "Where Dell Went Wrong: In a Too-common Mistake, It Clung Narrowly to Its Founding Strategy Instead of Developing Future Sources of Growth," *BusinessWeek*, February 19, 2007, pp. 62–63.

5. See Yuval Rosenberg, "Measured Progress: Investors Are Figuring It Out: Short Term Numbers Don't Tell the Whole Story," *Fast Company* (April 2007): 79–86, for examples of how short-term success does not lead to long-term success. Predicts integration of "long-term research plus fundamental equity analysis" will be hard to do but will happen. The article cites an Accenture study that shows that intangible assets account for about 70% of the value of the S&P 500, up from 20% in 1980.

6. See Erick Schonfeld and Chris Morrison, "The Next Disruptors," *Business 2.0,* 8, no. 8 (September 2007): 56ff., for a cover story summarizing 10 "game-changing startups" most likely to overhaul existing industry business models and accepted wisdom.

7. William Donaldson was quoted by Joseph McCafferty in "The Long View," *CFO* magazine, May 1, 2007, pp. 48–52 (joemc-cafferty@cfo.com). Donaldson suggests that companies simply stop giving quarterly earnings guidance. McCafferty points to Gillette, which stopped issuing earnings guidance at all in 2001, at the suggestion of board member Warren Buffett. After that, Coca-Cola, Intel, and McDonald's also abandoned earnings guidance to investors. By 2006, only 52% of companies provided public earnings guidance. Google has refused to offer earnings guidance from day one of its public status. So did Hanesbrands, which focuses on three- to five-year goals; its stock has been relatively less volatile than the industry. The downside, says McCafferty, citing Baruch Lev at New York University's Stern School of Business, is that companies that move away from quarterly earnings guidance often see a decrease in analyst following.

8. Although we will not devote much discussion to it in our main text, it should be noted that whenever we refer to future projected value (e.g., of a customer), translating that future value to current value will require discounting it, using a discount rate that appropriately reflects financial and other risks.

9. A personal letter from Steve Jacobs to one of the authors, January 16, 2007, quoted Peter Wuffli at UBS. Wuffli continues: "In the last three years, we have improved the relationship ratio towards the CEOs of the Fortune 500 from 11 to nearly 80% and are now No. 3."

10. Chip Heath and Dan Heath, in a deceptively simple but actually profound little book called *Made to Stick: Why Some Ideas Survive and Some Die* (2007), say "The takeaway [of the need for "credibility"] is that it can be the *honesty and trustworthiness* of our sources, not their *status,* which allows them to act as authorities," p. 131.

11. Netflix has been hugely successful in weaning customers off rental stores. Customers sign up online for a certain number of DVDs to have out at any one time, pay that fee monthly, and set up a "queue" online —the movies they want to see. The company sends out the DVDs, and as soon as you watch and return them (in the postage-paid envelopes provided), it will send out another. Turnaround for

each DVD is usually less than a week and sometimes only 48 hours, and you can take advantage of the company's peer recommendations (similar to amazon.com) to set up your own "queue" of movies you want to see next. If you don't want to wait for the mail, you can order up a pay-per-view download right away, which makes Netflix competitive with Blockbuster's claim that you swap its movies at the Blockbuster store the same day. See www.netflix.com. An intriguing conversation is attributed to Andy Grove and Gordon Moore, when the two were managing a troubled Intel in 1984. Grove asked Moore: "If we got kicked out and they brought in a new CEO, what do you think he would do?" They both knew, of course, that an entirely new CEO would discontinue a large part of Intel's current business altogether. So Grove answered his own question with another question: "*Why shouldn't you and I walk out that door, come back in, and do it ourselves?*" Cited in *Creative Destruction: Why Companies That Are Built to Last Underperform the Market—And How to Successfully Transform Them* by Richard Foster and Sarah Kaplan (2001).

12. In case you're wondering, everything we are talking about in this book applies equally to business-to-business organizations and business-to-consumer organizations, and for that matter, to government, nonprofits, and institutions, as well.

CHAPTER 3   CUSTOMERS ARE A SCARCE RESOURCE

1. Sometimes companies use up customers with technology. Jill Dyché, author of several excellent books on customer data coordination and management, including *Customer Data Integration: Reaching a Single Version of the Truth* (2006) which she cowrote with Evan Levy, explains how CDI (customer data integration) would help distinguish between John Smith (the very valuable customer) and John Smith Jr. (the deadbeat) so we don't turn down the former for a high-profit loan. Getting the process right is as important as getting the philosophy and the compensation right.

CHAPTER 4   IN THE LONG TERM, THE GOOD GUYS REALLY DO WIN

1. At the most basic level, when you trust someone, it means you're willing to put your own vulnerability in that person's hands, confident that you will not be taken advantage of.

2. Although we are not going into a full discussion here, the value of the preference customers give a business on the basis of their trust of that business amounts to something we call trust equity.

3. We like the way Lester Wunderman, the revered direct marketing guru, puts it: "Create relationships. Trust is the basis." From his keynote at the Forrester Marketing Forum, April 12, 2007, reported by Marianne Richmond.

4. Luc Bondar, vice president of loyalty for Carlson Marketing Worldwide, puts it this way: "To drive loyalty, you must be able to see your business from the customer's perspective. It's about finding out what could make your product or service even more relevant to their lives" (quoted in *Hoover's*, September 2007). Andy Wright, executive vice president at Carlson Marketing Worldwide, says: "Loyalty programs should be held to this standard: If companies can successfully use the data they collect through loyalty programs to meet customer needs, then they will lock in a truly loyal relationship" (quoted in John Gaffney, "The Myth of Customer Loyalty," *1to1 Magazine*, February 23, 2006).

5. Progressive Insurance serves customers and shareholders with this policy of transparency. To provide rate quotes, Progressive has to learn a bit about a prospect. If the prospective customer seems like a high risk, then it can protect other Progressive customers and shareholders by quoting that customer a higher premium. So Progressive can use the system to be fair and, in the process, to select its customer base.

CHAPTER 5   INCREASING THE VALUE OF YOUR BUSINESS

1. For a discussion of today's value of the customers you don't yet have, see pp. 88–89 of our book, *Return on Customer: Creating Maximum Value From Your Scarcest Resource* (2005).

2. The final word goes to the many companies, only a few of which are cited in this book, that are driving current revenue as well as building future success by focusing on increasing the value of every customer. Just one example: BNSF Railway took top honors in the Excellence in Enterprise CRM category for the Gartner CRM Excellence Awards 2006; it drove enterprise-wide customer strategy it credits for a 41% growth from 2001 to 2006 (reported by Ginger Conlon in "Customer-Centricity Delivers Revenue Gains to BNSF Railway," *1to1 Weekly*, October 9, 2006). We will not attempt in this book to exhaust the academic and professional literature on "customer equity." Excellent work has been conducted by a coterie of theorists, modelers, and researchers. To begin your own review, you may want to start with the listing of research on LTV in our *Return on Customer*, pp. 225–231. Also see Vadim Melnichuk, "Change in

Customer Lifetime Value and Forecast Accuracy," unpublished white paper (September 2006); Edward Malthouse and Robert Blattberg, "Can We Predict Customer Lifetime Value?" *Journal of Interactive Marketing* 19, no. 1 (2005): 2–16. Marie Leone, in "Capital Ideas: Back to the Future of Valuation," CFO.com, April 8, 2005, reviews *Value Your Business and Increase Its Potential* by Jay B. Abrams, (2003). You may also want to think about Balanced Scorecard applications in this context; Robert S. Kaplan (along with partner David Norton) now believes that "strategy maps" are an important prerequisite to the scorecard, as stated by Kaplan in "Five Questions About... Strategy Maps," *Harvard Management Update* (November 2004): 12. In *The EVA Challenge* (2002), Joel M. Stern and John S. Shiely point out that standard accounting doesn't give the true picture; also see James Singer and Richard Drobner, "Apply Customer Value Analytics to Boost Your Stock Price," white paper from Stern Stewart & Co. (2004). And see Cynthia Rodriguez Cano, Francois A. Carrillat, and Fernando Jaramillo, "A Meta-Analysis of the Relationship between Market Orientation and Business Performance: Evidence from Five Continents, *International Journal of Research in Marketing* (Amsterdam), 21, no. 2 (June 2004): 179; thanks to our colleague Linda Vytlacil for calling this to our attention.

3. Milton Friedman suggests that business should be more explicit in making the connection between its activity and our well-being. How many lives have Merck, Pfizer, and Lilly saved? Wal-Mart saves American shoppers $30 billion each year. And so on. Found in "Business Is the Best NGO," www.chiefexecutive.net (December 2006).

4. In recent years, we are gratified to see an increase in "marketing accountability." Whether it's because marketers believe they have a greater responsibility to contribute to building shareholder value, or it's because the finance folks have finally had it with marketing results they view as soft and squishy, we've seen a rush on the part of marketing managers to make sure their marketing spend has positive ROI. Excellent work by Roland T. Rust and his colleagues have helped to recenter the marketing spend on monetary results. (See, e.g., Roland T. Rust, "Seeking Higher ROI? Base Strategy on Customer Equity: Why CMOs Need to Pay Closer Attention to a New Metric to Focus Investments on the Most Profitable Actions," *Ad Age,* September 10, 2007; access at http://adage.com/cmostrategy/article?article_id= 120268.) Whether you call it RMR (return on marketing resources) or ROMI (return on marketing investment) or anything else, it's a good idea to understand the return your firm is getting from the cash

you invest in marketing. But like any other ROI measure, RMR and ROMI assume that the monetary budget allocated to marketing is more constrained than the number of customers available for the firm to make money from now and in the future. As with any other part of the company, the marketing department that considers only the return on the *money* it invests will be subject to making dead-wrong assumptions. This is stated eloquently by Tim Manners, "Measuring Marketing: Beyond ROI," Fastcompany.com, February 25, 2007, who notes that if what really matters is sheer ROMI, then Marlboro is the most accountable brand alive because it has the highest return. Not allowed by the government to compete freely in mass media, cigarette brands are pretty much locked in to market share. (Marlboro's share is 40%.) Instead of investing millions in mass media, Marlboro spends on direct communication to 26 *million* customers in its opt-in database. So "accountability in marketing" must also mean financial management, design, customer service, social responsibility, leadership—that is, *accountability to one's consumer.* We should also note that in a study out of Monash University, Australia, J. Scott Armstrong and Kesten C. Green discovered that, despite the evidence from many lab and field studies showing that "market-share" objectives harm performance, economic losses and profit losses continue from marketing managers who continue to hold themselves accountable for current profit rather than being better competitors ("Competitor-Oriented Objectives: The Myth of Market Share," Working paper 17/05 [July 2005]. We believe Return on Customer offers a financial measure: a way to balance ROI and short- and long-term value creation from customers.

5. A number of academic articles and books have begun to link customer lifetime value and shareholder value. See Robert C. Blattberg, Gary Getz, and Jacquelyn S. Thomas, *Customer Equity: Building and Managing Relationships as Valuable Assets* (2001) and Heinz K. Stahl, Kurt Matzler, and Hans H. Hinterhuber, "Linking Customer Lifetime Value with Shareholder Value," *Industrial Marketing Management,* 32 (2003): 267–279, who were among the first to view customers as financial assets. Also see Sunil Gupta and Donald Lehmann, *Managing Customers as Investments: The Strategic Value of Customers in the Long Run* (2005). And see Rust, mentioned in previous note, "Seeking Higher ROI? Base Strategy on Customer Equity."

CHAPTER 6   CULTURE RULES

1. "Culture" has been getting a lot of attention in the business press. See the special double issue of *BusinessWeek* for August 20 & 27,

2007, "The Future of Work," with notable articles on managing the new workforce, technology in the workplace, finding and keeping good talent, and globalization, for instance. A poll of middle and top managers ("Ten Years from Now," edited by Peter Coy) predicts that bosses will have less power over workers than they do now. The issue contains excellent articles by Michael Mandel, Pete Engardio, Bruce Einhorn, Jena McGregor, Jack Ewing, Michelle Conlin and Jane Porter, Brian Hindo, Steve Hamm, Michael Arndt, Joseph Weber, Gail Edmondson, Carol Matlack, Robert D. Hof, Louise Lee, and Elizabeth Woyke. Also see Scott Liebs, "Building a Better Workforce: How Technology Can and Can't Help Companies Optimize Their Most Valuable Asset," *CFO* magazine (Fall 2005): 20–25. Liebs emphasizes that workforce optimization means the right person, at the right place, right time, and right price, and points out that human capital management includes providing technology tools needed for what we are in this book referring to as "enabling." Also see Richard S. Gallagher, *The Soul of an Organization: Understanding the Values that Drive Successful Corporate Cultures* (2003). Why is all this important? Because "some employees are more equal than others," as Chris Banescu points out in *Orthodoxy Today,* July 6, 2007, www.orthodoxytoday.org/articles7/BanescuWork.php.

2. Cisco, like many companies, claims that customers are important. But at Cisco, the company means it. How do we know? Starting a decade ago, the customer service reps were called "customer advocates," and customer support began answering directly to the CEO. Reported in Kathy Chin Leong, "Customer Service Gets Royal Treatment," *InternetWeek*, September 14, 1998.

3. Robert Reppa and Evan Hirsh, "The Luxury Touch," *Strategy + Business,* April 3, 2007 (reported in strategy-business.com), described a recent survey by Booz Allen Hamilton, which found that superior customer service separates "good" luxury goods from "great" ones—and this superior customer service sprang from a *culture* of keeping customers happy. Nordstrom, Ritz, and Lexus "use a rigorous process to instill a customer-centric philosophy in all levels of the organization, and systematically train and reward employees to focus on keeping customers happy. . . .[This] can translate into business success: Each customer-centric company consistently outperformed its peers," even during industry slumps. "Once customers have grown accustomed to high levels of service, they are often willing to pay a premium for it and tend to remain loyal to the brands that provide it." The study concludes with steps to make your own company great:

1. Create customer-centered culture.

2. Use rigorous selection process to populate organization with superior staff.

3. Constantly retain and improve employees.

4. Measure and reward customer centric behavior.

4. Anne Mulcahy, chair and chief executive officer of Xerox Corporation, attributes the success of Xerox's recent successful turnaround to several strategies, one of which is to "Align! Focus all your employees on creating company value." From her keynote address, "The Customer Connection," World Business Forum, October 25, 2006, Frankfurt, Germany. And Andrew Mann, who heads the Clubcard program for U.K.-based discount retailer Tesco, points to the unified mission of all Tesco employees—even the hundreds who are paid minimum wage: "Create value for customers and earn their loyalty." From a presentation by Mann at the Gartner CRM Symposium, London, 2007.

Chapter 7   Capitalism Redux: Greed Is Good, But Trust Is Even Better

1. Many of our readers and the executives we talk to point out that not all customers play fair, and therefore companies have to protect themselves. Companies that differentiate customers by value are likely already taking into consideration some of the characteristics and indicators of customer trustworthiness as a part of the customer valuation process. Sprint generated headlines and controversy for "firing" 1,000 customers in 2007. And one urban legend has it that Filene's Basement used to send letters to customers who developed a reputation for buying a ball gown, wearing it, then returning it for a full refund; the letters asked the customers not to shop at the store anymore. It's possible that companies eventually may get to the point that they exchange information about the trustworthiness of different customers in the same way they already check customer credit ratings. This would serve not only to preserve shareholder value, but to protect good customers, as well. In essence, it would mean "*trusting* different customers differently."

2. Research has also shown a strong relationship between people's attitudes toward markets and market mechanisms and their charitable instincts. One study of cultural values, for instance, found that people who believe it should be the government's job to redistribute income through higher taxation and social spending (about a third

of Americans) are far less likely to give voluntarily to charities of any kind, relative to those who believe in less government and more individual responsibility (about 40% of Americans). Moreover, people who donate to charities are three times more likely to give money to friends and strangers, as well. See Arthur C. Brooks, "Charitable Explanation," *Wall Street Journal,* November 27, 2006.

3. To see the deck, search "Yours is a Very Bad Hotel" on Google. It includes such priceless witticisms as:

   - Lifetime chance of dying in a bathtub: 1 in 10,455 (National Safety Council)

   - Chance of Earth being ejected from the solar system by a passing star: 1 in 2,200,000 (University of Michigan)

   - Chance of winning the UK Lottery: 1 in 13,983,816 (UK Lottery)

   - Chance of us returning to the Doubletree Club Houston: worse than any of those (and what are the chances you'd find rooms for us anyway?)

   See www.craphound.com/misc/doubletree.htm for an example of an attempt by Doubletree's parent company to contain the problem. Of course, it's still easy to get a copy of the PowerPoint deck, and this kind of heavyhanded effort just makes Doubletree look even worse. The original disaster could be construed to be the responsibility of poor local customer service at one unit. But this threat is from corporate headquarters. We should all take a lesson.

4. The "un-Google" quote came from Linda Kaplan Thaler, CEO and chief creative officer of Kaplan Thaler Group (who brought us the Aflac duck; she coauthored *The Power of Nice*), quoted in "What's Next?" *Fortune* magazine, February 5 2007, p. 28: "People are fed up with greed and opportunism. . . . I think the Internet is a very big part of it. You can't un-Google yourself. Gone are the days when snappy campaigns could mask bad behavior."

5. We think businesses whose business models focus on one-time sales are inherently flawed. Oh, yeah? you say. What about wedding planners? Leaving aside the fact that half of all marriages end in divorce and one if not both parties will need to plan another wedding, the fact is that a good wedding planner should be planning the anniversary parties, kids' birthday parties, bar mitzvahs, office events, and so on for this couple for the rest of their lives. If you think you know of a business that really, truly can only sell once to a customer, why don't you try to "stump the authors" by posting a comment on our blog at www.1to1media.com/weblog/?

6. According to Wikipedia: "*Microcredit* is the extension of very small loans (*microloans*) to the unemployed, to poor entrepreneurs and to others living in poverty who are not considered *bankable*. These individuals lack collateral, steady employment and a verifiable credit history and therefore cannot meet even the most minimal qualifications to gain access to traditional credit. Microcredit is a part of microfinance, which is the provision of a wider range of financial services to the very poor." Wikipedia, "Microcredit," http://en.wikipedia.org/wiki/Microcredit.

7. See Jena McGregor's fascinating article, "Sweet Revenge: The Power of Retribution, Spite and Loathing in the World of Business," *BusinessWeek*, January 22, 2007, pp. 64–70. Two executives fired from Handy Dan Home Improvement Centers developed their own revenge: By 1988, their new company, Home Depot, had 96 stores and $2 billion in sales. The search for poetic justice can be a powerful motivator, and made a star out of Erin Brockovich.

CHAPTER 8   CUSTOMERS AND HONEYBEES

1. Not only is a network difficult to reproduce; for most organizations, it's difficult even to see. For an excellent overview of how to broaden the vision you have of the world your customers inhabit, see George S. Day and Paul J. H. Schoemaker, *Peripheral Vision: Detecting the Weak Signals That Will Make or Break Your Company* (2006).

2. We like the way Regent Cruise Lines has started "Circles of Interest"—cruises on their beautiful ships to gorgeous destinations, with a particular theme that interests the passengers, such as wine-tasting, antiques, food and drink, and many others. Sophie Vlessing, VP Customer Strategy and Marketing, Carlson Cruises Worldwide, led the initiative and points to its success in getting repeat business from travelers. Note: Co-creation of products and experiences is a good thing, but co-creation of television commercials is at best clever—and at worst, bogus, really. If customers help create an ad that's company-sponsored, then so what? The company has absolute veto power over what everybody sees and hears, right? The fact is, *customers do not need the help of a company and their ad agency to create messages for each other about products and companies.*

3. Wikipedia, http://en.wikipedia.org/wiki/Bastard_pop, accessed on 19 Feb. 2007.

4. October 2, 2007, closing price of Chipotle's Mexican Grill (symbol: CMGB): $104.90. Closing price on October 5, 2006, the first day

of trading: $48.50. We see similar if less dramatic success from other companies using word of mouth. Rick White, VP of Brand and Marketing Management at Scotiabank in Canada, realized that Canadians don't love banking, but they do love *hockey*. The bank has sponsored hockey league events and gets people started talking to each other about it. Sponsorship, blogs, two-way email, texting and the like is now one-third of Scotiabank's promotions budget. One immediate payoff: Scotiabank used to be rated number 5 on the attribute of being seen as "active in the community." Now it is consistently rated number 2 or number 1. (Telephone interview August 27, 2007.)

5. The Net Promoter Score (NPS) has generated some controversy. See, for instance, the blog discussion "NPS—Valid or Not?" (August 2007), at www. 1to1media.com/weblog/2007/08. Also see Timothy L. Keiningham et al., "The Value of Different Customer Satisfaction and Loyalty Metrics in Predicting Customer Retention, Recommendation, and Share-of-Wallet," *Managing Service Quality* 17, no. 4 (2007): 361–384.

CHAPTER 9   OOPS! MISTAKES HAPPEN: RECOVERING LOST TRUST

1. Not long after the JetBlue's Valentine's Day fiasco, we saw an interesting editorial ("The Politics of JetBlue," *Wall Street Journal*, February 24, 2007) and it got us to thinking: If Congress were to write a "Customer Bill of Rights" for airlines or any other industry, would that really help customers make better choices? Think about it: If all companies have to follow a government-mandated Bill of Rights for customers, then don't "honesty," "goodwill," "reciprocity," and "trust" become mere compliance issues? If companies decide for themselves whether they will take the customer's point of view, then, as a customer, I can actually see the difference between companies more easily than I can when regulations produce the appearance of universal rights.

2. Sometimes governments can lose a lot of credibility, even when nobody really thinks they want anything other than the best for their citizens. When money is unaccounted for, or when people who need rescue are left to fend for themselves, or when ballots may have been miscounted, people are shaken in their trust for their government. To be trusted, a parent, a company, a government, a teacher, an executive, a charity must be determined to do good *and* to be good at doing it.

3. Simple and strong: If you want to learn more about how to apologize in any part of your life where you make a mistake, see Ken Blanchard and Margret McBride, *The One Minute Apology: A Powerful Way to Make Things Better* (2003).

4. Privacy is, in many ways, the most tangible manifestation of "trust," and how everyone in the company thinks about privacy and data protection says a lot about a company's commitment to looking out for its customers' best interests as well as its own. See the work by Larry Ponemon and The Ponemon Institute (www.ponemon.org) as well as *The Privacy Payoff: How Successful Businesses Build Customer Trust*, by Ann Cavoukian and Tyler J. Hamilton (2002). For more on privacy issues, see the Web site for the International Association of Privacy Professionals: www.privacyassociation.org.

5. The 2002 McKinsey study is cited in Eric Beinhocker *The Origin of Wealth* (2006), pp. 261–262.

CHAPTER 10   INNOVATE OR DIE

1. Actually, there is debate about who really said these words. They could easily have been said first by Herbert Spencer, who chronicled Darwin's accomplishments and converted many of them to his own theory of "social Darwinism." If you Google the phrase yourself, you'll find no sure agreement on who said the words, but apparently they do not appear in any of Darwin's original published works.

2. See Paul Romer, "The Growth of Growth Theory," *Economist*, May 18, 2006. Based on Romer, it follows that even when patents are plentiful and well written, this is still true. Consider the flurry of accessories businesses that have arisen to support iPods, or look at the number of people getting rich from eBay, all without violating a single patent but using someone else's very good idea.

3. Springwise newsletter (at springwise.com) is a great way to see what the wildest thinkers are creating. There are many crazy ideas, but some that have real merit. In New York City, the newest restaurants are often big hits, but then the popularity dies down once everyone's been seen there. So Park Avenue—a restaurant at East 63rd and Park, closes every season and reopens with a new look and a new menu. Park Avenue Fall will offer new place settings, staff uniforms, and wall panels, different from the old Park Avenue Summer. Reported in springwise.com/weekly (June 26, 2007).

4. In the 1950s, Robert Solow won a Nobel Prize for suggesting that governments can hasten economic growth by reducing taxes,

increasing the savings rate, subsidizing capital investments, and the like. Policies like this all tend to raise the ratio of capital to labor—in effect, giving each individual worker more tools and devices with which to produce things. But Solow and other economists knew full well that such policies also had diminishing returns. Buying two tools for twice the money might make an employee *more* productive but not *twice* as productive. So every additional dollar spent on "deepening" the capital earns somewhat less growth, which means that in the absence of some other force, some other explanation, even the most efficient economy would simply stop growing sooner or later. That other force—the linchpin that *can* keep the economy growing—is technological innovation and progress. Because it couldn't be explained, technological advancement was considered an "exogenous variable" in Solow's model, which simply means the developments in technology happen outside the control of the policymakers. But technology is in fact what really drives an economy's growth over the long term as inexorably as a 12-year-old gets too big for his britches, regardless of tax policies, savings rates, or investment climate.

5. In a fascinating book, Tom Kelley (with Jonathan Littman) identified the 10 types of people you need to keep your organization creative (Caregiver, Storyteller, Anthropologist, Set designer, Experimenter, Hurdler, Cross-pollinator, Director, Collaborator, Experience architect) so you can engage in "being innovation" and not just "doing innovation." See *The Ten Faces of Innovation: IDEO's Strategies for Beating the Devil's Advocate and Driving Creativity Throughout Your Organization* (2005).

6. It goes without saying that the more innovative you are, the more you will have to deal with change. You may want to see Peter J. Flatow, "Unappreciated Task: Managing Change—Yet It Should Be a Core Competency," *Ad Age*, March 27, 1995, p. 14; Paul Branstad and Jan Miecznikowski, "Can You Change Your Organization's DNA? (Caterpillar Did.) The Cat That Came Back," *Strategy+Business*, no. 40 (Fall 2005): 32–45. Also see Ranjay Gulati and James B. Oldroyd, "The Quest for Customer Focus," *Harvard Business Review*, Reprint R0504F (April 2005): "Getting close to customers is not so much a problem the IT or marketing department needs to solve as a journey that the whole organization needs to make." The article identifies four stages of customer focus: Communal Coordination (collate information), Serial Coordination (get insight from customers' past behavior), Symbiotic Coordination (understand likely future behavior), and

Integral Coordination (real-time response to customer's needs), citing Continental Airlines, Royal Bank of Canada, Harrah's, and SBC.

CHAPTER 11   ORDER AND CHAOS

1. Eric Beinhocker summarizes some of the leading thinking on this subject in his article "Adaptable Corporation," *McKinsey Quarterly,* no. 2 (2006), www.mckinseyquarterly.com/The_adaptable _corporation_1757. Beinhocker notes that Tom Peters and Bob Waterman were among the first popular writers to draw attention to the managerial implications of this challenge, in 1982's *In Search of Excellence,* where they argued that organizations must simultaneously be "tight" in executing and "loose" in adapting. Beinhocker continues: "This dialectic has been a central theme in management literature ever since: James Collins and Jerry Porras, for example, note the importance of both control and creativity in *Built to Last*; Richard Foster and Sarah Kaplan examine the need to balance operating versus innovating in *Creative Destruction*; and Michael Tushman and Charles O'Reilly paint their vision of an "ambidextrous" organization that can operate as well as innovate in *Winning through Innovation.* One of the best-known and most-cited academic papers on the topic, written in 1991 by Stanford's James March, used the memorable terms 'exploration' versus 'exploitation.'"

2. Just to illustrate how the culture trumps the mission statement: At the time of its downfall, Enron's mission statement was:

   We have four values:

   • Respect: We treat others as we would like to be treated ourselves . . .

   • Integrity: We work with customers and prospects openly, honestly, and sincerely . . .

   • Communication: We take the time to talk with one another . . . and to listen . . .

   • Excellence: We are satisfied with nothing less than the very best in everything we do. We will continue to raise the bar for everyone.

   From Charles Green, "The Trusted Advisor" workshop, September 2007.

3. We are indebted to Lt. Gen. (Ret.) J. W. Kelly, who made comments about the inelasticity of integrity in his commitment dinner speech

to USAFA Class of 2007, on August 9, 2005, USAFA, Colorado Springs, as reported in the *Association of Graduates Magazine.*

CHAPTER 12 THE WISDOM OF DISSENT

1. Irving Janis didn't coin the term "groupthink," but he wrote a book on the topic in 1961, and on p. 9 of *Victims of Groupthink* he defines groupthink as "a mode of thinking that people engage in when they are deeply involved in a cohesive in-group, when the members' strivings for unanimity override their motivation to realistically appraise alternative courses of action." See http://en.wikipedia.org/wiki/Groupthink.

CHAPTER 13 ENGAGED AND ENABLED

1. The parent company of Peppers & Rogers Group is Carlson, based in Minneapolis. Named for each of the past seven years as one of the "100 Best Companies for Working Mothers," Carlson is led by the extraordinary and inexhaustible chairman and CEO, Marilyn Carlson Nelson, daughter of Carlson's founder. She is the recipient of numerous prestigious and international awards, but it is particularly fitting that she has been named the 2007 Working Mother Family Champion. She says: "As a family-owned company, it is consistent for us to care about our employees and their families . . . and without question, [that] leads to a more creative and productive workplace culture" (Reported on Carlson Epicenter intranet and in *Working Mother* magazine.)

2. The Gallup Employee Engagement Survey reported on October 12, 2006, that "engaged employees inspire company innovation," in an article from *Gallup Management Journal:* "National Survey Finds that Passionate Workers Are Most Likely to Drive Organizations Forward." http://gmj.gallup.com/content/24880/gallup-study-engaged-employees-inspire-company.aspx. We notice that, in many ways, the Gallup survey is the "employee" counterpart to the Satmetrix Net Promoter Score for customers. Just as NPS subtracts detractor customers from advocates, Gallup enumerates three levels of engagement for employees: engaged, not engaged, and actively disengaged.

3. In 1937, Thomas Rowe Price Jr. followed a very simple business principle in building the company T. Rowe Price: "What is good for the client is also good for the firm." http://en.wikipedia.org/wiki/Thomas_Rowe_Price,_Jr. And George W. Merck, the son of the founder of Merck Pharmaceuticals, believed that "placing

patients before profits is not only good medicine, but also good business." http://www.merck.com/cr/values_and_standards.

4. From Mila D'Antonio, "Inside the Ritz-Carlton's Revolutionary Ser-
    vice," *1to1 Magazine* (March 2007): One reason that employees stay is
    that they're empowered to deliver the level of service Ritz mandates.
    Jeff Hargett discussed empowerment next. He cited a statistic to em-
    bellish his point: Sixty-seven percent of customers leave you because
    of indifference with how they're treated. Customers judge the quality
    of the institution, he said, by the responsiveness of the first person
    they come in contact with to discuss their problem. Given that, the
    Ritz empowers and trains the front-line service to resolve conflicts.
    Part of this entails allowing employees to spend up to $2,000 per guest
    per day to "fix" any problems, as well as giving employees ongoing
    problem-resolution training. They learn things like how to "person-
    alize the resolution to truly delight the individual" and to "let the
    individual vent."

5. Now, here's an important question that will get the attention of your
    VP of human resources, the CFO, and all your employees at the
    same time: When many of your employees can't be evaluated by
    whether they follow a rulebook or a stated policy, can't be evaluated
    on number of hours worked at a desk or assembly line, can't be
    evaluated solely by tallying up how many products they get out the
    door, then *How do you evaluate the performance of your nonroutine decision
    makers?* You already know the answer. Start reading at Chapter 2 again.
    When the company has to rely on engaged and enabled employees
    operating beyond any foreseeable rules, then the best way to know
    that these valuable people are creating revenue from customers today
    and building equity in these same customers for tomorrow's enterprise
    growth, helping you beat the Crisis of Short-Termism, is to evaluate
    them using *Return on Customer*. We've already started work on our
    next book, which will address, among other things, how to reward
    your conceptual-age workers.

CHAPTER 14   LEADERS NEEDED. INQUIRE WITHIN

1. We need to buckle our seat belts. Accounting rule makers are promis-
    ing an overhaul of how companies calculate financial statements. Ac-
    cording to David Reilly, writing for the *Wall Street Journal*, May
    12–13, 2007, one possible result "may be the elimination of what
    today is known as net income or net profit, the bottom-line figure
    showing what is left after expenses have been met and taxes are paid."
    But balancing long- and short-term results are easier if we use the
    ROC metric and approach.

References

CHAPTER 1   FALSE ASSUMPTIONS

Page 1: According to *Ward's Auto Yearbook*, the total worldwide production of cars and light trucks in 2000 was 57,427,303. In 2006, the U.S. Bureau of Labor Statistics reported 154,490 registered and licensed chauffeurs in the United States.

Page 2: Thomas Watson, former CEO of IBM, has been credited with predicting in 1958 that the world would never need more than about five large computers. Of late, that quote has been questioned, but in 1985, the story was discussed on Usenet (in net.misc), without Watson's name being attached. The original discussion has not survived, but an explanation has; it attributes a very similar quote to the Cambridge mathematician Professor Douglas Hartree around 1951: "I went to see Professor Douglas Hartree, who had built the first differential analyzers in England and had more experience in using these very specialized computers than anyone else. He told me that, in his opinion, all the calculations that would ever be needed in this country could be done on the three digital computers which were then being built—one in Cambridge, one in Teddington, and one in Manchester. No one else, he said, would ever need machines of their own, or would be able to afford to buy them." Quotation from an article by Lord Bowden, *American Scientist* 58 (1970): 43–53, cited on Usenet. (From Wikipedia, Thomas Watson, September 2007.)

Page 5: In his *Wall Street Journal* article, Scott Thurm quotes Stanford business professor Robert Sutton, as pointing out in his book *Hard Facts, Dangerous Half-Truths, & Total Nonsense* that many companies have practiced the business techniques of "faith, fear, superstition, and mindless imitation."

Page 9: When we wrote *The One to One Future: Building Relationships One Customer at a Time* in 1993, there was not yet a "world wide web."

CHAPTER 2   "VALUE" IS THE NEW "PROFIT"

Page 16: Clockspeeds are discussed in Charles H. Fine, *Clockspeed: Winning Industry Control in the Age of Temporary Advantage* (1998), and Michael J. Mauboussin, *More Than You Know: Finding Financial Wisdom in Unconventional Places* (2006), pp. 121–22.

Page 16: GM's faster go-to-market is detailed in Glenn Rifkin, "GM's Internet Overhaul," *Technology Review* (October 2002): 62–67, cited in Mauboussin, *More Than You Know*, p. 120.

Page 16: Check out Scion.com to build your own Scion car. The Web site tells the customer, "We relinquish all power to you."

Page 16: The article about scanning data caught our attention because of the very important question it asks in the title. See "If Brands Are Built over Years, Why Are They Managed over Quarters?" by Wharton's Leonard Lodish, August 22, 2007, cited at http://knowledge.wharton.upenn.edu/article.cfm?articleid=1790.

Page 17: The study about S&P life span was from McKinsey, cited in Richard Foster and Sarah Kaplan, *Creative Destruction: Why Companies That Are Built to Last Underperform the Market—And How to Successfully Transform Them* (2001), and also in Charles A. O'Reilly III and Michael L. Tushman, *Ambidexterity as a Dynamic Capability: Resolving the Innovator's Dilemma* (2007), cited at www.hbs.edu/research/pdf/07-088WP.pdf. The study examined 6,800 firms in 40 industries over a 25-year period.

Page 19: We found the quote about restating four years of earning results in an article by Christopher Lawton and Don Clark, "Dell to Restate 4 Years of Results," *Wall Street Journal*, August 17, 2007, cited at http://online.wsj.com/article/SB118729623365900062.html?mod=hpp_us_whats_news.

Page 19: For more about the impact of VLSI, see Eric D. Beinhocker, *The Origin of Wealth* (2006), p. 333.

Page 23: A complete discussion of lifetime value (LTV) is beyond the scope of this book, but you can find a listing of great work by the academic community in our last book: See Don Peppers and Martha Rogers, *Return on Customer: Creating Maximum Value From Your Scarcest Resource* (2005), pp. 225–231. Also see Vadim Melnichuk, "Change in Customer Lifetime Value and Forecast Accuracy," unpublished white paper (September 2006); Edward Malthouse and Robert Blattberg, "Can We Predict Customer Lifetime Value?" *Journal of Interactive Marketing* 19, no. 1, 2–16.

Page 25: Jeff Bezos was quoted in "Good Profits," *Net Promoter* newsletter, January 3, 2007, www.netpromoter.com.

Page 26: Personal interview with John Stumpf, February 1, 2007.

Page 26: Personal letter from Steve Jacobs to one of the authors, January 16, 2007, quoted Peter Wuffli at UBS. Wuffli continues: "In the last three years, we have improved the relationship ratio towards the CEOs of the Fortune 500 from 11 to nearly 80% and are now No. 3."

Page 27: The "final resolution" for Ameriquest was found on the company's Web site: "Ameriquest Announces Agreement with States, Jan. 23, 2006," Ameriquest company press release, available online at www.ameriquestmortgage.com/releaseArticle.html?news=news 20060123 (accessed July 1, 2007).

Page 28: Employees were quoted on the transcript from National Public Radio program about Ameriquest, *Morning Edition*, May 14, 2007.

Page 29: One of our favorite writers, Carol Hymowitz, shared some lucid thoughts about cultures of bad management in her astute article "Lessons to Be Learned on Corporate Values from Year's Blunders," *Wall Street Journal*, December 17, 2003.

Page 30: Alice O'Keeffe, "The Age of Spend, Spend, Spend," *The New Statesman,* November 24, 2003, cited at www.newstatesman.com/ 200311240015. O'Keefe notes that "[l]ast month, the House of Commons Treasury select committee questioned five bank chief executive officers about misleading credit offers and high rates of interest. During the hearing, the Barclays CEO, Matt Barrett, admitted that he advised his own children against borrowing on Barclaycard because it was "too expensive." Meanwhile, the Royal Bank of Scotland was found to have sent an application form for a gold card, which carries a £10,000 credit limit, to a dog called Monty."

Page 31: Larry Zine is quoted by Tim Reason in "Late Fees, Lost Profits," *CFO* magazine (March 2005), cited at http://findarticles.com/ p/articles/mi_m3870/is_4_21/ai_n15784948.

Page 31: The actual quote from Samuel Johnson: "Depend upon it, sir, when a man knows he is to be hanged in a fortnight, it concentrates his mind wonderfully." From Boswell's biography of Johnson, cited at www.worldwideschool.org/library/books/hst/biography/ LifeofJohnson/chap25.html.

Page 31: The number of Blockbuster retail outlets was written up in http://en.wikipedia.org/wiki/Blockbuster_video#Retail_operations (accessed in July 2007).

Page 32: See Jim Harris, *Blindsided: How to Spot the Next Breakthrough That Will Change Your Business Forever* (2002).

Page 34: Carol Hymowitz was right on target with her article from *Career Journal Today* in the WallStreetJournalonline: "'Making the Numbers' Is Not a Management Strategy" (March 2005).

Page 35 See Jagdish N. Sheth, *The Self-Destructive Habits of Good Companies: . . . And How to Break Them* (2007).

CHAPTER 3 CUSTOMERS ARE A SCARCE RESOURCE

Page 37: See Eric D. Beinhocker, *The Origin of Wealth* (2006), pp. 182–181, for an excellent discussion of how the structure of the traditional "limit order" book at a stock market contributes to the short-term unpredictability of share prices.

Page 38: Fischer Black's comment about stock prices in an "efficient" market is cited in James Surowiecki, *The Wisdom of Crowds* (2004), p. 235.

Page 41: Peter F. Drucker, *The Practice of Management* (1993), originally published in 1954, pp. 316–317, as cited in James H. Gilmore and B. Joseph Pine II, *Authenticity* (2007), p. 124.

Page 41: See also Ron Swift, Sam Gragg, and Brian Handly, "Increase Your Company's Shareholder Value Using Enterprise Analytics to Drive Customer Equity Optimization (CEO) Strategies," *DM Review*, published in DMReview.com, October 21, 2005.

Page 41: Anne Mulcahy, chair and chief executive officer of Xerox Corporation, is quoted from her keynote address, "The Customer Connection," World Business Forum, Frankfurt, Germany, October 25, 2006.

Page 42: The comment about capital being the scarce resource appeared in Lowell L. Bryan and Claudia I. Joyce, "Better Strategy Through Organizational Design," *McKinsey Quarterly* (May 2007).

Page 52: Amy Merrick, "Chico's Falls Out of Favor with Investors," *Wall Street Journal*, July 28, 2006, pp. C1, C4.

Page 53: Amy Merrick, "Chico's Falls Out of Favor with Investors," *The Wall Street Journal*, July 28, 2006, p. C1, C4.

Page 54: We have seen an increase in academicians studying differences. For example, see Shawndra Hill, Foster Provost, and Chris Volinsky,

"Network-Based Marketing: Identifying Likely Adopters via Consumer Networks," *Statistical Science* 21, no. 2 (2006): 256–276.

CHAPTER 4   IN THE LONG TERM, THE GOOD GUYS REALLY DO WIN

Page 58: For books on the subject of trust, see David H. Maister, Charles H. Green, and Robert M. Galford, *The Trusted Advisor* (2000) and Stephen M. R. Covey, *The Speed of Trust: The One Thing That Changes Everything* (2006) just to get started.

Page 60: You can find these religious references to reciprocity in Wikipedia, http://en.wikipedia.org/wiki/Ethic_of_reciprocity (accessed on July 6, 2007).

Page 61: "The man with the folding chair" story is based on an anecdote told by Dr. Klaus Kleinfeld at the Siemens Ascent customer conference in Berlin, October 2006. The facts were verified in a phone call with Matthias Kraemer, Siemens Corporate Communications, January 24, 2007.

Pages 62–63: Gerald Zaltman, *How Customers Think: Essential Insights Into the Mind of the Market* (2003).

Page 64: "Finance Forum 2004 Focuses on Customer Loyalty and Cross-Channel Best Practices: New Research Unveils Financial Services Winners and Losers in Customer Advocacy Ranking," press release from Forrester Research, Inc., June 10, 2004.

Page 65: Fred Reichheld is quoted in an interview with Gartner fellow Richard Hunter, July 24, 2003, available at www.gartner.com/research/fellows/asset_53711_1176.jsp. Also see "Love Those Loyalty Programs: But Who Reaps the Real Rewards?" Knowledge @ Wharton, April 4, 2007.

Page 66: We noted the lopsided communication policy of cable companies according to Kim Plimal of the Waterville, OH, Time Warner cable service office April 2007.

Page 68: Here's how Cantwell at Big River puts it: "All my customers have my home phone number, and all my employees know it." The Big River story came from "2006 Customer Champions Revealed," *1to1 Magazine* (April 2006), cited at www.1to1media.com/View.aspx ?DocID=29465&m=n, as well as a personal interview with Cantwell, September 18, 2007, at the Gartner Customer Relationship Management Summit 2007, Hollywood, Florida.

Page 68: You can learn more about getHuman.com in James H. Gilmore and B. Joseph Pine II, *Authenticity: What Consumers Really Want* (2007), p. 14.

Page 69: The quotes from Fred Reichheld came from an interview with Gartner Fellow Richard Hunter, July 24, 2003, available at http://www.gartner.com/research/fellows/asset_53711_1176.jsp.

Page 69: The quote from Vince Burks came from a telephone interview November 27, 2006.

Page 71: The Amazon.com reminder about a previous purchase was cited in *1to1 Weekly*, December 20, 2006. One of the authors also personally received such a reminder.

Page 71: We originally told the story about RBC in our book *Return on Customer: Creating Maximum Value from your Scarcest Resource* (2005), p. 97. The details here are from Cathy Burrows's presentation to the Executive Education Program on "Managing Customer Value" at Fuqua School of Business at Duke University, September 13, 2004, and from a subsequent telephone interview with Burrows and Mark Vermeersch at Centra Bank.

Page 72: We found the story about John Lewis department stores in Chris Blackhurst, "High Street Highflier," *Evening Standard* newspaper (London), December 6, 2006. The "trust and honesty" quote is attributed in this article to Tyler Brulee, style guru and founder of *Wallpaper* magazine.

Page 72: Motiva card information pulled from the Discover.com Web site, accessed July 25, 2007:

Page 73: Fred Reichheld is quoted in an interview with Gartner fellow Richard Hunter, July 24, 2003, available at www.gartner.com/research/fellows/asset_53711_1176.jsp. You may also want to have a look at Robert B. Reich, "The Company of the Future: It's a Revolutionary Notion: Talented People are Joining Up with Fast Companies to Create 'Social Glue'—The Essence of Both a Winning Business and a Humane Workplace," *Fast Company*, October 1998, pp. 124–150.

Page 73: Chris Argyris's reference to "inauthentic behavior" was cited in James Surowiecki, *The Wisdom of Crowds* (2004), p. 207.

Page 74: The ethics and trust bullet points came from Stephen M.R. Covey, *The Speed of Trust: The One Thing That Changes Everything* (2006), p. 11

Page 74: See Harvard Business School professor Michael C. Jensen, "Paying People to Lie: The Truth about the Budgeting Process," Harvard Business School working paper 01-072 (2001).

Page 75: The quote beginning with "Two things are sure to happen" came from the work of Michael C. Jensen, Harvard Business School professor, quoted in James Surowiecki, *The Wisdom of Crowds* (2004) p. 209.

Page 75: The idea that happy employees are a prerequisite for happy shareholders is upheld over and over. For an excellent overview, see Brendan Coffey's article, "Do Happy Employees Equal Happy Shareholders? New Studies Prove Motivation's Effectiveness," *Motivation Strategies,* Motivation Show 2005, p. 13.

Page 76: The healthcare information on these pages is taken from Al Stubblefield, *The Baptist Health Care Journey to Excellence* (2005), quote on p. xiv and bulleted list on p. 16 of the book.

CHAPTER 5   INCREASING THE VALUE OF YOUR BUSINESS

Page 80: We quoted Jack and Suzy Welch from "That's Management!" *BusinessWeek,* February 19, 2007, p. 94.

Page 82: See Fred Reichheld, *The Ultimate Question: Driving Good Profits and True Growth* (2006), for a well-developed discussion of "good profits" and "bad profits." Also see "Marketing Metrics . . . Making the Connection to Financial Outcomes: An Interview with Dr. Dave Reibstein, William Stewart Woodside Professor, Professor of Marketing, Wharton," Teradata magazine.com, September 16, 2004.

Page 83: For a complete list of books by Don Peppers and Martha Rogers Ph.D., please see the listing at the front of this book.

Page 84: Verizon's publicly reported figures, which include a break-out for its Verizon Wireless joint venture, can be found on the "investor relations" section of Verizon's Web site. Available at http://investor.verizon.com/financial/quarterly/index.aspx. Note: On December 15, 2006, Verizon Wireless repaid all of its outstanding public debt. Consequently, effective December 18, 2006, Verizon Wireless ceased to be a reporting company under the Securities Exchange Act of 1934 and to make SEC filings: http://news.vzw.com/investor/index.html

Page 84: In our back-of-the-envelope calculation of Verizon Wireless's customer equity and Return on Customer, we assumed that profit per customer was proportional to revenue per customer in the same ratio as overall operating margin to gross revenue, using a rolling-average figure to dampen yearly fluctuations, and we used a 10% financial discount rate to value future profits. We also made the simplifying assumption that new customer acquisition costs were roughly equal to the LTVs of the new customers acquired.

Page 85: For an overview of the directions pursued by players in the telecom industry, see Adam Braff, William J. Passmore, and Michael Simpson, "Going the Distance with Telecom Customers," *McKinsey Quarterly*, no. 4 (2003).

Pages 85–86: The leading indicators of LTV change and calculations are discussed at length in our book *Return on Customer: Creating Maximum Value From Your Scarcest Resource* (2005), Chapter 6.

Page 88: For more detailed discussion of TSR, see our book *Return on Customer*, pp. 15–16 and 161–162, which makes the point that TSR usually is calculated retrospectively, based on actual stock prices, while we are proposing that ROC be estimated prospectively, as an evaluative tool. For a more detailed discussion of how to value future customers, see *Return on Customer*, pp. 68–69 and 232–233.

Page 88: Find more about TSR, ROC, and the cost of capital in Don Peppers and Martha Rogers Ph.D., "Loyalty and Customer Value Intersect in the Boardroom," *Return on Customer Monthly*, March 30, 2006: Customer loyalty is only an effective metric if it relates to customer value. "The measure of brand loyalty is not only misleading, it can actually be dangerous," says Harvard Business School professor Jeffrey Rayport.

Page 89.: For more about balancing ROI with ROC, in order to balance short- and long-term actions, see Don Peppers and Martha Rogers, Ph.D., "Return on Customer: A New Metric of Value Creation—Return on Investment by Itself Is Not Good Enough," *Journal of Direct, Data, and Digital Marketing Practice* 7, no. 4 (2006): 318–331.

Page 93: Shaw Wu is quoted in "AmTech: Apple 'Rare' Company Building Customer Trust," by Prince McLean, posted on www.appleinsider.com/article.php?id=1687, April 20, 2006. Also see Larry Selden and Geoffrey Colvin, "5 Rules for Finding the Next Dell: Sure, Companies Say They Put Customers First. But Only a Few Do. They're the Ones Whose Stock You Want to Own," *Fortune*, July 12, 2004; they note that Royal Bank of Canada and Best Buy concentrate on raising their "returns on specific customer segments." Available online at http://money.cnn.com/magazines/fortune/fortune _archive/2004/07/12/375872/index.htm. Also see James Singer and Richard Drobner, "Apply Customer Analytics to Boost Your Stock Price," white paper, Stern Stewart and Co., March 2004.

CHAPTER 6   CULTURE RULES

Page 97: The reference to training and the "key" for Baptist Health Care comes from Al Stubblefield, *The Baptist Health Care Journey to*

Excellence (2005), p. 17. The "first key" in BHC's method for upgrading service, now taught in monthly "Baptist Leadership Institute" training sessions that have been attended by more than 6,000 healthcare workers from 49 states, is "Culture will drive strategy or culture will drag strategy."

Page 98: If you do a Google search of "corporate culture" and "DNA" together, you'll get more than 100,000 hits. See Gary Neilson and Bruce Pasternak, *Results: Keep What's Good, Fix What's Wrong, and Unlock Great Performance* (2005) as well as Sara J. Moulton Reger, *Can Two Rights Make a Wrong?: Insights from IBM's Tangible Culture Approach*, (2006) in which Tom Davenport is quoted on p. 6: "Think of culture as the DNA of an organization—invisible to the naked eye, but critical in shaping the character of the workplace."

Page 98: The definition of culture as "the way we do things around here" is based on the business practices in effect at a company found in *Organizational Culture and Leadership*, by E. H. Schein (2004), pp. 12–13, cited in *Do Two Rights Make a Wrong?* by Sara Moulton Reger, 2006, p. 11. Reger makes the case that conflicting cultures are the primary reason why change management and alliance efforts so often fail.

Page 102: Daniel H. Pink, *A Whole New Mind: Why Right-Brainers Will Rule the Future* (2005), pp. 36–37.

Page 103: The statistics about non-routine decision makers and both quotes which follow are from "The Next Revolution in Interactions" *McKinsey Quarterly* (2005, No. 4), by Bradford C. Johnson, James M. Manyike and Lareina A. Yee, p. 21.

Page 104: The IBM/PWCC merger was described in *Can Two Rights Make a Wrong*, by Sara J. Moulton Reger, 2006.

Page 105: *Can Two Rights Make a Wrong*, by Sara J. Moulton Reger, p. 5; p. 8.

Page 106: Evan Ramstad, "Pulling Rank Gets Harder at One Korean Company," *Wall Street Journal*, August 20, 2007, pp. B1, B3.

Page 106: Gerard Fairtlough, *The Three Ways of Getting Things Done: Hierarchy, Heterarchy, and Responsible Autonomy in Organizations* (2005), www.triarchypress.co.uk./pages/book1.htm.

Page 107: BCG partner Philip Evans, quoted in Loren Gary, "The Next Ideas: The Rise of Hyperarchies," *Harvard Management Update* (March 2004): 12.

Page 108: Lucas Conley provides a great review of Ori Brafman and Rod A. Beckstrom, *The Starfish and the Spider* (2006), in "NextBooks" *Fast Company* (October 2006): 50: "A salute to the power of the open-source revolution which has dismantled industries and utilized the creativity of the masses to create new ones." The title of the book indicates an important distinction: If you crush a spider's head, it dies, but if you cut a starfish in half, you get two.

Page 110: The story about the Sunset Direct memo was reported in *Business 2.0*, "101 Dumbest Moments in Business," Jan/Feb 2004, p. 81, by Adam Horowitz, Mark Athitakis, Mark Lasswell, and Owen Thomas.

Page 110: For more about toxic cultures and how not to have one, see Ori Brafman and Rod A. Beckstrom, *The Starfish and the Spider*, (2006) and Nikos Mourkogiannis, *Purpose: The Starting Point of Great Companies* (2006).

Page 113: The anecdote told by Lincoln is paraphrased from Doris Kearns Goodwin, *Team of Rivals: The Political Genius of Abraham Lincoln* (2005), p. 620. (The way Lincoln actually told the story, as documented here, was "There's a man in it!") The "Mechanical Turk" even accounts for the origin of the German word "geturkt" which translates, approximately, into "faked out." See www.kyb.mpg.de/bs/people/gb/other.html.

Chapter 7 Capitalism Redux: Greed Is Good, But Trust Is Even Better

Page 117: We found some of our information about "doing business like a Quaker" in James Surowiecki, *The Wisdom of Crowds* (2004).

Page 118: To see the complete Quaker "Testimony of Integrity," see http://en.wikipedia.org/wiki/Testimony_of_Integrity.

Page 118: In the 1987 movie *Wall Street* corporate raider Gordon Gecko (played by Michael Douglas) made an impassioned speech to the shareholders of Teldar Paper, a firm he was attempting to take over: "I am not a destroyer of companies. I am a liberator of them! The point is, ladies and gentleman, that greed—for lack of a better word—is good.

"Greed is right.

"Greed works.

"Greed clarifies, cuts through, and captures the essence of the evolutionary spirit.

"Greed, in all of its forms—greed for life, for money, for love, knowledge—has marked the upward surge of mankind." Cited at www.americanrhetoric.com/MovieSpeeches/moviespeechwall street.html.

Page 118: We foresee a day when companies will be "rated" on their trust-worthiness. See Ronald Alsop, "Ranking Corporate Reputations," *Wall Street Journal*, December 6, 2005, pp. B1, B14.

Page 119: We found a lot of insightful commentary about China's "Quality Crisis." For a start, see "Chinese Quality Crisis Creates 'Import Czars,'" July 5, 2007, cited at http://money.cnn .com/2007/07/05/magazines/fortune/china_products_boyle.fortune/ ?postversion=2007070512. Also see http://observer.guardian.co.uk/ magazine/story/0,2113754,00.html. Lucy Siegle, "Should I Reject Chinese Shoes?" *The Observer*, July 1, 2007; Holman W. Jenkins Jr., "Yes Logo: China Learns Why Brands Matter," *Wall Street Journal*, May 30, 2007; Emily Parker, "Made in China," *Wall Street Journal,* July 12, 2007.

Page 120: See www.angieslist.com.

Page 120: We found information about epinions in Emanuel Rosen, *The Anatomy of Buzz* (2000), pp. 18–19.

Page 121: We started our listing of consumer-rant Websites when we read Rebecca Buckman, "Web Sites Put the 'Vent' Into 'Venture Capital,'" *Wall Street Journal,* August 7, 2007, cited at http://online. wsj.com/article/SB118644800916989977.html?mod=hps_us_editors _picks.

Page 123: The quote from Alan Greenspan came from a speech he gave on corporate governance, May 8, 2003, found at www.federalreserve. gov/boarddocs/speeches/2003/20030508/default.htm.

Page 123: Stephen M. R. Covey's story about Berkshire Hathaway, as well as his trust equation, came from his book *The Speed of Trust: The One Thing That Changes Everything* (2006), p. 13, 15.

Page 125: The idea of prosocial behaviors is found in Surowiecki, *The Wisdom of Crowds,* citing Bowles and Gintis, "Prosocial Emotions," Santa Fe Institute working paper, 2003, p. 116.

Page 126: Microlending payback was reported on American Public Radio: Mark Austin Thomas and Gretchen Wilson, "Character-Based Loans Grow in Kenya," *Marketplace,* aired on NPR May 16, 2007.

Pages 126–127: Ultimatum Game contrasts reported in Surowiecki, *The Wisdom of Crowds,* pp. 120, 125–126.

Page 127: Axelrod cited in *The Wisdom of Crowds* (2004), by James Surowiecki, p. 117.

Page 128: Read more about Prosper.com in Michael A. Prospero, "A Borrower or Lender Be," *Fast Company* (April 2007): 24. Also see

Renuka Rayasam, "Loans from Strangers Can Help a Start-Up Prosper," *US News & World Report,* March 12, 2007, p. 42.

Page 129: The 2007 survey of Web sites was the "Social Commerce Report 2007" from e-consultancy and Bazaarvoice, detailed in eMarketer's article "Customer Reviews Increase Web Sales," August 7, 2007, cited at http://customerevangelists.typepad.com/blog/ on August 16, 2007.

Page 129: You can find the Kevin Wise quote and study in "Building a Better Online Community," University of Missouri-Columbia news release, November 6, 2006, cited at http://munews.missouri. edu/NewsBureauSingleNews.cfm?newsid=11922.

Page 129: When you start thinking about how to pull together information in your organization, you may want to have a look at a book by Jim Davis, Gloria J. Miller, and Allan Russell, all of SAS: *Information Revolution: Using the Information Evolution Model to Grow Your Business* (2006).

CHAPTER 8   CUSTOMERS AND HONEYBEES

Page 132: Take a look at Michael Steckler, "Social Networks: The New Face of Customer Power," *Customer Management* (July/August 2007): 10–13. Also see *Social Networking: The Essence of Innovation*, by Jay Liebowitz (2007), and *Marketing to the Social Web: How Digital Customer Communities Change Your Business* (2007).

Page 133: The two events in 2006 were chronicled in Anya Kamenetz, "The Network Unbound," *Fast Company*, no. 106 (June 2006): 68, cited at www.fastcompany.com/magazine/106/open_social-networks.html.

Page 133: Brizendine's book *The Female Brain* was published in August 2006. Brizendine was quoted in "The World of Personal Friendship," *The Week,* August 19, 2006, p. 11.

Page 134: Associated Press, "Death Row Inmates' Pages on MySpace draws criticism," *Arkansas Times,* November 12, 2006, cited at www. arktimes.com/blogs/hoglawyer/2006/11/death_row_inmates_pages _on_mys.aspx.

Page 134: Granovetter's work has been cited in a number of books, including Malcolm Gladwell's *The Tipping Point: How Little Things Can Make a Big Difference* (2002), pp. 53–54), and Albert-Laszlo Barabasi's *Linked: How Everything Is Connected to Everything Else and What It Means* (2003), p. 42.

Page 135: We pulled this generic social network diagram from http:// trust.mindswap.org/images/output.png.

Page 135: Malcolm Gladwell, *The Tipping Point,* pp. 46–50 and ff.

Page 136: Learn more about preferential attachment in *Linked: How Everything Is Connected to Everything Else and What It Means,* by Albert-Laszlo Barabasi (2003), p. 42.

Pages 136–137: Some surprisingly influential people are documented in Jamon Warren and John Jurgensen, "The Wizards of Buzz: A New Kind Of Web Site is Turning Ordinary People into Hidden Influencers, Shaping What We Read, Watch and Buy," WSJ.com, February 10, 2007, accessed at online.wsj.com/public/article/ SB117106531769704150-zpK10wf4CJOB4IKo.

Pages 138–139: Examples of customer co-creation pulled from several sources, including Patricia B. Seybold, *Outside Innovation: How Your Customers Will Co-Design Your Company's Future* (2006). See also James H. Gilmore and B. Joseph Pine II, *Authenticity: What Customers Really Want* (2007), and www.myjones.com.

Page 139: We first wrote about Procter & Gamble's co-creation in "Give Your Bees Dancing Shoes," *Sales and Marketing Management* (September 2006).

Page 139: Hotspex was written up in Jason Compton and Elizabeth Glagowski, "Customer Feedback: The Next Generation," *Inside 1to1* newsletter, May 22, 2006.

Page 140: Appropriately, we didn't read about the Toppy story on the mass media news; We heard it from a Toppy user. Details here are based on email and personal interview with Richard Hornby, Toppy user, by one of the authors in London 2006.

Page 141: Thanks to our colleague Phil Dervan for calling our attention to the story about HSBC found in Sean Coughlan, "Bank's U-turn on Student Charges," BBC News, August 30, 2007. Cited at http://news.bbc.co.uk/2/hi/uk_news/education/ 6970570.stm.

Page 142: "Prosumers" discussion and reference to the co-creating teenagers can be found in Don Tapscott and Anthony D. Williams, *Wikinomics: How Mass Collaboration Changes Everything* (2006), p. 125. Also see Alvin Toffler, *The Third Wave* (1980).

Page 142: Learn more about SETI at http://setiathome.berkeley. edu/sah_about.php

Page 143: Stories about Steve Fossett's collaborative rescue effort abound, but see "Turk and Rescue," *Economist,* September 22, 2007, p. 97.

Page 144: We first found the Chipotle's story in Michael Arndt, "Burrito Buzz—And So Few Ads," *Business Week*, March 12, 2007, pp. 84–85.

Pages 144–145: We learned about Steve Wynn in Elizabeth Glogowski, "Wynn, Home Depot Talk Trust, Employees, and Enablement," *1to1 Weekly*, April 26, 2007. Wynn is also learning Mandarin Chinese so when he visits China, he can talk to his Chinese employees and customers to increase *their* trust.

Page 145: Spending estimates on social network advertising are cited at www.marketingvox.com/archives/2007/08/16/social-network-advertising-to-keep-growing/, accessed October 3, 2007.

Page 145: Andy Sernowitz, *Word of Mouth Marketing: How Smart Companies Get People Talking* (2006), pp. 29 ff.

Page 146: We first wrote about the MCI Friends & Family program in *Enterprise One to One Future* (1997), pp. 125–126. We discussed this program and a number of other innovative MCI customer-loyalty initiatives in *Enterprise One to One* (1997), pp. 79–134.

Pages 146–147: See Alana Semuels, "Friendly Advice or Secret Ad?" *Los Angeles Times,* August 17, 2007, cited at www.latimes.com/business/la-fi-wordmouth17aug17,1,3006736.story?page=1&coll=la-headlines-business. See also various blog comments and discussion strings, including Jeremy Nedelka, "Staples Speak Easy Is Hard to Swallow," www.1to1media.com/weblog/2007/08/staples_speak_easy_is_hard_to.html#more; Susan Gunelius, "Manufactured Word-of-Mouth Marketing," www.marketingblurb.com/2007/08/manufactured_wordofmouth_marke.html; and Valeria Maltoni, "Speak Easy and Other Clever Marketing Acts a Conversation Makes," www.conversationagent.com/2007/08/speak-easy-and-.html.

Pages 147–148: The Jupiter results were reported in Jupiter Research analyst Emily Riley's *Bringing the Message to the Masses,* cited in *1to1 Weekly*, October 15, 2007.

Page 147: Influencer behavior is described in Heath Row, "Influencing the Influencers: How Online Advertising and Media Impact Word of Mouth," a DoubleClick Touchpoints IV Focus Report, December 2006.

Page 149: The NetPromoter Score is based on Fred Reichheld's book, *The Ultimate Question: Driving Good Profits and True Growth* (2006) and work by the marketing research firm Satmetrix. It is based on asking customers a single question: "Would you recommend this company or product to a friend or colleague?" See http://www.customercast.com/pdfs/sm_np_fast_start_ds.pdf.

Page 149: Customer dissatisfaction is a much better predictor of defection than customer satisfaction is of loyalty. See Frank Kirwan, "Making Customer Dissatisfaction Profitable," *Customer Management* (July/August 2007): 24.

CHAPTER 9   OOPS! MISTAKES HAPPEN: RECOVERING LOST TRUST

Pages 151–153: See Scott McCartney, "Stuck on a Plane: Why Nightmare Delays Happen: FAA Rules, Company Policies Prod Airlines to Wait It Out; Calling in the Red Cross," *Wall Street Journal*, February 20, 2007; Nick Timiraos, "Considering a Passengers' Bill of Rights," *Wall Street Journal*, February 24, 2007; Maria Bartiromo, "Neeleman Explains Himself," *BusinessWeek*, March 5, 2007; Don Peppers and Martha Rogers, "JetBlue Steps Up to Rebuild Trust," *Inside 1to1 Newsletter,* February 26, 2007; Susan Carey and Paulo Prada, "Course Change: Why Jet Blue Shuffled Top Rank," *Wall Street Journal*, May 11, 2007.

Page 153: James H. Gilmore and B. Joseph Pine II, *Authenticity: What Customers Really Want* (2007), p. 103.

Page 154: Aristotle quote cited online at www.quotationspage.com/search.php3?homesearch=actions&page=1.

Page 154: Stephen M. R. Covey, *The Speed of Trust: The One Thing That Changes Everything* (2006), pp. 30–31.

Page 155: The ChoicePoint story begins in "101 Dumbest Moments in Business," by Adam Horowitz, Mark Athitakis, Mark Lasswell, and Owen Thomas, *Business 2,0*, Jan-Feb 2004, But the happy ending is reported in "Choicepoint Gives Consumers a Voice," by Martha Rogers, Ph.D., *1to1 Weekly*, January 16, 2007, at www.1to1media.com/printview.aspx?ItemID=29998.

Pages 156–157: For a complete discussion of these issues and a review of the relevant academic literature, see Maurice E. Schweitzer, John C. Hershey, and Eric T. Bradlow, "Promises and Lies: Restoring Violated Trust," *Organizational Behavior and Human Decision Processes* 1, no. 101 (September 2006): 1–19. This paper can also be downloaded at http://knowledge.wharton.upenn.edu/papers/1321.pdf.

Page 157: Honesty and competence are both important, but of the two, honesty is essential for recovery of a breach in trust. See "Promises and Lies: Restoring Violated Trust," by Maurice E. Schweitzer, John C. Hershey, and Eric T. Bradlow, *Organizational*

Behavior and Human Decision Processes, September 2006, Volume 1, Issue 101, pp. 1–19, downloaded at http://knowledge.wharton .upenn.edu/papers/1321.pdf, 2006, p. 26. Also see the same paper for a discussion about how binding contracts can undermine trust.

Pages 157–159: "The New ChoicePoint: A Privacy Success Story," 1to1 Media.com (December 2006).

Page 159: See "Eli Lilly Settles FTC Charges Concerning Disclosure of Email Addresses of Prozac Users," *The Computer and Internet Lawyer* (2002), Aspen Publishers, LexisNexis Current Developments; Privacy; Vol. 19, No. 4, p. 27.

Page 160: If it were a country, Wal-Mart would be China's eighth largest trading partner. We found the fact describing the size of Wal-Mart in Jiang Jingjing, "Wal-Mart's China inventory to hit US$18b this year" *China BusinessWeekly,* updated November 29, 2004, cited at www.chinadaily.com.cn/english/doc/2004-11/ 29/content_395728.htm. The 2002 McKinsey study is cited in Eric Beinhocker, *The Origin of Wealth* (2006): 261–262.

Pages 160–162: Personal interview with Chris Atkinson, Singapore, (November 1995), and phone call with Ali Jabeel, December 13, 2006.

Page 162: Personal interview in Redmond, Washington, with Jon Roskill, Microsoft corporate vice president, June 2007.

Page 162: "Microsoft Lengthens Xbox 360 Warranty," http://videogames. yahoo.com/printview_article?eid=521686. One of the editors for this book has a son who paid for a repair to his Xbox just out of warranty and when the extended warranty was announced, received a rebate on the repair.

Pages 162–163: See Alan Murray, "How Microsoft Rebooted Its Reputation," *Wall Street Journal*, March 1, 2006, at http://online.wsj.com/ article/SB114117076411385895-search.html?KEYWORDS=micro soft+trustworthy&COLLECTION=wsjie/6month.

Page 164: For the information about Southwest Airlines, see "Good Profits," *Net Promoter*, January 3, 2007, www.netpromoter.com.

Chapter 10   Innovate or Die

Page 167: Eric D. Beinhocker, *The Origin of Wealth* (2006).

Page 168: The short-lived success period of companies is mentioned in Robert R. Wiggins and Timothy W. Ruefli, "Hypercompetitive

Performance: Are the Best of Times Getting Shorter?" paper presented at the Academy of Management annual meeting 2001, March 31, 2001, cited in Michael J. Mauboussin, *More Than You Know: Finding Financial Wisdom in Unconventional Places* (2006), pp. 120–121. Also see Beinhocker's *Origin of Wealth,* pp. 331–332.

Page 169: Eric Beinhocker is quoted from his book *Origin of Wealth* (2006), p. 333.

Page 169: Lake Wobegon was created by Garrison Keillor and *A Prairie Home Companion*® airs on National Public Radio.

Pages 169–170: For a discussion about the cash effect of innovation, see Peppers & Rogers Group and SPSS, "The Predictive Enterprise," from "The Customer-Driven Innovation Series, Part 1," a white paper, available at www.1to1.com.

Page 171: Commodity hell quote from Jeffrey Immelt was cited by Louis Columbus, among others, in "Can CRM Avoid Commodity Hell?" *CRM Buyer,* May 1, 2005, cited at www.crmbuyer.com/story/41928.html.

Pages 171–172: Innovation that works for customers is the only valid innovation for business. Philips had to engage in "Design Intervention"; see Jennifer Reingold, "Design Intervention," *Fast Company* (October 2006): 88–96. Also see "How to Be a Smart Innovator: Nicholas Carr talks about the Right Way to Be Creative—and the Wrong Way," *Wall Street Journal,* September 11, 2006, p. R7. And see James P. Andrew and Harold L. Sirkin, *Payback: Reaping the Rewards of Innovation* (2007), reviewed in Michael Arndt, "Turning Ideas into Dollars," *BusinessWeek,* February 26, 2007; the authors insist that innovation is pointless unless it leads to profit. Smart ideas are smart only if you are able to turn those great ideas into business. Reena Jana emphasizes that innovation needs to secure flexibility that pays off for a company and its customers, and not just for its own sake or because innovation is cool: "**in**backlash," *IN* (March 2007): 28.

Page 172: See Paul Romer, "The Growth of Growth Theory," *Economist,* May 18, 2006.

Page 173: Bill Campbell is quoted in Lenny Mendonca and Kevin D. Sneader, "Coaching Innovation: An Interview with Intuit's Bill Campbell," *McKinsey Quarterly,* no. 1 (2007): 67–75.

Page 173: "Lessons from Apple: What Other Companies Can Learn from California's Master Of Innovation," *Economist,* (editorial) June 7, 2007.

Pages 173–174: For failures that led to success, see www.wd40.com/ AboutUs/our_history.html. Also see Jena McGregor et al., "How Failure Breeds Success," *BusinessWeek*, July 10, 2006.

Page 174: Jim McCann is a fascinating business philosopher who has built a culture of trust and innovation in his very successful family business. See the 2007 special produced by WBGU for PBS: "Entrepreneurs: An American Treasure."

Page 174: One of the authors heard Isdell give a speech at the annual Carlson corporate meeting in March 2006. The quote came from the *BusinessWeek* article by Jena McGregor *et al*, in *Business Week,* published at www.businessweek.com/magazine/content/06_28/b3992001.htm? chan=search July 10, 2006. Also see "Recharging Coca-Cola: Recruited from Retirement, Isdell Adds New Fizz To Giant But Still Faces Challenges," by Chad Terhune, *Wall Street Journal*, pp. B1-B2, April 17, 2006.

Page 175: For a useful definition of creativity, as well as a good list of out-of-the-box ways to innovate, see Robert I. Sutton, *Weird Ideas that Work: 11-1/2 Practices for Promoting, Managing and Sustaining Innovation* (2002).

Page 175: "You'll know obscenity when you see it." This was from a 1964 opinion on the kind of obscenity that is not to be protected as free speech. See www.law.umkc.edu/faculty/projects/ftrials/ conlaw/obscenity.htm

Page 176: The research about androgynous people came from Csikszentmihalyi and was cited in Dan Pink, *A Whole New Mind: Why Right-Brainers Will Rule the Future* (2005), p. 132

Page 176: Was Einstein creative because he was a "German Jew" in an era when that was an oxymoron? See Walter Isaacson, *Einstein: His Life and Universe* (2007).

Page 176: The personality traits of creative and innovative people are enumerated and analyzed widely. See, for instance, Michael J. Mauboussin, *More Than You Know: Finding Financial Wisdom in Unconventional Places* (2006) pp. 155–156, reviewing the creative traits needed for good investment management.

Page 176: For the relationship between creativity and sense of humor, see Dan Pink, *A Whole New Mind: Why Right-Brainers Will Rule the Future* (2005), pp. 188ff.

Page 176: Campbell's viewpoint is found in Lenny Mendonca and Kevin D. Sneader, "Coaching Innovation: An Interview with Intuit's Bill Campbell," *McKinsey Quarterly*, no. 1 (2007): 67–75.

Page 177: We interviewed Trimble for one of our "Face to Face" columns. See "In Dissent We Trust," *1to1 Magazine* (July/August 2007).

Pages 177–178: For a complete overview of Clayton Christensen's "Disruptive Innovation," theory, see www.12manage.com/methods_christensen_disruptive_innovation.html.

Page 178: Toyota's size and scope, as of May 2007, was ascertained from its official Web site, found at www.toyota.co.jp/en/about_toyota/manufacturing/worldwide.html.

Page 179: The five characteristics of Toyota's culture can be found in a survey report called "Inculcating Culture," in *Economist* (print edition), January 19, 2006, in a sidebar entitled "The Toyota Way." Takis Athanasopoulos is quoted in this article.

Page 180: Toyota's culture allows managers and employees to network together. See "Teaming with bright ideas," *Economist* print edition, Jan 19th 2006.

CHAPTER 11 ORDER AND CHAOS

Page 183: Michael Kanellos, "Where Dell Went Wrong: In a Too-common Mistake, It Clung Narrowly to Its Founding Strategy Instead of Developing Future Sources of Growth," *BusinessWeek,* February 17, 2007.

Page 184: Emerson Electric: Jeffrey Rothfeder, "The CEO's Role in Innovation: Can a leader personally drive new ideas? Yes," *Chief Executive* (November 2005).

Page 185: Govindarajan was quoted in Brian Hindo, "At 3M, a Struggle Between Efficiency and Creativity," *BusinessWeek*, June 11, 2007, cited at www.businessweek.com/print/magazine/content/07_24/b4038406.htm?chan=gl.

Page 186: The analyst was quoted by John Parkinson, "The Conflict Between Six Sigma and Innovation," *CIO Insight*, July 23, 2007, cited at www.cioinsight.com/article2/0,1540,2159181,00.asp.

Page 186: "New to the world" stats from Robert G. Cooper, "Your NPD Portfolio May Be Harmful to Your Business Health," *PDMA Visions 2004* (January 2005), cited in "Closing the Gap: Balancing Big I and Small i Innovations," a paper by Wharton professor George S. Day (July 2002).

Page 186: M. J. Benner and M. L. Tushman, "Process Management and Technological Innovation: A Longitudinal Study of the Photography and Paint Industries," *Administrative Science Quarterly,* 47 (2002)

676-706, cited in "At 3M, A Struggle Between Efficiency And Creativity," by Brian Hindo, *BusinessWeek*, June 11, 2007.

Page 186: Incremental vs breakthrough study: "Closing the Gap: Balancing Big I and Small i Innovations," paper from Wharton by Prof George S. Day, July 2002, p. 2.

Pages 186–189: The facts and quotes in our story about 3M came from Brian Hindo in his article "At 3M, A Struggle Between Efficiency And Creativity," *BusinessWeek*, June 11, 2007. There's no doubt that firing 8,000 workers streamlined costs and increased stock price, but did it make 3M a less creative company? The "invention machine" slowed from one-third of sales coming from new products to only one-quarter. Unfortunately, "new" looks bad in the context of Six Sigma. Hindo quotes Stanford's Charles O'Reilly: "If you take over a company that's been living on innovation, clearly you can squeeze costs out. The question is, what's the long-term damage to the company?" Hindo points out that 3M was BCG's #1 Most Innovative Co. in 2004, #2 in 2005, #3 in 2006, and #7 in 2007. 3M increased its R&D budget 20% in 2007.

Pages 187–188: Mike Harry and Richard Schroeder, *Six Sigma* (2000), cited at http://www.pqsystems.com/eline/2000/04/qualitytip.htm.

Page 188: We paraphrased Boyd a bit, for style. His exact quote is: "You're supposed to be having something that was going to be producing a profit, if not next quarter, it better be the quarter after that." From Brian Hindo in his article "At 3M, A Struggle Between Efficiency And Creativity," *BusinessWeek*, June 11, 2007.

Page 188: *BusinessWeek* article quoting Michael Mucci, "who worked at 3M for 27 years before his dismissal in 2004. (Mucci has alleged in a class action that 3M engaged in age discrimination; the company says the claims are without merit.)" Mucci and Cuckley quotes from Brian Hindo in his article "At 3M, A Struggle Between Efficiency And Creativity," *BusinessWeek*, June 11, 2007.

Pages 189–190: You can find lots of very good insights about innovation, leading innovation, and innovation that is customer-based. Here is an incomplete list of good reads on the subject:

Carlson, Curtis R., and William W. Wilmot. *Innovation: The Five Disciplines for Creating What Customers Want* (2006).

Christensen, Clayton, Michael Overdorf, Ian McMillan, and Rita McGrath. *Harvard Business Review on Innovation* (2001).

Collins, Jim, and Jerry Porras. *Built to Last* (1994).

Foster, Richard, Pierre Van Beneden, and Sarah Kaplan. *Creative Destruction* (2001).

Mendonca, Lenny, and Kevin D. Sneader. "Coaching Innovation: An Interview with Intuit's Bill Campbell," *McKinsey Quarterly*, no. 1 (2007): 67–75.

O'Reilly, Charles A. III, and Michael L. Tushman. *Winning Through Innovation: A Practical Guide to Leading Organizational Change and Renewal* (2002).

O'Reilly, Charles A. III, and Michael L. Tushman. "The Ambidextrous Organization," *Harvard Business Review* (April 2004), summarized in Paul Michelman "Today vs. Tomorrow: Are You Striking the Right Balance?" *Harvard Management Update* (July 2005): 1–4.

Peters, Tom, and Robert H. Waterman. *In Search of Excellence* (1982).

Pohle, George, and Michael DeMarco. "Become an Activist CEO: Unlock Value by Building a Culture of Innovation," *Chief Executive* (December 2006).

Pages 190–191: Examples and quotes in this section from Jim Collins and Jerry Porras, *Built to Last* (1994), pp. 37–38, 43, 55, 71, 147, 162.

Page 192: W. Chan Kim and Renée Mauborgne, *Blue Ocean Strategy: How to Create Uncontested Market Space and Make Competition Irrelevant* (2005), p. 13.

Page 192: Long-lasting success described in Christian Stadler, "The 4 Principles of Enduring Success," *Harvard Business Review* (July-August 2007): 62–72.

Page 195: We found it useful to see Carol Hymowitz's article, "Rewarding Competitors Over Collaborators Doesn't Make Sense," *Wall Street Journal,* February 16, 2001, online at www.careerjournal.com/columnists/inthelead/20060216-inthelead.html?cjpos=home_whats new_major.

Page 196: Bethany McLean and Peter Elkin, *The Smartest Guys in the Room: The Amazing Rise and Scandalous Fall of Enron* (2003).

Page 197: Beinhocker's norms are proposed in a wide-ranging discussion of the importance of a company's culture, in his book *The Origin of Wealth* (Harvard Business School Press, 2006), p. 371.

CHAPTER 12   THE WISDOM OF DISSENT

Page 199: Nonengineers solving engineering problems? See Daniel H. Pink, *A Whole New Mind: Why Right-Brainers Will Rule the Future* (2005), p. 132. Also see J. Edward Russo and Paul J. H. Schoemaker,

Winning Decisions: Getting It Right the First Time (2002). The authors admonish the reader to "make sure you are deciding about the *real* issue, improve your options, convert expert/conflicting opinions into insights, *cherish diversity,* foster group decision making, and learn from the past (within limits)" (italics ours).

Page 199: The April 2005 IBM survey of CEOs was cited in "Employees as Assets: The New Innovation Paradigm," a white paper from Carlson Marketing Worldwide, by John Gaffney, Jennifer Rosenzweig, and Ann Pryor, August 3, 2006. It can be downloaded at www.1to1media.com/view.aspx?DocID=29689.

Page 199: Christoph-Friedrich von Braun, in his 1997 study *The Innovation War.*

Page 199: The Booz-Allen study was written by Alexander Kandypin and Martin Kihn, "Raising Your Return on Innovation Investment," *Strategy + Business,* May 11, 2004.

Page 200: Eric D. Beinhocker, *The Origin of Wealth* (2006), p. 9: Beinhocker suggests that primitive hunter-gatherer societies may have had an economy based on a few hundred SKUs, while the modern economy is based on 10^{10} SKUs.

Page 200: The academic article quoted here is by John Seely Brown and John Hagel III: "Creation Nets," *McKinsey Quarterly,* no. 2 (2006).

Page 200: For the 3M story, see Eric Beinhocker, *The Origin of Wealth,* p. 250. The penicillin story is well documented in medical tests and easily available online, but go to www.botany.hawaii.edu/faculty/wong/BOT135/Lect21b.htm for a typical version.

Page 200: Art Fry's views about 3M and Post-it Notes are quoted from Brian Hindo, "At 3M, a Struggle Between Efficiency and Creativity," *BusinessWeek,* June 11, 2007.

Page 200: See Nassim Nicholas Taleb, *The Black Swan: The Impact of the Highly Improbable* (2007), p. 168.

Page 200: See "The Accidental Innovator," Q&A with Robert Austin, by Sarah Jane Gilbert, published in "Working Knowledge for Business Leaders," a series by Harvard Business School, July 5, 2006. Also available at www.manyworlds.com/default.aspx?from=/exploreCO.aspx &coid=CO712061871856.

Pages 200–201: All well-documented accidental innovations. Viagra was originally for hypertension, see www.chemsoc.org/chembytes/ezine/1999/viagra.htm, and story of corn flake discovery at www.ideafinder.com/history/inventions/kelloggcf.htm, and a good

general review of how accidents often lead to innovation at www.
manyworlds.com/default.aspx?from=/exploreCO.aspx&coid=CO
712061871856.

Page 201: According to Wikipedia's entry on the subject, collective intelligence is "an intelligence that emerges from the collaboration
and competition of many individuals, an intelligence that seem-
ingly has a mind of its own." It is, in other words, an emergent
behavior exhibited by a system of independently acting agents. See
http://en.wikipedia.org/wiki/Collective_intelligence.

Pages 201–202: Mixing "laymen" with experts results in better decisions.
See James Surowiecki, *The Wisdom of Crowds* (2004), p. 31.

Page 202: "Exploration and Exploitation in Organizational Learning,"
Organizational Science 2 (1991): 71–87, by James G. March, cited in
The Wisdom of Crowds by James Surowiecki, 92004 p. 31.

Page 202: Nassim Nicholas Taleb, *The Black Swan: The Impact of the Highly
Improbable* (2007) pp. 147, 152–153.

Page 203: Ninety percent of managers think they're in the top 10% according to a poll of middle and top managers cited in the special double issue of *BusinessWeek* for August 20 & 27, 2007, "The Future of
Work." (See "Ten Years from Now," edited by Peter Coy, in that issue.)

Page 203: Jack Welch is quoted at www.1000ventures.com/business
_guide/crosscuttings/culture_corporate.html.

Page 203: The power of markets to make accurate predictions is argued
persuasively in Daniel Gross, "The Disaster Market," *Slate*, August
8, 2003, www.slate.com/id/2086811 and in Rob Cross and Andrew
Parker, *The Hidden Power of Social Networks: Understanding How Work
Really Gets Done in Organizations* (2004).

Page 203–204: See Michael T. Maloney and J. Harold Mulherin's
excellent study about the *Challenger* in "The Stock Price Reaction
to the Challenger Crash: Information Disclosures in an Efficient
Market," December 7, 1998, which can be found at http://papers.
ssrn.com/sol3/papers.cfm?abstract_id=141971.

Page 204–205: Rite-Solution's "Mutual Fun" was written up by William
C. Taylor, "Under New Management," *New York Times,* March 26,
2006.

Page 205: The brain being able to include 150 people in it is a tidbit
we found in Malcolm Gladwell's excellent book, *The Tipping Point:
How Little Things Can Make a Big Difference* (2000), pp. 175 ff.

Page 205: Gore-Tex®is a registered trademark of W. L. Gore & Associates.

Pages 205–206: We found the quote from Malcolm Gladwell about Gore in his book *The Tipping Point: How Little Things Can Make a Big Difference* (2000), pp 183 ff.

Page 206: "100 Best Companies to Work For," Press release from W.L. Gore, February 28, 2007, "W. L. GORE & Associates Acquires Amesil," cited at http://salesandmarketingnetwork.com/news_release .php?ID=2016796.

Page 206: Gore associate Jim Buckley is quoted in Gladwell's book, *The Tipping Point*, p. 186.

Pages 207–208: Columbia details from *The Wisdom of Crowds*, by James Surowiecki, (2004), pp. 182ff.

Page 208: You may want to take a look at Christina Bielaszka-DuVernay, "How to Get the Bad News You Need: If Your Company Doesn't Welcome Disagreement and Punishes Truth Tellers, You May Pay a High Price in Customer Satisfaction," *Harvard Management Update* (January 2007): 8–10, January 2007.

Page 208: A happy ending for *Endeavor*: Kenneth Chang, "Caution over Shuttle Shows Shift at NASA," *New York Times*, August 20, 2007, cited at www.nytimes.com/2007/08/20/science/space/20shuttle .html?hp.

Page 209: "Ben Franklin Forum on Innovation: What Can You Learn from the World's Top Innovators?" February 27, 2006, in Knowledge@Wharton, cited at http://knowledge.wharton.upenn. edu/article.cfm?articleid=1398.

Page 209: Tom Kelley and Jonathan Littman identified the 10 types of people you need to keep your organization creative (Caregiver, Storyteller, Anthropologist, Set designer, Experimenter, Hurdler, Cross-pollinator, Director, Collaborator, Experience architect) so you can engage in "being innovation" and not just "doing innovation." *The Ten Faces of Innovation: IDEO's Strategies for Beating the Devil's Advocate and Driving Creativity Throughout Your Organization* (2005). Excerpted in *Fast Company* (October 2005): 74–77.

CHAPTER 13 ENGAGED AND ENABLED

Page 211: Don Tapscott and Anthony D. Williams, *Wikinomics: How Mass Collaboration Changes Everything* (2006), p. 246.

Page 212: See the special double issue of *BusinessWeek* for August 20 & 27, 2007, "The Future of Work." With notable articles on managing the new workforce, technology in the workplace, finding and keeping good talent, and globalization. Also see the special issue of *CFO*

Magazine (Fall 2005), for the article "Building a Better Workforce: How Technology Can and Can't Help Companies Optimize Their Most Valuable Asset," Scott Liebs, pp. 20–25.

Page 212: We pulled the term "unique intangibles" from Lowell L. Bryan and Michele Zanini, "Strategy in an Era of Global Giants," *McKinsey Quarterly*, no. 4 (2005): 47ff.

Page 212: 2006 ExxonMobil sales of $365 billion, according to the company's 10-K. 2005 GDP of the Republic of China, according to International Monetary Fund, is $346 billion, cited at http://en.wikipedia.org/wiki/List_of_countries_by_GDP_(nominal).

Page 212: "Strategy in an Era of Global Giants," by Lowell L. Bryan and Michele Zanini, McKinsey Quarterly (2005, No. 4) p. 56.

Page 213: Knight was quoted from "The CEO's Role in Innovation: Can a leader personally drive new ideas? Yes." Roundtable discussion conducted by *Chief Executive Magazine* (November 2005), by Jeffrey Rothfeder.

Pages 213–214: Market cap facts as well as Bryan and Joyce quote came from Lowell L. Bryan and Claudia I. Joyce, "Better Strategy Through Organizational Design," *McKinsey Quarterly* (May 2007).

Page 215: Robert Cross, "The Hidden Power of Social Networks," a slide presentation based on the book of the same title by Rob Cross and Andrew Parker (May 2004).

Pages 215–216: Bell Canada statistics came from "The Hidden Workplace," *Fortune Magazine,* July 18, 2007.

Page 216: Motivation for work has been explored extensively by Jennifer Rosenzweig of Carlson Marketing Worldwide. We started our list of motivators when we saw her presentation "Reinventing Motivation," October 25, 2006. We think it's important to add "responsibility and authority" to her very good list.

Pages 216–217: Carlson Marketing Worldwide CEO Jim Schroer, as well as others, has expressed the opinion that teams should be rewarded intrinsically for the most part, while individuals will need both intrinsic and extrinsic rewards. We like the way Fay Beauchine put it; she's the executive vice-president of incentives, meetings and events at Carlson Marketing: "Engagement provides fulfillment money can't buy." (From her article "The Best Things At Work are Free," *1to1 Magazine,* December 2007, p. 46. Beauchine's article cites a series of studies reported in "The Psychological Consequences of Money," a study at the University of Minnesota's Carlson School of Management, led by Kathleen Vohs, which offers the hypothesis that "money makes people self-sufficient—increasing pursuit of their own goals but impairing relations with others." Also see "Beyond Employee Engagement: Motivating and Enabling Individual and Team Performance," a presentation by Mark Royal, Senior Consultant, Hay Group Insight, and Tom Agnew, Senior Consultant, Hay Group Insight, delivered as a Webinar, October 25, 2006. Major points are summarized in the Hay Group Insight Selections newsletter, April 2007, Selection 12, available at http:// www.haygroup.com/downloads/ww/Hay_Group_Insight_Selections_April_2007.pdf

Pages 218-129: Clare Hart is quoted in Jeffrey Rothfeder, "The Innovation Imperative: Mysteries of Innovation," *Chief Executive* (January/February 2006), posted at www.chiefexecutive.net/ME2/dirmod.asp?sid=&nm=&type=Publishing&mod=Publications%3A%3AArticle&mid=8F3A7027421841978F18BE895F87F791&tier=4&id=A61D5C59BCE4420196A2A9359512A2C7.

Page 219: The changing expectation of recruiters and those who make hiring decisions, who are now looking at the character and values of new hires, is covered in Jeffrey Pfeffer, "Why Resumes Are Just One Piece of the Puzzle," *Business 2.0* (December 2005): 106.

Page 220: The "poverty" insight came from Eric D. Beinhocker, *The Origin of Wealth* (2006), p. 315.

Page 220: See Martin Seligman's book, *Authentic Happiness* (2004), which began the "positive psychology" movement.

Page 220: The Carlson Positive Engagement Model is explained in Rosenzweig's presentation "Reinventing Motivation."

Page 220: Al Stubblefield, *The Baptist Health Care Journey to Excellence* (2005), p. 13.

Page 220: The Gallup Management Journal survey write-up was cited at http://gmj.gallup.com/content/24880/Gallup-Study-Engaged-Employees-Inspire-Company.aspx. "Gallup Study: Engaged Employees Inspire Company Innovation," October 12, 2006.

Page 222: Brian Grubb at the Ritz-Carlton was quoted in Ginger Conlon, "Culture Wins at Ritz-Carlton," *1to1 Weekly*, August 13, 2007.

Page 222: The startling finding that 50% of disengaged employees admit they have personally acted unethically with customers was reported in research by Associates Advancing Relationship Marketing/Relationship Management (AARM), cited in a letter to the editor of *1to1 Weekly*, from Andy Lorin, Marketing Analyst, Bonasource, Toronto, Canada.

Page 223: www.allbusiness.com/periodicals/article/901365-1.html. Kovacevich is quoted in "Bank's Culture Impacts Customer Trust," *Hoosier Banker* (February 2004). Also see Sara Gulbas, "A Simple Equation: Employee Satisfaction = Customer Satisfaction," *IMC Research Journal* (2002): 40–43.

Page 223: Jim Sinegal was interviewed by Kris Hudson in the *Wall Street Journal*, August 27, 2007.

Page 224: Mark Royal and Tom Agnew, Senior Consultants, Hay Group Insight, "Beyond Employee Engagement: Motivating and Enabling Individual and Team Performance," delivered as a Webinar, October 25, 2006.

Pages 224–225: Cited in James Surowiecki, *The Wisdom of Crowds* (2004), p. 212.

Page 225: Stena Ferry Lines' policy allowing all 600 employees to grant vouchers or cash up to £1,000 in value to a customer in order to redress a service problem was verified in a personal phone interview with Stena executive Alan Gordon, September 17, 2003.

Page 225: The Richard Lee and David Mangen survey "Customers Say What Companies Don't Want to Hear" was cited in a Gartner presentation at the annual Gartner CRM conference in September 2006, attended by one of the authors, who heard Ed Thompson's "empowering employee" remark at the same conference.

CHAPTER 14   LEADERS NEEDED. INQUIRE WITHIN

Page 232: The blistering pace of technology reminds us of a neat little column by Seth Godin: "If it's Urgent, Ignore It," *Fast Company* (April 2004): 101, which reminds us that we should never confuse the urgent with the *important*.

Index